CREATING PARTICIPATORY RESEARCH
Principles, Practice and Reality

Louise Warwick-Booth, Anne-Marie Bagnall
and Susan Coan

I0146429

P

First published in Great Britain in 2021 by

Policy Press, an imprint of
Bristol University Press
University of Bristol
1-9 Old Park Hill
Bristol
BS2 8BB
UK
+44 (0)117 954 5940
bup-info@bristol.ac.uk

Details of international sales and distribution partners are available at
policy.bristoluniversitypress.co.uk

British Library Cataloguing in Publication Data
A catalogue record for this book is available from the British Library

ISBN 978-1-4473-5236-5 hardcover
ISBN 978-1-4473-5237-2 paperback
ISBN 978-1-4473-5238-9 ePub

Cover design: Qube Design Associates, Bristol
Front cover image: iStock/smartboy10

To all of the people we have worked with
in participatory ways, thank you

Contents

List of tables, figures and boxes

Tables

Figures

Boxes

List of learning tasks

List of case studies

About the authors

Louise Warwick-Booth is a Reader and Associate Director of the Centre for Health Promotion Research, Leeds Beckett University. She has a background in sociology and specific interests in health and social policy. Louise has conducted research with vulnerable women, drawing on feminist participatory approaches to data collection. Her evaluation research is used in practice to further develop interventions, and to capture the voice of service users. Louise has published several text-books such as *Social Inequality, 2nd Edition* (2019), *Global Health Studies: A Social Determinants Perspective* (co-authored with Ruth Cross; 2018) and *Contemporary Health Studies: An Introduction* (co-authored with Ruth Cross and Diane Lowcock; 2012). Louise is also the author of numerous journal articles.

Anne-Marie Bagnall is Professor of Health & Wellbeing Evidence and Director of the Centre for Health Promotion Research at Leeds Beckett University. Her research interests lie in developing and using innovative methods to determine 'what works, for whom and in what circumstances' to improve people's health and wellbeing and reduce inequalities. Recent work focuses on routes to and measurement of community engagement and community wellbeing, including: evaluations of initiatives to improve collective control and reduce social isolation and loneliness; systematic and scoping reviews on community wellbeing and social relations; and mechanisms of community-based support.

Susan Coan is a qualitative researcher working with marginalised groups of people. Susan is experienced in programme evaluation where she incorporates participatory and creative methods to enhance the research experience for participants and to produce richer data. She also leads the CommUNIty team, supporting the development of sustainable community partnerships between third sector organisations and Leeds Beckett University. Her work promotes knowledge exchange, fosters collaborative research and enterprise, and opens up opportunities for participation in higher education.

Acknowledgements

The authors would like to thank the following people.

Policy Press for commissioning us to work on this book and supporting us in developing and refining our ideas.

The reviewers for providing constructive feedback on the development of the book proposal, and the draft manuscript.

The members of the Centre for Health Promotion Research team for their support, commitment to participatory research (and broader approaches, of course), as well as their ongoing engagement in critical, reflective discussions about data collection when working with communities.

The diverse range of community partners, peer researchers and participants with whom we continue to work, because you challenge us to keep learning, to develop our practice and to refine our approach on a continuous basis. We look forwards to continuing to work with you and hope to keep learning alongside you for many years to come.

How to use this book

This book is designed to provide you with insight into participatory research and the many ways in which it can be done. In writing this book we aimed to provide insight into participatory approaches as well as many practical examples, drawing from our own experiences in health promotion as well as the work of others in similar fields. The examples we use may be largely drawn from health-related projects (this is what we do in reality), but we have written about these in a way to enable a wider audience to benefit from the book by making connections into their own fields.

We have produced a book that introduces readers to the basics in a practical and accessible way, providing a 'how to' approach to doing participatory research in practice. Drawing on evidence from a range of contexts as well as our own experiences, we explore the nature of participatory research, by discussing its principles and ethos, its relationship to co-production, the practicalities of design, methods, ethics, analysis and dissemination, then end the book with critical and reflective chapters about the realities of such approaches.

We introduce the basics of participatory research in a clear and accessible way, with this broader focus intended to help any contemporary researchers who are using participatory approaches within their own practice. This may be students doing small-scale data collection, as well as professionals in universities and other sectors who are working to build longer-term partnerships underpinning community-based research. Therefore, if you are thinking about adopting participatory research as part of your own work, this book aims to inspire ideas and provide examples to help you to go about doing it.

We have pitched the book at an introductory level as many students and indeed professionals are new to participatory research. In recognition of this, the book is designed to be used in several different ways. It can be read as a whole – from start to finish – since the chapters are organised in an order that allows readers to take this approach. Alternatively, readers might wish to select certain chapters for attention depending on their interests and what might be relevant to their own research requirements. The book is also divided into three coherent parts and each part can be read independently of the whole. The book is structured to logically move through principles underpinning participatory research (Part I), into practice (Part II) and then concludes with broader reflections on the reality of working in such ways (Part III). We provide an overview of each of these areas as well as examples of the many methods that can used as part of participatory research, in boxes throughout the chapters.

We begin each chapter with learning outcomes and a brief introduction to allow readers to select the most appropriate content for their perusal. We have also cross-referenced content throughout the book so that readers can follow ideas and topic areas without needing to read the whole book in its entirety.

Given that the book is written as an introductory-level text, we appreciate that readers may require more information; therefore, there are useful references to further reading and resources in each chapter. Each chapter contains learning tasks which readers can complete if they are relevant to their own practice, with feedback on these available via the companion website. We have also provided additional material on the companion website, again allowing scope for those who wish to explore in more depth. Each chapter contains a detailed case study at the end, and the companion website provides an additional case study related to each of the chapter topics. Grounding the book in case studies, we move beyond discussing theory, principles and providing lists of do's and don'ts as these examples reflect practice. Given that each chapter in the book contains a series of pedagogical features, these will also be of use for those who wish to teach about participatory methods, therefore summary lecture slides are also available on the companion website.

The following overview of the book's contents explains what you will find in each of the three parts, as well as the chapters.

Overview of contents

Part I focuses on principles and comprises two chapters. The first chapter defines participatory research, compares it with more traditional approaches, highlights the principles of participatory models and provides some brief detail about the history of such methods. The chapter illustrates a range of contexts in which participatory methods have been used, reflects on the importance of relationships for all involved and ends with a discussion about inclusivity. Chapter 2 moves on to co-production as an approach because this term is increasingly being used in relation to participatory research. The chapter outlines the principles of co-produced research and provides examples of what it looks like, in a range of contexts. Co-production as an approach that offers a mechanism for being inclusive is discussed, with experiences for both researchers and the researched drawn on to offer examples of how this operates.

The second part of the book is titled 'Practice' and provides five chapters related to the praxis of participatory methods. Chapter 3 focuses on research design, covering research questions/objectives and methodology, illustrating participation within each aspect of the research design process. Chapter 4 moves the reader on to ethics, specifically related to participatory approaches. This chapter discusses how ethics can be managed within participatory research approaches that have not been tried before or that are evolving. The chapter illustrates ethical dilemmas that can arise in participatory projects and their associated management through a variety of examples. Chapter 5 details data collection approaches that can be used within participatory research, outlining a range of methods and associated examples of tools that accompany these. The chapter discusses the use of qualitative and quantitative approaches, as well as more creative techniques that lend themselves to participatory approaches. The chapter emphasises the importance of inclusive practice to ensure that research methods are accessible for all of those involved. Chapter 6 introduces the reader to approaches to analysis that are participatory. A range of analysis approaches are discussed with accompanying examples provided to bring this area of the research process to life. The chapter also discusses how collaboration can work within analysis approaches and notes the challenges that can occur. The final chapter included in this second part of the book is Chapter 7, on dissemination. Chapter 7 explores dissemination models that include and involve participants, using practical examples to illustrate successes. The chapter details a range of dissemination approaches enabling non-academics to be involved, but also discusses the limitations to some models.

Part III considers the realities of doing participatory research and contains three chapters. Chapter 8 provides reflection on the reality of applying participatory approaches, discussing what 'doing' participatory research means, as well as what happens when principles are applied in reality. This chapter notes the tensions between principles and practice and discusses what is realistic. The potential conflicts and dilemmas arising from commissioned participatory research sometimes compromise such approaches and affect the project delivery, so reflection on these challenges is detailed in this chapter. Chapter 9 discusses community-campus partnerships as a model for creating longstanding relationships between universities and their surrounding communities and as a potential foundation for participatory research involving trusted partners. The chapter debates if these community-campus partnerships are able to overcome some of the challenges that have been noted throughout the book. The chapter also provides the reader with clear guidance on how to work with partners such as research commissioners, community partners and universities. Detailed discussion about the impact of participatory research is provided in Chapter 10 to conclude the volume. This chapter outlines the context of participatory research within the participants' lives and the impact of taking part, for example in terms of skill building and empowerment. The chapter explores the impact on community members, academics and other professionals. Impacts related to learning and knowledge, wellbeing, social change and communities are also noted. The chapter ends by drawing on the voice of participants to show outcomes from their point of view.

Much of the literature in participatory research as well as our own work is based on physical proximity. In the wake of COVID-19, we have included a postscript on the implications of this as well as discussion of digital approaches for this sort of research.

Teaching and learning resources to accompany this book can be found at https://bristoluniversitypress.co.uk/creating-participatory-research-website

PART I

Principles

1

Defining participatory research

Key learning outcomes

By the end of this chapter, you should be able to:

- Define participatory research and understand why it is so important

- Demonstrate awareness of the principles and values underpinning participatory approaches to research

- Identify several contexts in which participatory approaches to research are used

Introduction

The chapter begins by defining participatory methods and outlining what they do and don't include, as well as detailing the principles of such approaches. We are writing this book at an exciting time for research approaches in general, with data collection developing in a range of ways. Researchers are looking for new and innovative ways in which to explore and understand the social world. There is also more data available (digital data and big data being two such examples). Participatory approaches have been written about for many years, which is why we start this chapter by providing a brief history of community-based participatory research (CBPR). Publications about participatory approaches are increasing, so there is a wealth of information available to increase our understandings and aid our own practice as participatory researchers. As the field is changing so rapidly, we provide ways for you to think about how to use these approaches rather than a comprehensive overview of the field in its entirety. This chapter distinguishes between traditional approaches to research by drawing out comparisons to illustrate how participatory approaches are different. The chapter then discusses the contexts in which to use participatory methods, and the importance of relationships for all of those involved within the process. Participatory research operates according to a number of principles, including inclusivity, so we outline these to enable you to consider them in relation to your own ideas and research questions. The chapter ends with a case study on the use of participatory research approaches with children.

What is research?

We have structured this book around aspects of the research process such as ethics, data collection, analysis and dissemination, writing about them in a linear, organised way but the reality of 'doing' research is complex as these areas overlap and challenges do arise (see Chapter 8 for more on the reality of participatory approaches). Even defining research is not an easy task because when we look at the literature, it is defined in numerous ways. In general it is an active and systematic process of inquiry used to explore the social world and to gather information, to discover, interpret or revise facts, events, behaviours or theories. Research is a process by which questions can be both explored and answered. Research is therefore a tool to explore, describe, understand, explain, predict, intervene (change), evaluate and assess impact.

Traditional research is usually defined as involving expert researchers, who gather data using a variety of methods from research subjects whose involvement ceases following the data gathering component of the research process (Danley and Langer 1999). For example, people complete a survey, answering the questions that have been created by the researcher, or some agree to be interviewed either one-to-one or in a group of others (focus group). So involvement is limited and short term for those defined as respondents or participants. In many instances traditional research is also about making practical applications with the help of the information gathered through the research process. So what works? What does not work? Researchers can address these questions; for example, by asking patients receiving certain types of treatment and by evaluating interventions. In traditional research, the process is driven by questions, objectives or hypotheses. In traditional approaches, these questions, objectives and hypotheses are usually designed by professionals who have been specifically trained as researchers. Sometimes researchers label the starting point of a project (the questions, objectives and hypotheses) as the problem. Different research questions, objectives, hypotheses ('problems') can be addressed by differing research designs and methods. For example, if a researcher wishes to explore the attitudes of a population then a quantitative design using a questionnaire is an appropriate design. If researchers are assessing the effectiveness of a new medication, then an experimental design such as a randomised controlled trial will enable them to achieve this. A study that needs to explore an issue in depth, is more likely to adopt a qualitative design, in which methods such as interviews and observation are appropriate tools (see Chapter 3 for more on research design and Chapter 5 for discussion of data collection approaches). Therefore, there are many different methods available to researchers, depending on what information they are looking for, the types of questions that need to be addressed, as well as the time and resources available. Most of these methods involve people responding or participating in the study but this does not mean that they are defined as participatory research. Furthermore, all research approaches whether they are traditional or participatory have limitations in addressing the questions that have been set. Take time now to complete Learning Task 1.1 to reflect on the limitations of traditional research.

LEARNING TASK 1.1 LIMITATIONS OF TRADITIONAL RESEARCH

Use the internet, and any other relevant resources that you have (for example, books and articles). Explore the question 'what are the limitations of traditional research?' Make some notes on the following.

1 Why do some professional researchers reach inaccurate conclusions? What gets in the way?
2 What does the relationship between the researcher and those providing the data look like in terms of involvement, power and the value of knowledge?
3 Can traditional researchers provide community-wide knowledge, values and relationships as external social actors?

Having completed this learning task, you will have debated these questions and perhaps not been able to come to a clear conclusion. These issues are widely debated in the academic literature and have in part influenced the development of participatory research approaches, which are an attempt to deal with some of the identified problems with more traditional approaches to research.

What is participatory research?

Participatory research contrasts to the traditional approaches outlined above in terms of its approach and the values that underpin it. Participatory research focuses less on scientific and academic interests (Sclove 1997) and emphasises the participation and influence of non-academic researchers in the process of creating knowledge (Israel et al 1998). There is, however, no specific 'type' or model for a participatory research approach. All approaches generally involve the collaboration of community members, organisational representatives and researchers. This approach is an orientation to research with a heavy accent on trust, power, dialogue, community capacity building and collaborative inquiry, working in combination with 'non-experts' and sometimes attempting to facilitate social change (Minkler and Wallerstein 2003). The main difference between participatory research and traditional approaches is in relation to the principles underpinning them and the philosophical values informing them, as outlined later in this chapter. Table 1.1 provides an overview of the main differences between traditional and participatory research approaches.

The phrase 'participatory research' is a much-discussed term, so what exactly is it? Defining participatory research has led to much debate in the literature, in part because participation by non-researchers, service users and community members has often been variable. Some non-traditional approaches have high

Table 1.1 Overview: differences between traditional and participatory approaches

Traditional research	Participatory research
Academics (university staff) conduct research	Community members conduct research (alone or with the support of the academic community).
The research is about the needs of the university and the interests of the academics; for example, it is about contributing to a particular topic area.	The research is intended to help improve issues within the community and is usually linked to social change, and social justice, so is more likely to serve the needs of the local community. It can also serve academic needs at the same time.
The academic is the expert (e.g. the university, or research organisation) 'owns' the research.	The community member is the expert and owns the research.

Source: Adapted from Strand et al (2003) and University of Delaware (2016)

degrees of involvement but are still not considered to be participatory (Nelson 2017). Participation has been at varying levels from dissemination right through to design and, in some instances, full control. Furthermore, participatory appraisal techniques are often used in lower-income countries with accompanying arguments that they contribute positively to both community development and empowerment (Laverack 2006). In some instances, participatory research has been driven by funding agencies who ask for research that is collaborative and community based (rather than community placed), because many contemporary social problems are complex and arguably ill-suited to traditional outside expert approaches to research (Minkler and Wallerstein 2003). Bennett (2004) also criticises the ways in which traditional research findings are presented using research jargon, which is unintelligible to many non-academics, as well as irrelevant in terms of what communities require.

Participatory research has a long history and diverse origins reflected in its various labels, illustrated and defined in Table 1.2.

Table 1.2 illustrates how the wider academic literature provides some discussion about these labels, as well as associated definitions. These traditions have distinct origins and histories but overlap in terms of their meanings and the principles that underpin them. This umbrella of approaches has emerged from an interesting history, associated with creating 'alternatives' to traditional methods of research.

The history of participatory research

There is a long history associated with 'alternative' research paradigms, as traditional approaches have not always been able to address all research questions. Traditional approaches have been criticised for using the principles of neutrality and objectivity as well as being used by professionally trained people from sections of society who are advantaged, while over-researching marginalised groups (Bennett 2004). Macaulay (2017) describes participatory research as emerging

Table 1.2 Labels given to types of participatory research and associated definitions

Label/tradition	Definition
Participatory research	'An umbrella term for a school of approaches that share a core philosophy of inclusivity and of recognising the value of engaging in the research process (rather than including only as subjects of the research) those who are intended to be the beneficiaries, users and stakeholders of the research' Macaulay (2017:256).
Co-inquiry approaches to research	A collaborative form of inquiry is about all of those involved engaging together in democratic dialogue as co-researchers and as co-subjects (Heron 1996).
Participatory action research	This approach seeks to understand and improve the world by changing it. The process is both collective (involving researchers and community members) and uses self-reflection so that all of those involved can understand and improve their research practice. Action taken is linked to the local context in which the research is being done (Baum et al 2006).
Action research/ inquiry	Action research is about creating strategies to address and improve specific issues, using action to develop services and organisations (Danley and Langer 1999).
Co-production in research	'Co-producing a research project is an approach in which researchers, practitioners and the public work together, sharing power and responsibility from the start to the end of the project, including the generation of knowledge' (Involve 2018:4).
Collaborative inquiry	DeLuca et al (2017:67) describe collaborative inquiry as engaging 'teachers as learners within their own teaching contexts with the aim of transforming teachers' conceptions of professional learning and promoting enhanced pedagogical effectiveness'.
Community-based research	Community-based research is defined as a collaboration between community groups and researchers for the purpose of creating new knowledge or trying to understand a community issue in order to bring about change. The topic or issue is generated by the community and community members participate in all aspects of the research process (Hills and Mullett 2000).
Inclusive research	The term 'inclusive research' is used when doing research *with* people who have learning disabilities (Nind 2017). Walmsley and Johnson (2003:10) define this as an approach that 'involves people who may otherwise be seen as subjects for the research as instigators of ideas, research designers, interviewers, data analysts, authors, disseminators and users'.

from both global north and global south traditions, referring to the geographical locations of key thinkers associated with the early beginnings of these approaches. These traditions are summarised in Table 1.3.

Table 1.3 History of participatory research approaches

Global north	Global south
• Lewin worked in both the UK and the US, during the 1940s to develop what is now known as action research. This cycle of continuous inquiry and associated action was conducted by society's marginalised communities, rather than on them.	• Paulo Freire (1970) questioned the values underpinning both education and research in the *Pedagogy of the Oppressed*.
• Lewin's (1948) action research approach noted the importance of promoting empowerment and social equality.	• Freire's (1970) ideas outlined the social construction of knowledge and the importance of emancipatory learning.
• Other researchers then used these approaches, developing them within broader contexts such as in organisational research.	• His ideas have been used by international agencies such as UNESCO (United Nations Educational, Scientific and Cultural Organization) to work with communities who had been excluded from the research process, in attempts to enable them to change policy and secure funding.
	• His ideas have also been used by research practitioners to create space for communities to study and understand their own social conditions, to then act and try to implement change.

Source: Adapted from Macaulay (2017) and Wallerstein et al (2017)

These methods have developed over many years and have been used across the globe, and some commentators argue that these different traditions still exist today. For example, in the US traditional research approaches remain dominant, and it is only recently that participatory approaches are starting to be recognised. Comparatively, in locations such as Brazil, participation in research is more obvious, having been used within World Health Organization approaches underpinning community development (Wallerstein et al 2017). Despite any differences, the methods are based on trying to increase social justice for those who are disadvantaged, as well as working with them and not simply doing research on them (Macaulay 2017).

Participation within health research by community members has been drawn from the Ottawa Charter (WHO 1984), which called for communities to mobilise for health justice. Some participatory research in health started within Indigenous communities in North America, when local healthcare practitioners became concerned about traditional researchers 'parachuting' in with their own agendas, then leaving without sharing their findings with community members (Macaulay 2017). During the 1990s, in this field of public health and health promotion, an approach to research started that was based on the co-production of knowledge (Israel et al 2013). This approach embraces an asset-based approach to community involvement in attempts to tackle health disparities (see Heckler 1985). Box 1.1 provides an overview of asset-based approaches.

In 2009, the International Collaboration on Participatory Health Research was established (icphr.org), and there are other collaborative networks in many locations. These networks illustrate how researchers are seeking both legitimacy

---

Box 1.1 Asset-based approaches

- Focus on the positive aspects associated with individuals; for example, what skills can they bring to a research project? This might be expert local knowledge that can be used to define the 'research problem' as well as local knowledge of an area and its many characteristics.

- Focus on the positive aspects associated with communities. For example, people may have a strong sense of belonging and feel connected to those who live within the same community.

- These 'assets' can be identified via a process called asset mapping at the start of a research project, and then used as the foundation to develop a project.

---

and more evidence about the impact of such approaches, which is a positive development for those who support participatory research (Wallerstein et al 2017). These developments have also been accompanied by changing terminology, with Hall et al (2015:26) recently writing about 'knowledge democracy', a term describing 'expertise residing in the world of practice, beyond academia'. This recognition of the importance of non-professional and non-academic expertise is one of several principles that underpin participatory research approaches.

What are the principles of participatory research?

Israel et al (2008) provide a summary of core principles, outlined in Box 1.2 below.

Box 1.2 Key principles of participatory research

- It involves participation by non-professional researchers
- It engages communities and researchers *equally* in a cooperative approach
- It is a process involving joint learning
- It involves local capacity building as well as systems development
- It is underpinned by empowerment, enabling participants to take control of their lives
- It balances research and action

Source: Adapted from Israel et al (2008)

The key principles of participatory research are outlined within the academic and practice literature and are argued to be both characteristic to such approaches as well as unchanging. Macaulay (2017:256) summarises the fundamental principles of participatory research as 'equitable co-ownership and co-decision making with full partnership engagement with academic researchers, locating power and ownership at every stage of the research process, or however the individual teams decided was equitable'.

Other authors note that community-based participatory research contrasts to traditional research paradigms by integrating non-academics into the production of research knowledge as key partners (Wallerstein et al 2008).

Epistemologically, participatory research is consistent with constructivist and critical theory paradigms, which understand knowledge as socially created (Israel et al 1998). Multiple, socially constructed realities exist, which are influenced by social, historical and cultural contexts. Therefore, participatory approaches to research acknowledge the value of multiple ways of knowing and, more significantly, recognise the value of knowledge contributed by community members (Hills and Mullett 2000). Furthermore, the researcher and the participant are interactively linked (Israel et al 1998). Therefore, participatory research approaches encourage the knower to participate in the known and generate evidence in many ways (Hills and Mullett 2000).

In ontological terms, participatory research arguably adopts a position influenced by politics. Participatory research can be used a mechanism to search for meanings that have traditionally been excluded, and often attempt to neutralise power differentials to enable participants' views to be heard (Stringer 1996). The inquirer and the participant are connected in such a way that the findings are inseparable from their relationship (Guba and Lincoln 1989), although this connection does not necessarily have to work for the benefit of the participant (see Chapter 8 for further discussion about the reality of such approaches).

In terms of methodology, the methods adopted as part of any participatory approach are said to emerge from the chosen principles and context of the project and the discussions held between those participating. Therefore, participatory research is not and arguably cannot be method driven. To provide research evidence that involves people (community members and/or service users) the people themselves should be involved in deciding what the appropriate methods are for collecting data and how the data should be analysed. Whether or not this is the always the case in practice varies according to individual projects, contexts and research approaches. Given these debates, it is useful to take some time to consider the concept of participation in Learning Task 1.2.

LEARNING TASK 1.2 WHAT IS PARTICIPATION?

Take some time to reflect on the concept of participation. What does it mean to you? Have you considered that participation may mean different things to people, and that there can be degrees and scales of participation within research projects?

Use the internet or other resources (books and journal articles) to locate examples and models of participation in the research process. Start with Arnstein's (1969) ladder, which depicts low to high levels based on involvement in the planning process in the US. Hart (1992) also has a similar model that can be applied to young people's participation. Can you see how these ladders can be applied to different research projects?

In your view, what would full participation in the research process look like?

Despite some research approaches claiming to allow community members to participate, critical scrutiny is required because of the complexities of defining the concept and achieving it fully. Participation as a concept within the literature is described as a continuum; some approaches allow it in the whole research process whereas others dictate a more limited level of participation (Goodson and Phillimore 2012). So 'full' participation varies.

Participatory research is also underpinned by principles associated with partnership working, aiming to integrate knowledge and to produce benefits to all partners involved in the research process. In an ideal model, there is shared articulation of all aspects of the research process from questions, through to data collection, analysis and the use of results. Community members and service users should ideally be involved at the earliest stages of the research, to design the research objectives and organise the project. However, partnerships in practice are not without problems, thus the principle of partnership working again requires critical scrutiny.

Participatory research approaches also rest on the principles of empowerment. They aim to build on strengths and resources within communities and to promote a co-learning and empowering process. Therefore, participants in the process arguably gain knowledge, skills, capacity and power (Israel et al 1998) resulting from their participation. However, different contexts serve to exclude participation and therefore empowerment. For example, language differences exist, and minority and vulnerable community members can be overlooked. Researchers with a lack of understanding of such groups can create problems, rather than empower.

In addition to these seminal principles defined by Israel et al (2008), others have emphasised the importance of recognising the intersectional nature of both power and privilege. For example, ethnicity, gender and sexuality, social class position and cultural heritage all affect the research process (Minkler et al 2012). Indigenous community members have also added principles related to tribal communities being afforded permission to control research processes, and highlighted the need for broader ethical principles (see Chapter 4 for further discussion of ethics). For example, they requested that all data be shared with them and suggested that they approve all publications to illustrate respect from the professionals (Walters et al 2009). While there are key principles underpinning participatory approaches, there is no single method, recipe or style that should be used when practising them.

Why is participatory research important?

Participatory research typically involves projects in which the topics explored relate to inequalities and oppression, and in sharing power between all of those involved, voice is given to groups who are socially silenced. For example, those using mental health services have clear contributions to make to research given that they have lived experience of illness (Danley and Langer 1999).

There has been a range of systematic reviews examining the evidence from participatory research in relation to health outcomes. For example, Cyril et al (2015) found that 88 per cent of the studies that they examined (n=24) had positive outcomes in terms of community engagement and health outcomes.

Those who advocate for the use of participatory research approaches also argue that they are intrinsically worthwhile because of the human benefits they create. Involvement in research, decision making and the social context in which the research is located are said to enable participants to flourish. Several beneficial results are outlined in the literature in relation to the use of participatory research approaches. These are discussed as being added extras when compared with traditional research approaches, and several of these are illustrated in Box 1.3.

Box 1.3 Benefits associated with participatory research

- The development of skills, confidence and employability among community members involved in the process (Green et al 2000).

- Those involved gain specialised knowledge (Whitmore 2001).

- Participation can also develop new social relationships, trust and social efficacy (Sclove et al 1998).

- Participation can lead to a feeling of increased control and therefore, empowerment (Papineau and Kiely 1996; Whitmore 2001).

- Involvement in research can also create leaders who represent a range of skills and functions (Greve 1975).

- Such research creates a focus on local agendas (Sclove et al 1998), allowing research to be steered in the direction of what people really want. Thus, it gives people a voice and space in which to share experiences (Watters et al 2010).

- The process of involving community members in disseminating any research findings may well lead to an increased acceptance and use of the results (Ayers 1987).

- Facilitation of change: programmes and services including those for marginalised groups often receive criticism for not recognising the reality of daily life for users, because they are designed by professionals according to their own routines, values and perceptions, or according to the organisational contexts in which they are located (Stringer 1996). Involving users allows for different views to be heard, and potentially leads to change.

- Such approaches can support the development of social capital. Participatory research involves the building up of useful contacts and the strengthening of social networks (Greve 1975; Warwick-Booth 2008).

In summary, the benefits of participatory research approaches are many, as illustrated in Box 1.3. This is not an exhaustive list, however, and outcomes are variable, therefore doing research in an inclusive manner needs careful consideration.

How can I use participatory research in an inclusive manner?

Nind (2017) uses the terms inclusive research to describe research *with* people, not *on* them in the field of learning disabilities. Her use of the concept is based on involving people in the design and conduct of the research about them, illustrating their lived experience and valuing different (non-academic and non-professional) ways of knowing. Complete Learning Task 1.3 to consider what inclusive research practice involves.

LEARNING TASK 1.3 INCLUSIVE RESEARCH PRACTICE

You are a researcher about to start working with community members as part of a participatory research project that aims to identify health needs of disabled individuals in an economically deprived neighbourhood, which is also underserved in terms of service provision. Consider the following questions.

1 How can you work to ensure that community member voices are included? In doing so, what issues do you need to consider?
2 What approaches can you take to ensure that your approach to practice is inclusive? As a starting point consider the context in which the study is being undertaken.
3 What topics may be inappropriate within such communities? It is useful to consider that in some contexts, it can be a mistake to try to engage community members in research that might further stigmatise some individuals.

Completing this learning task should have enabled you to reflect once again on the complexities, and practical issues associated with participatory research. Nind (2017) suggests that the question of what matters most in inclusive approaches really depends on the standpoint of the people involved and their views, and that there is always the opportunity to learn about such approaches for all participants (professionals and non-professionals alike). This illustrates the importance of the context in which participatory research takes place.

Importance of context

Participatory research has been used in a range of contexts (for example, education and health settings) within organisations as well as in a variety of local communities. Staley (2015) argues that in the field of health, researchers collaborating with patients/the public often acquire new knowledge in relation to the health condition, but also argues that involvement is unpredictable. Crowe et al (2015) support the need for patient involvement by illustrating the mismatch between what patients and health professionals want to study within research projects, arguing that the research community within medicine needs to make more effort to address issues of importance for patients and service users. Health is, however, just one area in which participation in research is important. Further, selected contextual examples are illustrated in Table 1.4.

Table 1.4 illustrates a small number of different contexts in which participatory research has been conducted; there are many more examples in the literature. Contextual influences are also important in terms of the support and funding provided for participatory research approaches, and the emancipation of

Table 1.4 Examples of participatory research in different contexts

Context	Research approach	Typology
Community mental health	Eight users of mental health services interviewed eight people who had also a mental illness diagnosis. They explored experiences, life goals and the influence of services on people's lives. The findings from this project were presented as a live performance, as well as within a report (Davidson et al 2010).	Action research/inquiry Users of a specific type of health service talked to other users. Their findings were used to suggest a change in the service approach as the need for a map to guide people back to ordinary life was suggested.
Co-production of online sexual violence support	Users of Rape Crisis services, and staff and trustees of the organisation were involved in a project titled Weaving the Web. Service users' views were gathered through structured events, designed to enable their participation in data gathering. These were seen as positive, useful mechanisms for ideas generation and capturing the views of those who were underserved. While the events were very successful in eliciting information, they were very structured and staff were sometimes more vocal than service users. Attendance at some of the service user events was also low (Fisher et al 2017).	Co-production in research and service development Service users views were gathered and used to co-produce the development, design and content of a new online platform for survivors of sexual abuse.
Indigenous community approaches	Visser (2012) discusses community research as a mechanism to explore HIV/AIDs in South Africa. Community researchers developed close relationships with their participants (a benefit and a challenge), and they were able to understand the local culture, arguably enhancing the validity of the research findings. However, the researchers experienced emotional trauma and had not been trained in counselling skills.	Community-based research Local community members explored the impacts of HIV on the lives of women diagnosed during pregnancy.

marginalised groups as per the principles outlined earlier in this chapter. Research is not and cannot be separate from the political context in which it exists. Political contexts can thus serve to support participatory approaches or to undermine them. Wallerstein et al (2017) noted the troubling presidential context in the US (2017–21) in which vulnerable groups were likely to be further excluded in a range of ways. Equally, the British social policy context of austerity and welfare state retrenchment is one in which poor and underserved communities are being further excluded (Alston 2018).

Universities as a context

The roles that researchers adopt when engaging in participatory approaches have been described as exceptions to typical research culture found in environments such as universities, because of the need for cultural change, commitment to participatory approaches, researcher interpersonal skills and different perceptions of the importance of ethnicity, power and privilege (Wang et al 2017). However, some universities do engage in participatory and community research, as do other non-university organisations such as private companies and consultants. Examples of such approaches in which university staff adopt non-traditional research roles are varied, but community research poses several challenges in terms of control, power, ownership (of the process and any associated data), time-lines and whether community researchers are really adopting the role of a researcher (Flicker et al 2007). To explore these issues in more depth, attempt Learning Task 1.4 which will facilitate reflection through the exploration of practical toolkits.

LEARNING TASK 1.4 UNIVERSITIES AND PARTICIPATORY RESEARCH

Staff and students at universities can and do engage in participatory research within community contexts, despite the challenges of doing this. Use the internet to find the following toolkits published by Beacon North East (2011, 2012). You can find these via Durham University web pages.

- Community toolkit: A guide to working with universities on research projects (www.dur.ac.uk/socialjustice/toolkits/community/)
- Co-inquiry toolkit: Community-university participatory research partnerships: co-inquiry and related approaches (www.dur.ac.uk/socialjustice/toolkits/coinquiry/)

Read one (or both) of these, making notes on the key points especially from the 'top tips' and 'other things to consider' sections.

What is your key learning from completing this activity?

In completing Learning Task 1.4, you will have had the opportunity to think about participatory research being about equal relationships between community members and others involved in the research process (for example, university staff and students). There are clearly many challenges when professionals and community researchers work together, and some of these are explored in detail in later chapters (see Chapter 9 for discussion about community–campus partnerships).

• •

CASE STUDY WORKING WITH CHILDREN IN PARTICIPATORY RESEARCH APPROACHES

The United Nations Convention on the Rights of the Child was ratified in 1992 (Unicef 2018) and has led to debates that are ongoing in terms of the participation of children. Participation in research is still under discussion to ensure that children are both protected during the process and enabled to give genuine voice (Samrova and Cummings 2017). Many researchers offer a political commitment to give voice to those who are marginalised (which is assumed to include children) via participatory approaches. However, others note that caution should be exercised given that childhood is not a homogeneous experience and not all child voices are equally valued and heard (James 2007).

Examples of participatory approaches with children include draw-and-write techniques, with these described as non-threatening and child-friendly. This approach has been used in research to explore children's views of health (Bradding and Horstman 2009). Woodall et al (2014) used the draw-and-write technique with 21 children aged three to five years old, to explore their views on oral hygiene while they were participating in scheme to encourage toothbrushing within school. This approach to data collection was developed in the UK during the 1980s (Hartel 2014) and is generally seen as a participatory method in which children of all ages can take part (Backett-Milburn and McKie 1999). The technique was pioneered by Wetton who used the technique to understand children's views on drugs (Wetton and McWhirter 1998). Data gathered from the draw-and-write activities that were used to explore the toothbrushing intervention consistently showed children smiling and enjoying toothbrushing (Woodall et al 2013). It is argued to be of use with school-aged children as most are used to drawing and writing, and it can support exploratory research aims while encouraging children's participation in an ethical and non-intrusive manner. Research based on draw and write can inform adults of children's views and thus enhance researcher understanding (Bradding and Horstman 2009). Furthermore, participation in research has been noted as resulting in positive outcomes for children in terms of increased knowledge of topics and better awareness of social justice, as well as skills development (Samrova and Cummings 2017).

Other approaches to encouraging the participation of children within the research process have used arts-based techniques. Mand (2012) describes research with Bangladeshi children in migratory circumstances, conducted in two London schools. The approach involved participatory activities, interviews, observation and art workshops. In one school, children were asked to sketch images of being at home and images of being away. These were then used to create bunting, which was hung in an exhibition space. In the other school, an artist was employed to work with children using graffiti to illustrate literal and spiritual journeys. These visual methods are argued to be child-centred, enabling participation via enjoyment. However, the accompanying researcher narrative provided in this instance was recognised as reasserting her authority over the voice of the children (Mand 2012).

Summary

- Participatory research approaches have a number of different labels and definitions, but they are different from traditional research in the ways in which they encourage the involvement of non-experts and community members within the research process. There is a long history associated with community-based participatory approaches within both the global north and south.

- Participatory research approaches are governed by a range of principles including involvement, participation, partnership working, empowerment, action and learning. Successfully applying these principles in practice can result in a range of benefits for all of those involved in the research process. However, this is not without challenges.

- The contexts in which participatory research takes place are varied in terms of location, the roles that researchers adopt, the nature of projects and the organisations involved. Context is an important factor in the application of participatory research.

Suggestions for further reading

1 Minkler, N. and Wallerstein, N. (2008) (eds) *Community-based participatory research for health: from process to outcomes*, 2nd edition, Jossey-Bass, San Francisco.
   These authors who lead the field in terms of writing about community-based research have produced this updated edited collection. It covers all of the principles of such approaches and offers detailed case studies to illustrate examples of research approaches.

2 Hind, M. (2014) *What is inclusive research?*, London: Bloomsbury Academic.
   This is a book that defines inclusive research, comparing it to participatory, emancipatory research and user-led approaches, as well as noting how this field has evolved. There are illustrated exemplars to show the reader how to do this and accompanying reflections about the challenges of such work.

3 Goodson, L. and Phillimore, J. (eds) (2012) *Community research for participation: from theory to method*, Bristol: Policy Press.

This is an edited book drawing up chapters from a range of different disciplines, introducing the reader to theoretical and practical debates. There are recommendations, debates and reflections throughout, providing useful insights for those new to this area.

Questions for reflection

1 How will you adapt your approach to ensure that you are using the principles of participatory research in practice? In your view, are some principles easier to achieve than others, and if so, how might this influence your approach?

2 In which research situations do you think participatory approaches can be used? Might some situations lend themselves more easily to such approaches?

3 Why are you considering using participatory research methods? In terms of your own identified topic area, reflect on the benefits and disadvantages of such approaches with specific reference to your own research project (for example, are you attempting to give voice to groups that are not usually afforded this?).

Top tips for practice

1 Consult manuals as a mechanism to support your own approach. There are many examples of manuals detailing participatory research, across a range of contexts. Those delivering in practice have shared their experiences, learning and practical approaches. So, use these as a starting point to help you.

2 Allow lots of time for your research study to develop through discussion. There will need to be space and time for conversations about all aspects of the research process; for example, in terms of the levels of involvement for community members, including them in the areas that they wish to participate in, hearing their ideas about how to 'do' data collection and listening to their views. There may be disagreements, power imbalances, criticisms and ongoing debates, all of which will take time to resolve – more so than in traditional projects, where the principal investigator can take the lead and make a decision.

3 Be flexible and be creative – you may well need to change your ideas and plans based on the dialogue that you have, and your approach is likely to need tailoring. For example, how will you train community researchers (assuming this is a need that they identify) and how will you support them while working alongside them? Participants are likely to have different needs, hence the need for flexibility.

Further teaching and learning resources to accompany this book can be found at https://bristoluniversitypress.co.uk/creating-participatory-research-website. The companion website includes:

- teaching slides for lecturers
- further information on learning tasks
- lesson activities
- further reading, links to websites and practical resources
- examples from practice
- additional case studies

2

Co-production as an approach

Key learning outcomes

By the end of this chapter, you should be able to:

- Define the concept of co-production and understand why it is important in relation to participatory research

- Demonstrate awareness of the principles and values associated with undertaking co-produced approaches to participatory research

- Identify several challenges associated with co-production as an approach to research

Introduction

This chapter will introduce the concept of co-production in research, because this is a term increasingly being used in a range of fields, though not always consistently. So, what does co-produced research look like? What are the principles of co-produced research? Co-production in service design in health and social care has been taking place with support from policy makers for many years, and co-production is now used within the field of research. This chapter will explore co-production in research, examining how it is defined, debated and used, and explore its relationship with participatory research. Co-production as a research approach is said to offer a mechanism for being inclusive. This chapter will explore how this works in practice, drawing on the experiences of those using it to offer examples of the operation of such approaches in reality.

What is co-production?

Co-production as a term has been gaining ground within public policy reform across the globe (OECD 2011). However, it is not a new concept. The term co-production refers to people working together jointly who traditionally would have been separated into different groups (Durose et al 2017), such as service user versus service provider and researcher versus participant. Co-production is a concept and term that was introduced to UK policy in the Department of Health's Putting People First policy for personalisation and transformation, and further developed by New Economics Foundation (among other organisations). Despite its recognition in policy terms, co-production lacks conceptual clarity – it has been identified as a 'woolly-word' in public policy (Osborne et al 2016:640), and described as having elasticity as a term (Durose et al 2017).

Co-production as a term has been historically used in the context of public service delivery but it is now increasingly being used in relation to research contexts (Durose and Richardson 2015). However, research methodologies that are based on co-production and/or seek to evaluate co-production are in their infancy. Box 2.1 provides some example definitions of co-production in research.

Box 2.1 Defining co-production in research

- Oliver et al (2019:33) provide the following explanation of co-production in the research process: 'a collaborative model of research that includes stakeholders in the research process'.
- 'Co-producing a research project is an approach in which researchers, practitioners and the public work together, sharing power and responsibility from the start to the end of the project, including in the generation of knowledge' (Hickey et al 2018:4).
- Flinders et al (2016:264) define the co-production of knowledge as 'the design, administration and dissemination of academic knowledge through collaboration'.

As Box 2.1 illustrates, there are several different definitions of term co-production and the wider literature offers more. Hickey et al (2018) note that the term is difficult to define because it emerges from a wide range of disciplines. For example, Metz et al (2019) note that the term 'co-creation' is also being used more frequently to describe close, collaborative working. Therefore, it is important to recognise that there are ambiguities attached to the term 'co-production' and others like it. Furthermore, similar to the history of participatory approaches, Holmes (2017) argues that the co-production or co-creation of research is not new because action-based research traditions lay claim to a long history, as outlined in Chapter 1.

Why is co-production important?

Co-production in research draws on the tenets of participatory action research (see Chapter 1) as well as knowledge exchange principles; therefore, collaboration between researchers and users aims to 'dissolve the boundary between producers and users – all forms of expertise (among academics, practitioners, business and the public) are considered valuable and contribute to knowledge production' (British Academy 2008:43). Flinders et al (2016) note that co-production in research has its origins in both the epistemological and methodological concerns that academic knowledge is too exclusionary because of the social and political environment in which it sits. There are a range of people beyond the confines of academia who are able to contribute to research legitimately. Co-production is then seen as a positive process in terms of opening up research and offering more equality. Co-production has also been described as an approach that can address the 'gaps' between different communities involved in research: for example, academics and policy makers (Wehrens 2014). Jasanoff (2004) offers a co-production framework for the development of scientific and political relations and suggests that such approaches are about interpreting complex phenomena through partnerships involving various social actors.

Similar to the promises associated with various modes of participatory research (again, see Chapter 1 for more on this), co-production promises to be transformative for those involved (Flinders et al 2016). Co-production also offers promise in terms of the outcomes associated with the research; for example, the findings are seen as more likely to be taken up and used (British Academy 2008). Co-production is therefore based on the assumptions that those affected by research are in the best position to design it, do it, be involved and that their skills are as important as those of professional researchers (Hickey et al 2018). Box 2.2 outlines reasons to co-produce.

Box 2.2 Why co-produce?

Oliver et al (2019) summarise the four main arguments in favour of using co-production that are used within the literature:

1 *Substantive* – engagement is undertaken to improve the quality of the research. In talking with others, researchers discover unknowns and create new knowledge via partnership involvement.
2 *Instrumental* – using co-production is a way to ensure that research outputs are more useable, with both research questions and findings described as being implementable.
3 *Normative* – co-produced research is seen as having more value intrinsically because universities should work with civil society, in the public interest. Co-productive approaches are also seen as being more ethical, and transformative as a result of collaborative working.
4 *Political* – co-production has been justified on political grounds by many researchers in the sense that involvement can be empowering for lay researchers and increase the relevance of the research. Working with communities who are seen as disempowered and marginalised is political because it is about trying to enact change.

As you can see from Box 2.2, there are a variety of reasons why researchers choose to work in a co-productive research context. Beebeejaun et al (2015:556) argue that 'co-production as a means of generating public value allows us to reimagine the role of communities in research and challenge the current model which sees minimal intervention into participants time [...] which limits their role to informants to increase our knowledge'. Co-production in research also matters because of the principles that underpin it as an approach.

What are the principles of co-production?

Hickey (2018) highlights that there is no one set way of co-producing research, because it is principle driven. The use of a principles-based approach means that co-production can take a range of formats. Box 2.3 illustrates the key principles underpinning co-production as discussed in the literature.

Box 2.3 Summary of key principles of co-production
- Hickey et al (2018) outline several principles underpinning co-produced research:
  Sharing power in key decisions – with people having joint ownership and working together.
  Inclusion – with research team members ensuring that those who can contribute are included, and that diversity is embraced.
  Equality – everyone involved has equal importance; therefore, they should be respected and the knowledge that they have should be valued.
  Reciprocity – the contributions made by everyone should be recognised, as everyone benefits from working together.
  Relationship building – there is emphasis on relationships as key to sharing power, which requires consensus and clarity in relation to roles and responsibilities.

- *Valuing knowledge as experience* – thinking differently about how academic knowledge can be generated and used is an important principle of co-produced research (Flinders et al 2016).

- *Politics of presence* – the inclusion of marginalised groups ensures representation of broader voice, noting that while such groups have their own biases, their involvement can reveal the unnoticed partiality carried by researchers (Young 2000). Politics of presence is therefore argued to transform the research process (Beebeejaun et al 2015).

- Nesta (2012) also outlines several principles based on 'people-powered health co-production':
  Reciprocity and mutuality – offering people a range of incentives to engage, enabling reciprocal relationships, mutual responsibilities and expectations.
  Blurring distinctions – removing distinctions between professionals and others.
  Asset recognition – transforming people from passive recipients into equal partners.

- The principle of openness should also be applied to co-productive approaches. Openness requires high levels of reflexivity and the willingness to modify perspectives/values in an ongoing learning process (Fisher 2016).

- Durose et al (2011) note the importance of empowerment as a principle underpinning co-production in research. In putting this into practice, researchers work 'with' community members who are given more control in the process, in comparison to traditional approaches.

Hickey et al (2018) acknowledge that the extent to which each co-produced research project can embrace the principles will vary, and that it is useful to view the principles as an underpinning pathway along the route to co-production in research. Complete Learning Task 2.1 to reflect on the relationship between co-productive principles and participatory approaches to research.

LEARNING TASK 2.1 CO-PRODUCTION AND PARTICIPATORY RESEARCH: DIFFERENT PRINCIPLES?

1 Revisit Chapter 1, specifically Box 1.2, and remind yourself of the principles that underpin participatory approaches to research.
2 Compare these principles with those discussed in Box 2.2. in this chapter.
3 In what ways are the principles the same?
4 Are there any differences?
5 If the principles underpinning both of these approaches are the same, does this mean that there are no differences between the ways in which these approaches work in practice?

Having completed the learning task, you will have seen that the principles underpinning co-productive and participatory approaches to research have much in common. Locock and Boaz (2019:409) discuss how different approaches to involvement such as participatory research, co-production and co-design 'sit alongside each other […] [but] they share some underpinning philosophies and all are prone to be challenged on the grounds of tokenism despite avowed good intentions'. However, some researchers while recognising these commonalities argue that applying these principles in practice results in differences. Kagan (2013) argues that co-production is more than participatory research because participation can be at one or many stages of the research process, and therefore can be seen as existing on a continuum. In contrast, while co-production has participation at the heart of the process, it is underpinned by sense making achieved through joint reflection. For Kagan (2013), co-production is therefore more than participation because it is about sense making in all of the following areas:

- Co-produced knowledge
- Co-produced ideas
- Co-produced methods
- Co-produced data collection
- Co-produced data analysis
- Co-produced dissemination

Similarly, Beebeejaun et al (2013:39) suggest that:

An understanding of co-production in research therefore has the following elements: a more equal partnership with communities and practitioners; working in a dynamic relationship to understand issues, create knowledge and then implement findings for transformational social change. This approach to research is underpinned by respect for different bases for expertise and claims to knowledge, a research production process that allows genuine participation at all stages, and transparency in the values informing the inception of the work.

In Beebeejaun et al's (2013:39) description of co-production, the approach is also argued to encourage reflexivity and reflection, as a mechanism to explore the ways in which research is socially situated and produced (Gillard et al 2012). Co-productive approaches still hold other commonalities with participatory research in that they are different from traditional research approaches because they offer another model via which to do research, in relation to decision making and joint enquiry (Oliver et al 2019).

How are co-produced approaches different from traditional research approaches?

Chapter 1 provides a detailed discussion about the differences between traditional research approaches that are controlled by professionals such as academic researchers, and participatory approaches which aim to broaden involvement and address power dynamics in the research process. Co-productive approaches to research have similarly emerged as a potential solution to the criticisms of traditional research of failing to meaningfully include community members (Durose et al 2011). Co-production is therefore different from traditional research approaches as it is less expert driven (Fischer 2000), and better informed by community members' preferences (Ostrom 1996). Perspectives of community members can be dismissed by researchers using traditional methods, illustrating that there are hidden power dynamics at play in the research process (Orr and Bennett 2009).

A recent and influential initiative of the N8 Research Partnership (N8) and of the Economic and Social Research Council (ESRC) titled *Knowledge that matters: Realizing the potential of co-production* (N8/ESRC 2016) asks researchers to abandon traditional research approaches in favour of flexibility, the blurring of boundaries, and for an expanded and altered understanding of research that sees all partners as experts with different forms of knowledge that are of equal value. The N8/ESRC document advocates a two-phase approach that focuses on partnerships and prioritises what is at stake (rather than being led by precise research questions).

Table 2.1 provides an overview summary of the differences between traditional research and those employing co-production. As Table 2.1 shows, co-production in the research process is based on redefining the role of the researcher in relation to

Table 2.1 Overview: differences between traditional and co-produced research approaches

Traditional research	Co-produced research
Academics (university staff) and or other experts remain in control of the research process.	Community members are much more involved in the research process, and knowledge production is interactive. Knowledge is created through the meeting of different social worlds and acknowledgement of the importance of lived experience. The presence of marginalised groups changes the dynamics of representation and transforms the nature of the research process.
The research is about the needs of the university/researchers and the interests of the academics. The value of the research is about its scientific contribution.	The merit of the research is located in the 'public value' that is brings. Researchers are accountable to those with whom they have built relationships (community members).
Research outputs are often presented in the form of reports, papers and conference proceedings, within contexts limited to professional researchers.	Co-productive outputs are about improving issues within the community, social change, and the achievement of social justice. The potential audience with interest in the findings is usually broader, with dissemination being in beyond-text format.

Source: Adapted from Durose et al (2011)

ways of working within communities. Coutts (2019) notes that the co-production of evidence involves co-designing the research at its development stage, the involvement of non-professionals in data gathering (for example, peer-to-peer interviewing), the involvement of all in analysis, and feedback into the community to put the research into action. Pohl et al (2010) suggest that co-production rests on developing a shared thought style, which is in stark contrast to the more traditional approaches in which academics lead. Furthermore, Beebeejaun et al (2013) also highlight that university research governance structures are largely immune to engaging with communities and their research needs and priorities, therefore co-production is a radical re-evaluation of the ways in which universities should engage with them. However, as earlier chapters showed, working in non-traditional ways raises a range of dilemmas and challenges.

Dilemmas and challenges when using co-production

Beebeejaun et al (2015) point out that while co-production is offered as a solution to some of the problems that arise when using traditional research approaches, it is not simply the answer to all issues. Co-production needs to be understood as a facilitator in attempts to create more relevant solutions. Considerable challenges in evaluating the impact of research co-production remain (Durose et al 2014; Loeffler and Bovaird 2016) for a range of reasons. Therefore, researchers need to acknowledge that not every research project can be co-produced (Kagan 2013).

Durose et al (2017) point out that despite the use of the term in policy circles, there is little formal evidence to support its use. In addition, the existing evidence is limited as it tends to be in the form of case studies, published by organisations committed to working in a co-productive manner. There is a lack of longitudinal evaluation data, and little exploration about why co-production is expected to produce the benefits that are described by advocates. Indeed, the subjective benefits attributed to using co-production (for example, enhanced wellbeing and participation) cannot be adequately assessed by methodologies that are reliant on measurement. Further, evaluating co-production requires a focus on processes rather than pre-determined outcomes. Gillard et al (2010) argue that based on their experiences, more research is needed to explore expertise, knowledge and knowing within co-production approaches, because knowledge and expertise shift over time as do the identities of those involved. Box 2.4 provides an overview of some of the challenges of using co-productive research.

Box 2.4 Challenges when using co-produced research

• Flinders et al (2016) offer reflections about the limits and risks linked to co-produced research, noting that those involved may have different expectations, the validity of the research may be compromised, and that there are likely to be power imbalances.

• Oliver et al (2019) note that challenges are likely to arise throughout the life cycle of any co-produced project, because the direction of the research cannot possibly reflect the values and priorities of all of those involved. It may also be the case that time is invested in relationships for no concrete output and tense relationships may well need to be managed throughout the research process.

• Durose et al (2017) note that many co-produced activities are small-scale, which can compromise validity.

• Kagan (2013) lists a range of challenges, including: issues with trust; the likelihood that people who are 'mouthier' get involved; difficulties with establishing genuine partnerships; limited funding opportunities (which usually come after initial investment in relationships and trust building); and negotiations about authorship and ownership.

• Kagan (2012) reports a range of obstacles to this type of research drawn from her own experiences. These include the power of gatekeepers in influencing the ways in which the research is framed and attempted control over the dissemination of findings from professionals.

• Kagan (2007) also discusses the tyranny of co-production, suggesting that sometimes people do not want to get involved, or are unable to. In such circumstances, do researchers then just go ahead, including only those who can/want to participate?

• Wolfson et al (2017) point out that researchers can often have 'lofty' goals in expecting community members to become engaged with interpreting the research results, and that they are often specifically interested in achieving outcomes for their own community, rather than thinking about the broader implications of the work.

Even those who advocate for the use of co-productive research approaches acknowledge that barriers exist (Martin 2010). The privileging of some forms of knowledge over others is an issue in terms of experts being perceived as knowing more that lay people (Porter 2010), with research often remaining exclusionary (Durose et al 2011). Practical issues and tensions mean that the time-scales of researchers and community members can be different (Martin 2010), and while the principles underpinning co-production are admirable, does intending to create social change always result in this happening (Riger 1992)? Co-productive approaches to research are also discussed as a way to work with 'hard to reach' and marginalised groups; however, these are constructed labels which reflect power within the research process, as it is usually researchers (the powerful) who define such categories (Durose et al 2011). Flinders et al (2016:266) argue that 'co-production is a risky method of social inquiry for academics. It is time-consuming, ethically complex, emotionally demanding, inherently unstable, vulnerable to external shocks, subject to competing demands and expectations, and other scholars (journals, funders, and so on) may not even recognise its outputs as representing "real" research.' Oliver et al (2019) argue that mindful engagement is needed when using co-production to ensure that ethical research is a reality because of the range of costs involved. These are illustrated in Figure 2.1.

Several questions remain in need of debate in recognition of the evident challenges associated with co-production in the research process. Indeed, Oliver et al (2019) can also be challenged in relation to the terminology used in their discussion of academic 'researchers' with 'skills and expertise' and 'lay people'

Figure 2.1 Potential costs of co-production

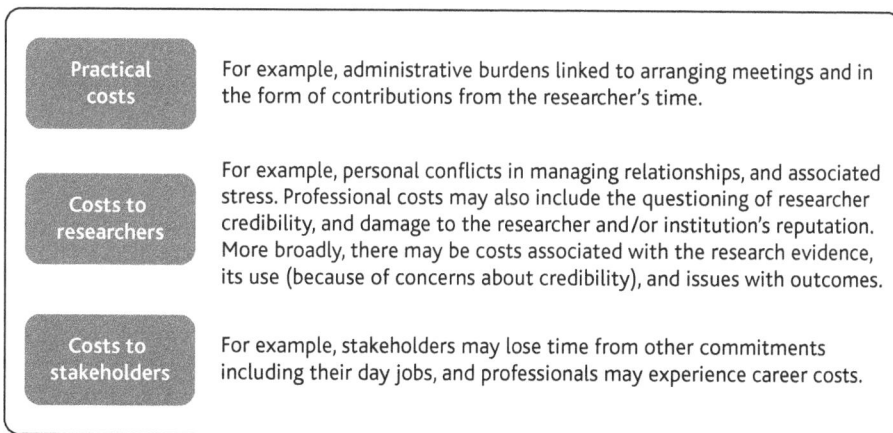

Practical costs	For example, administrative burdens linked to arranging meetings and in the form of contributions from the researcher's time.
Costs to researchers	For example, personal conflicts in managing relationships, and associated stress. Professional costs may also include the questioning of researcher credibility, and damage to the researcher and/or institution's reputation. More broadly, there may be costs associated with the research evidence, its use (because of concerns about credibility), and issues with outcomes.
Costs to stakeholders	For example, stakeholders may lose time from other commitments including their day jobs, and professionals may experience career costs.

Source: Adapted from Oliver et al (2019)

with their 'experiences', which does not accurately represent the reality of these approaches (see Chapter 8), or indeed the asset-based approaches discussed later in Chapter 9.

Complete Learning Task 2.2, to consider some of the key questions that remain unanswered when using co-productive approaches.

LEARNING TASK 2.2 EXPLORING QUESTIONS AND CHALLENGES WHEN CO-PRODUCING EVALUATION

You are a researcher who has been commissioned by a community group to evaluate an intervention that is aiming to improve the mental health of 'hard to reach' community members, in a specific geographical location. The community group has received external funding to deliver the intervention and is expected to employ an independent researcher to assess their success. They are keen to co-produce the evaluation.

Consider the following questions (adapted from Hickey et al 2018).

1 Can we really achieve power sharing? Current approaches to the funding of research projects often present significant challenges to co-productive approaches.
2 Do current structures support and enable co-production? For example, your own organisational governance protocols, may be a limiter. More broadly, can you co-produce and be a truly independent researcher, given that relationships are central to the process?
3 Can we judge and evaluate co-production? Given the definitional diversity noted in the literature, how can we assess whether a research project really has been co-produced? What benchmarks (if any) could you use in this situation?
4 Can we ensure that co-produced research is taken seriously and given credibility? If those delivering a service are also influencing its evaluation, does this make the findings less scientific? How might the funder expectations influence the research and compromise its integrity?

Having completed Learning Task 2.2, you will have had time to reflect on several questions and challenges in relation to the reality of using co-production. Researchers such as Flinders et al (2016) therefore discuss co-production as a risky method of social enquiry because it is time consuming, and is likely to be more ethically challenging and emotionally demanding than traditional research projects. Furthermore, they argue that the politics of co-production need further acknowledgement as broader societal inequalities may have negative consequences for researchers and participants, so there are risks associated with such approaches. In addition, these inequalities might serve to prevent co-produced research from achieving its promises of more equal social outcomes. Flinders et al (2016) are not denying the potential of co-produced research; rather, they are pointing out the importance of wider power relationships, expectations and priorities, which affect the research process. In their view, it is important to acknowledge that there is a rhetoric versus reality gap. In light of these challenges, Table 2.2 illustrates the importance of context in informing decisions about when to co-produce, especially as Martin (2010:217) outlines that 'what works best will vary according to the context'.

Table 2.2 Choosing when to use co-production

Co-production is less likely to work when …	Co-production is more likely to work when …
The area of research is controversial and the findings may be challenged.	The area of research is viewed positively and the findings are likely to be accepted.
Conflicts of interest will make it difficult to manage roles.	There are likely to be few conflicts of interest.
The findings are not going to be used directly in relation to policy and/or management decisions.	The goal of the project is to use the findings for either policy or management decisions.
Funders value expert knowledge and scientific approaches to research.	Funders are not concerned about types of knowledge or scientific findings.
The purpose of the research is well defined from the outset.	The purpose of the research needs to be refined, tested for feasibility and its acceptability considered.
There is limited time and resources for involving stakeholders at various points in the research.	Time and resources are available to involve stakeholders in the research process.

Source: Adapted from Oliver et al (2019)

Table 2.2 is a summary of some considerations that researchers need to make when deciding if co-productive approaches to research are feasible. Locock and Boaz (2019) also point out the importance of methodological and practical considerations in research projects. Furthermore, as Oliver et al (2019) note, it is important to be reflective about how co-production influences the process of research when such approaches are applied in practice.

Case studies of co-production in practice

Co-produced research is now much more widely discussed in the literature, and there are many case studies of example ways of working. Illustrative examples of co-production in practice can be found in a range of fields. Complete Learning Task 2.3 to find some examples of co-production described by those who have engaged with this approach to research.

LEARNING TASK 2.3 EXPLORING EXPERIENCES OF CO-PRODUCTION

There are now many reflections from people involved in co-production activities. Use the internet to find the Social Care Institute for Excellence web-site (www. scie.org.uk/co-production/). Navigate this website to find the section about co-production. SCIE has supported a national co-production week since 2017, and there are accompanying blogs from people involved. The 2019 blog focuses on 'designing, delivering and evaluating services in equal partnerships with people who use services'.

1 Explore the 2019 blog posts, and their content – reading the contributions that those involved in co-producing evidence have made.
2 Review the blog posts and the reflections that people offer about co-production in practice.
3 What is the key message that you gather from this activity, e.g. are those involved positive about their experiences? What does the reality of co-production actually look like?

Having completed Learning Task 2.3, you will have been able to see that there are many different ways in which evidence can be co-produced, across a range of fields. For example, the Dutch Academic Collaborative Centres for Public Health provide an infrastructure to support co-production, usually between public health services and universities. This framework has resulted in projects such as Healthy in the City. Healthy in the City focused on co-producing policy solutions to tackle the health disadvantages of the Rotterdam population (Wehrens 2014). Sherriff et al (2019) offer another example of successful co-creation in Aboriginal health research, describing SEARCH (Study of Environment on Aboriginal Resilience and Child Health). SEARCH has been used for a decade to build a sustainable partnership across policy, clinical, community and research settings, working as a mechanism to improve Aboriginal health. Table 2.3 provides further illustrative examples of how co-production has been used within several different research projects.

As well as offering examples of co-production in the research process, the literature is also a useful resource for advice on how to use co-production within research.

How can I use co-production within participatory research practice?

Hickey et al (2018) offer several tips to those who are co-producing a research project.

1. Ground rules need to be established.
2. There should be ongoing dialogue between all of those working on the research project.

Co-production as an approach

Table 2.3 Examples of co-production in the research process

Context	Co-productive approach	Outputs
A research project with Indigenous (Atikamekw) women in Canada, which involved co-production of the research design.	Basile et al (2018) discuss how their research project focused on Indigenous women's roles in land governance was co-produced. The research project was led by an Atikamekw woman. The project started with preliminary interviews being conducted with Atikamekw women, representing the communities of study. These women were asked to comment on the research process, and to discuss their preferred approach. Researchers asked community members about the best time to schedule research activities, the thematic content of the interview guide, and the consent form that had been designed by the researchers in line with their institution's ethics board requirements and in accordance with guidelines for working with Indigenous communities. Atikamekw women showed great interest in the design of the consent form and offered comments on the suggested measures for confidentiality and anonymity, confirming the importance of these principles within their communities.	Atikamekw women shaped the wording of the consent form and taught the researchers that consent is a process needed to build respectful relationships, not just a process to follow (see Chapter 4 for more on ethics). Basile et al (2018) argue that if research is to be decolonised then research tools should not be developed within universities but via collaborations with research participants.
Service user involvement in the development of a questionnaire.	Chambers et al (2016) describe their approach to seeking service user involvement in the development of a questionnaire for use within mental health research. Prior to service user involvement the research team generated a pool of statements for inclusion in the questionnaire based on themes that they had gathered from the academic literature. Service users were recruited to work on an expert panel and to offer their feedback to the researchers. They discussed the need for the statements to be personalised, which led researchers to include the words 'I' and 'me' in each of the statements. The tool was then tested with other service users who were already connected to the university. Service users provided feedback via a focus group discussion which used an informal 'think aloud' approach. This resulted in further changes to the wording, layout and structure of the questionnaire.	Service user contributions shaped the ways in which the survey questions were phrased and presented, so that their input contributed to the design of the therapeutic engagement questionnaire. Chambers et al (2016) argue that the development of this tool involving service users is positive because it can potentially benefit care and treatment for others, as well as enabling professionals to be better able to plan and allocate resources.

3. There needs to be joint ownership of key decisions.
4. There should be a commitment to relationship building.
5. Opportunities for personal growth and development should be available.
6. Flexibility is an important element in co-production to allow research ideas to evolve and develop.
7. Continuous reflection will be needed to allow research team members the space to consider how they are working together.
8. Evaluate the impact of the research while recognising that the end products of co-produced research projects are often different from those produced by a traditional academic process.

As noted earlier, co-production is significantly shaped by context. Nolan et al (2003) argued in favour of a 'senses' framework. All of those involved in the research should feel that what they do matters and that they are valued as a person of worth. To be clear 'the senses framework' is not synonymous with co-production but it has been identified a creating a social environment which supports co-production.

Oliver et al (2019) suggest being cautious in considering when to use co-production and paying attention to context (see Table 2.2). They provide a range of questions for consideration including:

1. In what ways are all of those involved contributing to the process? Funders give money, researchers have skills and expertise, and lay people contribute their experiences.
2. At what points of the research process are each of the contributions useful? For example, patients are better placed to talk about user experiences than to be placed in roles which require them to have methodological expertise.
3. What costs are involved and how are they going to be managed?
4. How will decision making be both conducted and governed?

While stating that co-production in research is exciting and has the ability to generate new and different outputs, Oliver et al (2019) in posing these questions note the importance of time, investment, skills and respect in such approaches. They also note that when engaging in co-production, much more reflection is needed about how this changes the research process from all of those involved.

Holmes (2017) argues that when researchers commit to co-production, this has to include them also recognising that it is challenging because of power imbalances and the need for difficult conversations. However, researchers can put mechanisms in place to support co-productive approaches to research. Boivin et al (2014) point to three areas that require attention in the co-production of research:

1. *Credibility* This comes from participants learning each other's language and understanding the value of all contributions. It can also be developed further by skill building during the research process.

2. *Legitimacy* Participants need to be clear about who it is that they are representing (those who use services, other professionals, patients and so on). There should be an understanding that access to community groups or related data is not the same as producing statistically significant research findings.

3. *Power* All participants must be able to influence decisions. To ensure that this is achieved, facilitation is a critical element of the research process, as well as the use of ground rules and agenda-setting.

Sherriff et al (2019) describe nine success factors in the use of a co-productive approach in an Aboriginal context. These factors include power sharing, shared goals, risk-taking, empowerment of the community, valuing local knowledge, investment in the collaboration and adaptation. They argue that co-creation in research is therefore possible, as well as necessary to improve health-related research.

Given the growing interest in co-production in research, funders have now started to create resources to support researchers who wish to co-produce evidence. Complete Learning Task 2.4 to explore these resources.

LEARNING TASK 2.4 EXPLORING RESOURCES THAT SUPPORT CO-PRODUCTION

Use the internet to find resources that funding agencies have made available for those who wish to engage in co-productive research. For example, the Connecting Communities programme website has a section on it labelled resources. This is funded by the Arts and Humanities Research Council. The National Institute for Health Research website also has a section titled 'Resources for co-producing research'.

1 Find these websites and explore their content.
2 Select one or more of these resources and read them.
3 Were the resources helpful in shaping your knowledge of how to co-produce research? What were the key points of learning that you gathered from this activity?
4 Is there a model of co-production that you could use to underpin your own approach in practice?

In completing Learning Task 2.4, you will have had the opportunity to think about some of the practical issues related to co-production, and despite the many challenges that are discussed in this chapter, and within the resources that are available on the internet, discussion of co-production is growing within the academic literature.

CASE STUDY SERVICE USER EXPERIENCES OF CO-PRODUCTION

Leanne is a patient champion who volunteers with a clinical commissioning group in the north of England. She has delivered co-production training to other patient champions and co-produced risk training to healthcare professionals.

What does co-production mean from a volunteer perspective?

Leanne stresses the 'problem' should be defined in collaboration. One of the most difficult aspects of this work in the health service is that the problem is defined by medical professionals/management and then they seek to co-produce a solution. When put on the spot to describe what co-production is, Leanne explains that it's

> 'Everybody working together and everybody's experiences being valued ... not dependent on what background they've got, so if they're somebody [...] who's in a paid role or somebody who's got lived experience or somebody who's an academic, who's got a different viewpoint, then I think it's valuing the person and their ideas without judging whose knowledge is more important.'

Why is co-production a good thing?

Co-production is important because it's more effective in bringing together different viewpoints you might not consider. Additionally, when it comes to using co-production to plan changes to services, people who have been part of the process will generally be more supportive of the results. The important thing is to be upfront about limitations and not rule out this approach because it can't be perfect, as Leanne explains:

> '[E]ven if it's not 100% gold standard co-production, it doesn't mean it's not worth doing because there are times when it's not practical for it to be one hundred per cent true co-production and there might be there may be time issues and resource issues ... but you can still consult people and value them.'

Change through co-production

Leanne co-produced the design and delivery of interactive clinical risk training, which included using her personal experience as a living case study. The participants had valuable learning experience from real situations, and Leanne found that being able to use personal experiences to improve things for other people was very therapeutic.

Warning!

The things Leanne has been involved in have been good examples of co-production but she is keen that people don't use it as a buzzword without really knowing what it means.

Leanne's experiences reflect those of other service users who work as peer researchers, within mental health contexts in the UK. Gibson (2013) illustrates the importance of service user involvement in the form of co-production, to shape the focus of research topics, to engage people as participants, in a supportive manner and to produce research findings that honour multiple perspectives, which therefore have greater relevance for service users.

Summary

- Co-production in research is not easy to define but involves approaches that are different from traditional research in terms of the involvement of non-experts and community members within the research process, in a reflective process.

- Co-production as a research approach is governed by a range of principles such as power sharing, valuing the knowledge of all of those involved, being inclusive and trying to achieve equality through relationship building. Successfully applying these principles in practice can result in a range of benefits for all of those involved in the research process. However, as this chapter illustrates, there are a range of challenges associated with co-producing research.

- The contexts in which co-production takes place in are varied in terms of location, the roles that researchers adopt, the nature of projects and the organisations involved. Context is an important factor in the application of co-productive research in practice.

Suggestions for further reading

1 Durose, C., Beebeejaun, Y., Rees, J., Richardson, J. and Richardson, L. (2011) *Towards co-production in research with communities*, Swindon: AHRC.
  This is a brief guide providing some tips on how to co-produce research with communities, discussing why it matters, some of the potential issues that can arise, and outlining some practical tools to support those wishing to engage in co-production.

2 Hickey, G., Brearley, S., Coldham, T., Denegri, S., Green, G., Staniszewska, S., Tembo, D., Torok, K., and Turner, K. (2018) *Guidance on co-producing a research project*, Southampton: INVOLVE.
  This is a basic and brief piece of guidance from INVOLVE offering principles and tips for those wishing to co-produce research. The guidance itself came from a co-produced process. It is a practical resource, including suggestions for how to achieve principles in reality.

3 Banks, S., Hart, A., Pahl, K. and Ward, P. (eds) (2019) *Co-producing research: a community development approach*, Bristol: Policy Press.
  This book offers a community development approach to co-production, discussing how to build collective capacity and working towards social change. Contributions come from various fields, and as a result there are examples from neighbourhood research, a prison setting and art contexts (as well as others).

Questions for reflection

1 How will you adapt your approach to ensure that you are using the principles associated with co-production in practice? Might some principles be more applicable than others?

2 In which research situations do you think co-production as an approach can be used? Might some research projects and contexts lend themselves more easily to such approaches?

3 Why are you considering using co-production? In terms of your own identified topic area, reflect on the benefits and disadvantages of co-producing research. In your view, do the benefits outweigh the disadvantages?

Top tips for practice

1 Consult toolkits and advice to support your own approach to co-production. There are now several manuals available on the internet, in which principles are laid out (how can you apply these to your study?), lessons learned are discussed (these may help you to anticipate hurdles and to better manage them). Use these existing resources as a starting point to help you.

2 Allow lots of time to build your approach to co-production in your research study. You will need to build time and space into your research plan for conversations about all aspects of the research to ensure that co-production can take place. There will be different ideas about co-production in research design, data collection and analysis, so allow for disagreements, power imbalances, criticism and ongoing debates.

3 Be flexible and be prepared to listen – you may need to change your ideas, your approach and grasp of power and control. For a research project to be co-produced, traditional models, language and standards are likely to be seen in different ways.

Further teaching and learning resources to accompany this book can be found at https://bristoluniversitypress.co.uk/creating-participatory-research-website. The companion website includes:
- teaching slides for lecturers
- further information on learning tasks
- lesson activities
- further reading, links to websites and practical resources
- examples from practice
- additional case studies

PART II

Practice

3

Research design

Key learning outcomes

By the end of this chapter, you should be able to:

- Outline the strengths and weaknesses of different research designs, define the key research designs and methods associated with participatory research, and those that are not generally associated with participatory research

- Demonstrate awareness of the principles and values associated with participatory research design and methods

- Identify several challenges associated with participatory approaches to research design

Introduction

How can research design be participatory? This chapter starts with research questions and objectives, and links these to decisions about methodology and study design. Participation within each aspect of the research design process is illustrated, with some discussion of whether pure participatory research projects can be designed fully in advance of the project starting, and noting the need for the use of some initial frameworks as a mechanism to get people involved. While the chapter refers to the need for ethical research practice, this is covered in detail in Chapter 4. Similarly, although data collection and analysis are referred to, these are each covered in detail in later chapters. Some example outputs are noted in this chapter, but again, dissemination is covered in full in Chapter 7.

What is research design?

Research design is synonymous with study design and refers to the overall structure or plan of the research; for example, whether an experimental or observational study will be conducted. The overall methodological approach to the research (qualitative or quantitative) informs the choice of research design (see Box 3.2) and, once this is decided, the specific research methods and data collection methods are chosen – in practice, these are very closely linked; see Chapter 5 for more on methods and how these link back to research design. Table 3.1 provides a comparative overview of the differences between traditional research design and participatory approaches.

Table 3.1 Traditional research design compared with participatory research design

	Traditional research design	Participatory research design
Research question, aims and objectives	Chosen by researchers, informed by published research literature and/ or funders' priorities.	Chosen by non-research stakeholders or co-produced by research and non-research stakeholders.
Methodology	Quantitative methodology is chosen when research questions are about effectiveness; qualitative methodology when research questions are about beliefs or experiences.	Either quantitative or qualitative methodology may be chosen, as for traditional research design, but the majority use qualitative methodology.
Study design	Wide range of designs: experimental or observational. Hierarchies of evidence are often used to rank study designs in terms of methodological robustness; these almost all favour quantitative methodology and experimental design.	Range of qualitative designs; many studies using multiple and creative approaches to participant engagement and data collection. Traditional evidence hierarchies are not commonly used. Quantitative designs or elements of design in mixed methods studies are usually observational (e.g. surveys).
Population and sampling	Usually people must meet tightly defined eligibility criteria to be included in the study. Checklists to assess methodological rigour favour representative sampling for quantitative methodology and purposive or maximum variation sampling for qualitative methodology.	Eligibility criteria for the study population are either broad (e.g. anyone living in a neighbourhood or using a community centre) or define a population group that is often overlooked in traditional research (e.g. homeless). Snowball sampling via peers is often used to recruit participants from vulnerable groups.

Research questions, aims and objectives

One of the first stages of research design is to decide on the research questions or hypotheses, aims and objectives of the study (Bowling 2014). Put simply, what are you trying to find out, or what question do you want your research to answer? Aims are broader than this, often incorporating both the research question and the reason for asking it (for example, to inform practice or policy in this area). Objectives are more specific 'operational tasks, which have to be accomplished in order to meet aims' (St Leger et al 1992:12). In participatory research, research questions and aims can be decided by the interested stakeholders who then commission the researchers, they can be co-produced by the research team and the other stakeholders, or they may be decided by the research team ahead of the involvement of other stakeholders (that is, a non-participatory element of the research design). Complete Learning Task 3.1 to consider how to work with stakeholders and community members in designing research questions.

LEARNING TASK 3.1 PARTICIPATION IN FORMULATING RESEARCH QUESTIONS

Research questions or objectives are the basis of all study designs, so before you start your participatory project, these will need to be clarified and agreed. All those involved in the study (professional researchers, stakeholders and community members) must have a clear understanding of the broader goals of the research project. Consider the following questions as a starting point for formulating questions for your own participatory study.

1 What is your research trying to accomplish?
2 What are the goals of the researcher and those of community members – are there common areas of overlap that can be used to inform the research questions?
3 What are the values of all of those involved, and how are these useful in informing the research questions?

In thinking about the questions posed in Learning Task 3.1, you will have a basis for defining research questions or objectives. Once these are created, the next step in research design is to consider the population you need to access in order to start addressing your research questions.

Defining the population and sampling

'Sampling' is the process of selecting research participants from the target population that we are studying.

In social research, sampling involves the selection of units; a sampling unit can be at many levels – for example, households, schools or individuals. The main reason for sampling is practical, as it is not usually possible to research every member of the population.

In quantitative research, a representative sample is drawn from a defined target population and has demographic and other characteristics that match those of the population as closely as possible. This allows extrapolation from the sample findings to the population – that is, they are generalisable, having high external validity. This is the main goal of sampling for quantitative studies.

Some examples of sampling techniques for quantitative studies include:

- *Random sampling* Every unit (for example, pupil, class or school) has the same theoretical chance of being selected into the sample. A sampling frame is needed, for instance a list of population members (units) from which the sample is drawn. Random numbers tables or computer-generated random numbers are used to select units randomly from the list.

- *Quota sampling* Not random selection, but quotas are set that mirror the population characteristics.
- *Convenience sampling* Also known as opportunity sampling, the researchers select whoever is available at a particular time, or responds to an invitation, and those who consent are then screened to check they match the target population.

In contrast, sampling principles for qualitative studies are dynamic and reviewed during the process. The main issues to consider are:

- Whose voices need to be heard or represented?
- When to stop sampling?

In *theoretical sampling*, groups or categories are selected to study on the basis of their relevance to the research questions, the researchers' theoretical position, or the argument they are developing (Glaser and Strauss 2017).

In *purposive or purposeful sampling*, the sample should be chosen because it illustrates a feature or process that we are interested in. For example, in a study of a health trainer service in general practice, we might want to choose participants who represented the health trainers, the patients who used the service, the general practitioners (GPs) who made the referrals, other stakeholders such as those commissioning the service, the GP practice manager, and patients who had been offered the service but chose not to engage with it. Within or across these categories, we might want to also consider whether the diversity of the target population was reflected in our study participants in terms of gender, ethnicity, age and other relevant characteristics.

Deciding when to stop sampling In qualitative research, there are few strict guidelines about when to stop data collection. Some criteria include exhaustion of resources, emergence of regularities, overextension or going too far beyond the boundaries of the research (Guba 1978). The decision to stop sampling must take into account the research goals, the need to achieve depth, and the possibility of greater breadth through examining a variety of sampling sites. Box 3.1 outlines sampling and recruitment considerations in relation to participatory research.

Box 3.1 Sampling and recruitment in participatory research

- A key issue in participatory research is inclusion. Participatory research studies, for the most part, aim to include data from and represent the views of all relevant stakeholders in the target population, and particularly those who are vulnerable, disadvantaged or at risk of health or social inequalities, as these are people who are often not included in traditional research.

- Traditional sampling methods are not necessarily enough, as even purposive sampling may only result in research participants who are already engaged with the intervention or situation in question.
- 'Snowball' sampling has been used in studies of vulnerable populations; for example, sex workers or people who are homeless. 'Gatekeepers' for the vulnerable group engage first with the research team, then contact and suggest members of the vulnerable group as research participants. If this goes well, these participants put other group members in contact with the research team, and so on. This relies on the target population being members of a group who are in contact with one another. It can be more difficult to recruit research participants who are vulnerable but are not part of a group and do not engage with services (for example, people who are socially isolated or excluded).
- It remains a challenge to ensure that all views are represented, as those who come forward as research participants may hold similar views to one another.

Choosing a study design

As you will be starting to understand from reading this chapter, there are many options for choosing a research design. Learning Task 3.2 encourages you to reflect on the differences between qualitative and quantitative designs.

LEARNING TASK 3.2 METHODOLOGY: QUALITATIVE OR QUANTITATIVE?

Qualitative methodology is chosen when the research is about understanding situations or the experiences or beliefs of individuals. In qualitative methodology, people or situations are observed and/or questioned to uncover what the phenomenon means to them. An inductive approach is used, which is based on the assumption that there is no one 'true' reality relating to that phenomenon, but there are multiple realities, as people experience it in different ways. In an inductive approach, we try not to 'lead' research participants by asking very specific or detailed questions, as we want to know what their experiences of the phenomenon are in their own words. In qualitative methodology, results are usually expressed in some form of words or pictures. Interviews are one example of a qualitative research method.

Quantitative methodology is chosen when we believe that there must be one true 'factual' result or range of values, and we want to find out what this truth is. A deductive approach is used, in which a theory or hypothesis is tested, and the concepts or constructs that we are trying to research are defined and measured, using common tools. In quantitative methodology, results are usually expressed numerically. Experimental studies are one example of a quantitative research design, but some observational study designs such as surveys are also quantitative.

Now take time to think about the following questions.

1 With reference to the two descriptions provided above, and considering your own participatory project idea, which of these methodologies is most suited to addressing your research questions?
2 Consider how you can introduce these different methodologies to lay researchers and support them in choosing the methodology most suited to the participatory research project you have in mind.
3 Have you considered how to resolve any differences of opinion in relation to methodological decisions?

The majority of participatory research that has been published has used qualitative methodology. Participatory research that uses quantitative methodology is less common, although when it is used, the research design is usually a survey (for example, Parrado et al 2005; Binet et al 2019). Therefore, participatory research rarely takes an experimental approach, although there are examples of lay researchers being involved in producing the research questions, advising on data collection methods and 'sense-checking' early findings of randomised controlled trials and other experimental studies. In fact, this is considered to be good practice and is recommended by many funding and regulatory bodies such as the National Institute for Health Research in the UK.

Different study designs

Study designs are chosen by following a process, such as the one depicted in Figure 3.1 for quantitative methodology, to select the most methodologically rigorous design that will give the most accurate and unbiased data (for quantitative methodology) or the richest and most relevant data (for qualitative methodology). In practice, the choice of study design often involves a compromise between methodological rigour and the resources (that is, time, funding, team capacity) available to the researchers and (in participatory research) the lay stakeholders. In Figure 3.1, the first choice that is made is between experimental and observational study designs, based on whether the research participants were assigned to treatment groups by the researcher.

Experimental study designs

In experimental studies, there is an intervention and manipulation under tightly defined or controlled conditions. If the researcher assigns people to groups receiving different interventions then this is an experimental study.

The 'gold standard' or most rigorous experimental study design in health research is the *randomised controlled trial* (RCT), in which participants are randomly allocated to one or more interventions or 'control' groups, in a process which

Figure 3.1 Flow diagram for choosing quantitative study designs

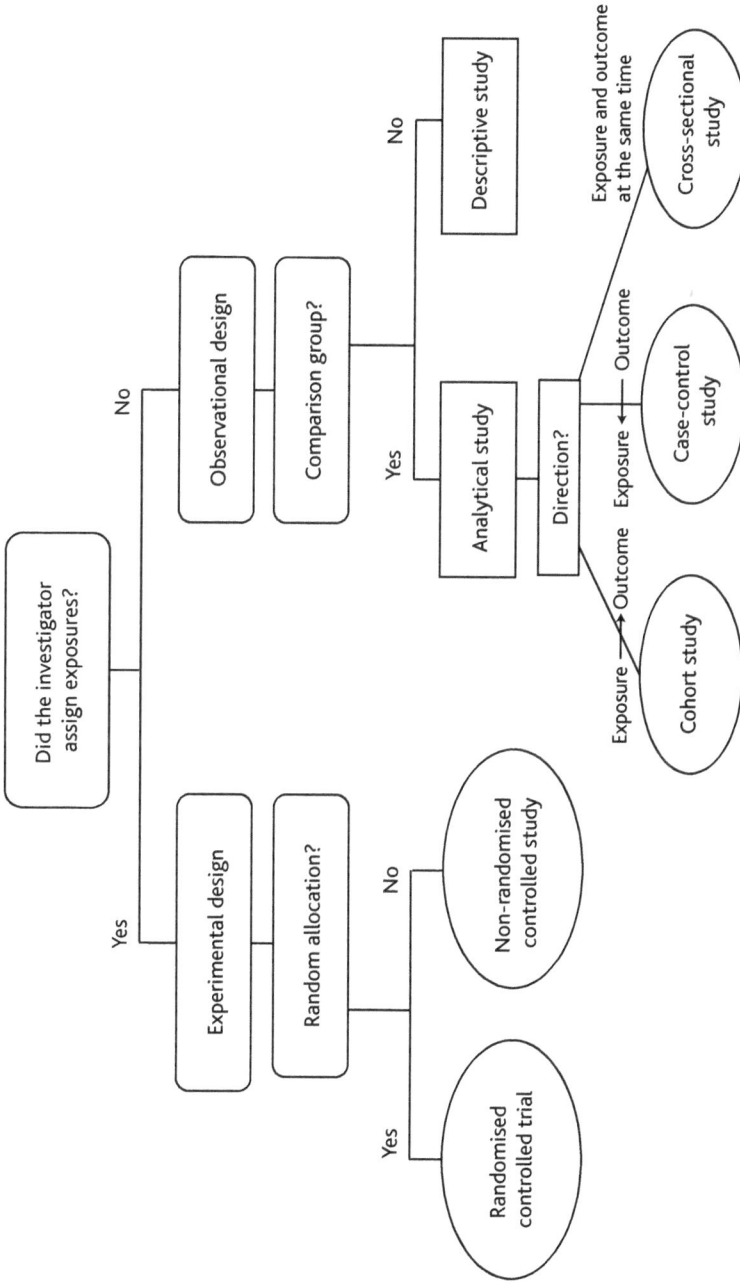

Source: Adapted from Grimes and Schulz (2002)

is characterised by unpredictability. This should ensure that both known and unknown participant characteristics and risks (genetic, biological, medical, lifestyle and so on) are evenly distributed between the groups, meaning that any differences seen in outcomes measured during or at the end of the trial are due only to the intervention, as this is the only thing that is different between the groups.

Less rigorous than the RCT is the quasi-randomised or non-randomised controlled trial. In a *quasi-randomised controlled trial*, participants are assigned to groups using a method that is not truly unpredictable; for example, alternate allocation or allocation by day or week attending the clinic. A *non-randomised trial* may also use these methods, or may allocate people into groups by patient or clinician choice, or by another method. Allowing people to choose which group they or their patients are allocated to will inevitably lead to uneven distribution of participant characteristics between the groups, so any differences in outcomes that we might see between the groups may be due to the intervention or may be due to different risk factors or biological responses in that group.

Natural experiments are a kind of non-randomised study but, as the name suggests, allocation into groups is not controlled by the researchers but by exposure to the intervention or control conditions. This exposure could be determined by nature (for example, a natural disaster) or by policy changes, and the researchers have no control over the exposure. Some argue that this effect is similar to randomisation, as exposure is determined by chance, but there is evidence that natural disasters or policy changes may happen first or worst in areas of deprivation (for example) and so participant characteristics would not be evenly distributed between exposed and non-exposed groups.

Before-and-after studies (also known as pre–post studies) involve just one group of participants, in which everyone is exposed to the intervention or change. Measurements are taken or observations are made before the change or intervention happens and at one or more points after the intervention or change has begun. Although these studies can show us how certain outcomes have changed over time, without a control group which remains unexposed to the intervention we cannot be sure whether observed changes are due to the intervention or to something else that was happening at the same time.

One-group 'after-only' studies collect observations or measurements from a single group of participants, all exposed to the intervention, at some point after the intervention or change has begun. These are very limited in what they can tell us, as we do not know how the 'after' measurements from this group compare with the 'before' measurements (that is, has there actually been any change?) or how they compare with measurements from participants not exposed to the intervention.

Box 3.2 illustrates some of the key elements that contribute to well-designed experiments.

Box 3.2 Features of well-designed experiments

- Random selection of participants into intervention and comparison groups.
- Comparison of groups at baseline to ensure balanced allocation (of known prognostic or confounding factors) between groups.
- Control of other (non-intervention) variables during the experiment.
- Blinding – to reduce the placebo effect, and other forms of bias related to knowing whether participants are receiving the intervention or not.
- Some assessment of how faithfully the intervention has been implemented or delivered.
- Full follow up of those receiving and refusing/no longer receiving the intervention (also known as 'intention to treat analysis').
- Assessment of statistical significance of results.

Observational study designs

Cohort studies recruit and follow up one large group of people over a number of years or decades to determine whether there is an association between exposure to potential risk or protective factors and development or prevention of an illness. Study participants usually fill in a detailed questionnaire at the start of the study period (also known as the 'baseline') and then regular follow-up questionnaires, which are less detailed and sometime focus on one particular topic. Often, biological measurements such as blood pressure or cholesterol are taken at the start of the study, and sometimes these are repeated at less frequent intervals. Many cohort studies track participants in national registries for illnesses or death. Study investigators are automatically informed when a study participant is registered as having died or been diagnosed with the trackable illness. Some well-known cohort studies are:

- Framingham Heart Study (1948–, n=5,209), www.framinghamheartstudy.org/
- Nurses' Health Study (all female, 1976–, n=280,000+), www.nurseshealthstudy.org/
- Health Professionals Follow-Up Study (all male, 1986–, n=51,529), https://sites.sph.harvard.edu/hpfs/

These cohort studies are known as *prospective cohort studies*, because people are recruited at baseline and then followed forwards. Prospective cohort studies are one of the most methodologically rigorous observational study designs, but they take a long time – often decades – to produce results.

There are also *retrospective cohort studies*, where investigators look back at the records of a group of people who were exposed or not exposed to potential risk or protective factors to see if these are associated with developing an outcome; these are less time consuming but more likely to be affected by inaccuracies and bias.

Case control studies are like retrospective cohort studies in that they look back, but participants are selected on the basis of having developed an illness. A matched control group of people who have similar characteristics but have not developed the illness is also selected, and then the two groups are compared in terms of levels of exposure to the potential risk or protective factors.

Descriptive epidemiological studies examine patterns of disease occurrence with regard to population, place and time. These are often carried out on a local level using relatively accessible data that are routinely collected. Bach et al (2017) developed a conceptual framework to illustrate the potential of participatory epidemiology to enhance the quality and effectiveness of research. Participants may be involved in designing relevant and meaningful research questions, defining the population, considering context, retrieving and synthesising data, managing and adapting the research process and disseminating findings.

Observational studies are less useful than experimental studies for investigating causal links because the observed associations may be due to confounding factors – that is, a third factor linked to the proposed causal mechanism. For example, in a study indicating that slightly overweight people live longer than thin people, the simple observation is that there is an association between weight and life expectancy. A potential confounding factor would be an illness that causes weight loss and also reduces life expectancy.

Qualitative study designs

Qualitative research is about meaning, rather than measurement or numbers. It does not provide a single answer; there are multiple meanings and interpretations as experienced by different people, and context is seen as an important contributor to this, rather than as a potential confounding factor or source of bias (Braun and Clarke 2013). A common feature of qualitative projects is that they aim to create understanding from the data as the analysis proceeds. This means that the research design of a qualitative study is more diffuse and less structured compared with quantitative research. The main methods of data collection are described in Chapter 5.

Mixed methods study designs

Mixed methods research is a purposeful approach where the investigators collect and analyse both qualitative and quantitative data within the same study, drawing on the potential strengths of both methodologies. Integration of the data is an important stage of a mixed methods research study (Shorten and Smith 2017). Mixed methods research may be used to improve understanding of similarities or differences between qualitative and quantitative data; they can provide opportunities for participants to share their experiences across the research process, and can lead to different areas of exploration that enrich the evidence and enable questions to be answered more deeply. The process of mixing methods within one study, however, often requires more time, a larger research team and additional research training, as multidisciplinary research teams need to learn different approaches to research (Wisdom and Creswell 2013). Table 3.2 illustrates a range of examples of different mixed methods research designs.

Table 3.2 Types of mixed methods research designs

Mixed methods type	Research processes	Examples
Explanatory sequential	Quantitative data are collected and analysed first, then qualitative data are collected and analysed to help explain quantitative data. QUAN → QUAL	AIM: Identify levels of stress among healthcare professionals (HCPs) working in community settings QUAN: National survey of HCPs working in community settings measuring levels of workplace stress. QUAL: Personal interviews with 15–20 HCPs working in community settings to discuss their experiences with stressful workplace situations. SYNTHESIS: Sequential. QUAL data help explain QUAN data.
Exploratory sequential	Qualitative data are collected and analysed first, then quantitative data are collected and used to test findings empirically. QUAL → QUAN	AIM: Identify highest sources of workplace stress for HCPs working in community settings QUAL: Focus group data collected from HCPs working in local community settings to discuss workplace stress. QUAN: QUAL data used to create a national survey administered to all HCPs working in community settings about sources of workplace stress experienced within the last year of practice. SYNTHESIS: Sequential. QUAL data inform collection of QUAN data, which verify QUAL data.
Parallel	Qualitative and quantitative data collected and analysed concurrently. QUAL + QUAN	AIM: Identify sources of stress for HCPs working in community settings, personal coping strategies used and types of programmes or support systems provided by employers. QUAN: National survey of all HCPs working in community settings, based on the literature, to identify common sources of stress and methods of support used by employers to reduce HCP stress. QUAL: Focus groups and interviews with a random selection of HCPs working in community settings to broaden understanding of different sources of stress and personal coping strategies used. SYNTHESIS: Data integration during interpretation phase after QUAN and QUAL data analyses.
Nested	Can be either QUAL or QUAN main design with the alternative paradigm embedded within the study to answer a complementary question. QUAL + quant or QUAN + qual	AIM: Test an online peer support programme designed to reduce workplace stress for HCPs working in community settings. QUAN: RCT to test online programme effect on stress levels and intention to remain working in the community setting. QUAL: Interview nested in the RCT, focused on user experiences of the online programme. SYNTHESIS: qual analysis embedded within the main QUAN study.

Source: Adapted from Halcomb and Hickman (2015)

Table 3.2 provides examples of several mixed methods designs, so now complete Learning Task 3.3, drawing on this table to consider how you could use these designs in a more participatory manner.

LEARNING TASK 3.3 PARTICIPATORY APPROACHES AND MIXED METHODS DESIGN

1 Consider one or two of the research designs listed in Table 3.2 above. How could you make them more participatory in their design?

2 What barriers to participation might you need to address? How could you approach this?

3 Do you have the skills within the team or might you need some more training or specialist support?

Now that we have considered potential mixed methods designs, let's turn to implementation research.

Designing implementation and realist research

In a report for the World Health Organization (WHO), Peters et al (2013:9) define implementation research as

> the scientific study of the processes used in the implementation of initiatives as well as the contextual factors that affect these processes. It can address or explore any aspect of implementation, including the factors affecting implementation (such as poverty, geographical remoteness, or traditional beliefs), the processes of implementation themselves (such as distribution of fully-subsidised insecticide-treated bednets (ITNs) through maternal health clinics, or the use of mass vaccination versus surveillance-containment), and the outcomes, or end-products of the implementation under study.

Implementation research is important because it helps us to understand how to use proven interventions in different settings and contexts. It can help in making adaptations when transferring an intervention from a high-income country to a low-income country, or when scaling up or rolling out an intervention from a local to a regional level, and aligns with participatory research because of its underpinning principles of learning and social change.

Participatory research methods are particularly relevant in implementation research, which is the scientific study of the processes used in the implementation of initiatives as well as the contextual factors that affect these processes.

Marie-Paul Kieny, writing in the foreword of the Peters et al (2013:5) WHO report says that

> [r]esearch on implementation requires the engagement of a wide range of stakeholders and draws on multiple disciplines in order to address complex implementation challenges. As this Guide points out, at its best, implementation research is often a collective and collaborative endeavor and in many cases it is people working on the front line [...] who ask the questions around which it is built.

Table 3.3 presents a range of realist and implementation research designs.

Table 3.3 Implementation and realist research design

Type of evaluation	Description	Application to participatory research
Process evaluation	Examines how an intervention is implemented and what was actually delivered, compared with what was intended to be implemented and delivered.	The UK Medical Research Council recommends combining outcome and process evaluation for complex interventions (Craig et al 2008). In community-centred interventions, research participants have 'insider' knowledge of what changed and what went wrong, which they are more likely to share if trust is built with the researchers.
Formative evaluation	Assessment and feedback is given before an intervention is rolled out or scaled up; often used in feasibility or pilot studies of new interventions that need testing and refining.	Research team works quite closely with the stakeholders and practitioners, and adaptations are made to the intervention in 'real time' in response to the findings of the formative evaluation.
Developmental evaluation	A kind of formative evaluation where the evaluation is ongoing and the evaluators are embedded within the project as members of the team (Patton 2010; Simister 2017).	This is clearly a participatory research design. The evaluator's role is to facilitate discussions about evaluative questions, and encourage project staff to collect, analyse and use information to support ongoing decision making.
Theory-based evaluation	Theories of change (Connell et al 1995; Fulbright-Anderson et al 1998) Realistic evaluation (Pawson and Tilley 1997) Both concepts are concerned with understanding the theory behind an initiative (Blamey and Mackenzie 2007).	Research participants should be involved from the start, as they have important insights into the context and intended pathways, mechanisms and outcomes of the interventions.

Action research

Winter and Munn-Giddings (2001:8) define action research as 'the study of a social situation carried out by those involved in that situation in order to improve both their practice and their quality of understanding'. Action research can be used to support organisational change and has been recommended by the UK National Institute for Health Research as a method to explore the gap between research and implementation and to build capacity in the health service (Whitehead et al 2003). It uses flexible methodology, drawing on both qualitative and quantitative approaches and using a range of resources to collect and analyse data. A systematic review of the use of action research in health suggested that action research is useful for developing innovation, improving healthcare, developing knowledgeable practitioners, and in the participatory involvement of users and staff in research (Waterman et al 2001).

Whitehead and colleagues (2003) reported that action research differs from other research designs because it aims to uncover and resolve problems rather than merely investigate them. The starting point is usually the description of a problem rather than a research question or hypothesis. They state that all action research adheres to specific processes that involve:

- Systematically collecting research data about an ongoing system relative to some objective, need or goal of that system.
- Feeding these data back into the system.
- Taking action by altering selected variables within the system, based both on the data and on assumptions about how the system functions.
- Evaluating the results of actions by collecting more data.

As Krimerman (2001:60) states, action research places great emphasis on a 'democratising social inquiry process that actively engages the subject in the design and conduct of the research' and demands that a collaborative team approach is used. This, together with its cyclic, dynamic nature, ensures that both the researchers and the research participants decide on the nature and scope of the research methodology, and amend the methods as the research progresses (Whitehead et al 2003).

Participatory research design

Systematic reviews of the effectiveness of community engagement for improving health and wellbeing and reducing health inequalities have reported that the most effective interventions are those where communities are involved in their design, delivery *and evaluation* (O'Mara-Eves et al 2013, 2015; Brunton et al 2015, 2017). As well as taking a more participatory approach to any of the research designs considered earlier (as in Learning Task 3.3), there are some research designs that have community participation built in. Some of these are described below.

Community-based participatory research (CBPR), as explained in *The guide to community-centred approaches for health and wellbeing* (PHE/NHS England 2015), involves partnerships between academic researchers, communities and services, usually with the aim of identifying community needs and working together to develop interventions and programmes to address them (Minkler 2010). In CBPR, community researchers are recruited and trained to gather data in their community and identify issues and potential solutions. A range of research designs and methods of data collection can be used, from questionnaire-based surveys to creative methods such as photovoice (see Chapter 5). Established methods of participatory needs assessment, such as rapid participatory appraisal, are complemented by asset-based methods (Rippon and Hopkins 2015). Israel and colleagues (2008) suggest that the CBPR principles adopted for each research study should be owned by the group and adapted to the local context, as not every CBPR principle will be relevant to the needs and goals of that community.

There are many examples of community-based participatory research in the literature (for example, Teti et al 2012; Ingram et al 2015; Mosavel et al 2016; Rink 2016; Elder and Odoyo 2018; Furman et al 2019). In a project to create inclusive practices for disabled children at two schools in Western Kenya, Elder and Odoyo (2018) combined CBPR with decolonising methodologies, building on local history of community-based approaches to social issues. There were three cycles of CBPR where inclusion committee members set, monitored and adjusted research goals at each school site.

CBPR is not always a practical option. In a CBPR study of the implementation of a sexually transmitted infection intervention for Greenlandic youth, the remote location of one of the places influenced the use of CBPR, both because the researchers were unable to travel to this location as often as to the other two locations, and because the residents were less used to engagement with people from outside the area. This in turn affected the uptake of the intervention (Rink 2016).

Rapid participatory appraisal is used to provide qualitative information, especially about deprived urban areas, using key informants with knowledge of the area to identify problems and contribute to solutions. As Murray and colleagues (1994) explain, the primary aims of rapid participatory appraisal are to gain insight into a community's own perspective on its main needs; to translate these findings into action; and to establish an ongoing relationship between local communities and the organisations that serve them. Information is collected on nine aspects, which are brought together to form an information pyramid, including: community characteristics and capacity; social determinants of health; local services; and national, regional and local policies. Data are collected from existing written records about the neighbourhood, interviews with a range of informants, and observations. The scientific rigour and validity of the approach depends on the concept of triangulation, with data collection from one source being validated or rejected by checking it with data from at least two other sources or methods of collection.

Participatory action research (PAR) It could be argued that all action research is participatory, involving close collaboration between researchers and other stakeholders. However, PAR is distinguished by a focus on power relationships.

Baum et al (2006) state that PAR advocates for those being researched to be actively involved in the process:

> [...] power to be deliberately shared between the researcher and the researched: blurring the line between them until the researched become the researchers. The researched cease to be objects and become partners in the whole research process: including selecting the research topic, data collection, and analysis and deciding what action should happen as a result of the research findings.

PAR focuses on research which aims to enable action and empowerment of those involved. Action is achieved through a reflective cycle, where participants collect and analyse data, then decide what action should follow. The action is then further researched and refined. PAR requires researchers to work in partnership with civil society and health policy makers and practitioners, requiring each to work together effectively and to manage their different and sometimes competing agendas (Sanders et al 2004).

Box 3.3 Example of participatory action research

A study of non-binary youths' experiences (Furman et al 2019) used a checklist developed by Singh et al (2013) for PAR. The checklist encourages researchers to choose a theoretical framework that centres the research on trans identities, to consider how to engage trans participants in empowering research; that is, provide opportunities to actively participate without placing a burden on them, and to conduct outreach to create authentic relationships and collaborations, connecting the research with advocacy and social change. In this study (Furman et al 2019), non-binary youth identified a need for spaces where they could express themselves, talk about their experiences and discuss avenues for engaging in their communities. Although the researchers' intention was to collaboratively develop a body-mapping workshop curriculum, limited funding to compensate non-binary participants for their time meant that the workshop was developed by two of the authors, and a draft version shared with participants who were interested in providing feedback.

Peer research is often thought of purely as a method of data collection, where members of the target population adopt the role of active researchers, interviewing their peer group about their experiences. It adopts the view that peers are 'experts' within their field of experience. However, peer researchers may be involved in the design of the study, having input into the research questions, sampling (knowing where potential research participants can be found), recruitment of research participants, design of data collection tools such as surveys, interview schedules and more creative methods, data analysis and dissemination. Peer researchers may be able to reach and communicate with groups not in touch with traditional services, in their own communities and social networks. There is evidence that people may be willing to discuss issues with peer researchers that they would not be willing to raise with academic researchers (Green and South 2006).

As the McPin Foundation for mental health research puts it:

> Peer research (sometimes called user focused research) is research that is steered and conducted by people with lived experience of the issue being studied. Peer research may be completely user-led, or it may be carried out by peer researchers working alongside non-peer researchers as part of a bigger research team.[1]

Peer research requires careful consideration of the nature and definition of 'peerness' – something that may vary from study to study. For example, the McPin Foundation defines their peer researchers as people with relevant 'lived experience of mental health problems', who are willing to draw on and share those experiences as part of the study. However, they also reflect that sharing an experience may not be sufficient to make people peers, and that differences in background, other life experiences or characteristics such as race or gender may be as or more important in some contexts. This reflection was also shared by a large study of peer roles in public health (South et al 2010), which found that peer status can be based on individual attributes (age, gender, ethnicity, neighbourhood) as well as types of experience and knowledge.

Lushey and Munro (2015) report on their experience of working with peer researchers in studies of children in and leaving care. The peer researchers (children) were first identified by social workers or managers as being willing and able to engage with the research project as peer researchers. Training took place over several one- and two-day workshops, and covered research ethical issues including obtaining informed consent and outlining the limits of confidentiality, as well as in interview skills, including building rapport, listening skills, and questioning and probing to elicit high-quality data. The young people then took part in workshops to help design the data collection tools and participant information sheets and had some training in data analysis. Ongoing support was provided by the children's social workers and the academic research team.

Done correctly, peer research can help establish rapport with participants and put them at ease, help researchers ask more relevant questions and place the answers into a broader context. It de-emphasises the power differential that has traditionally existed between researchers and their subjects, by emphasising their shared experience or identity (Guta et al 2013).

But there are also interesting ethical, practical and data quality challenges for academic researchers working with peer researchers. For example, Lushey and Munro (2015) reported the following main issues in their studies of participatory peer researcher methodology in research with children in and leaving care:

---

[1] https://mcpin.org/wp-content/uploads/McPin-PPI-slides-v1.1-july-2017.pdf

- *Confidentiality* Although a recognised benefit of peer research is shared experience, in this study the research team were concerned about potential research participants being friends or acquaintances of peer researchers living in their area. Therefore, the peer researchers travelled to their neighbouring area to recruit and interview participants.
- *Data quality* It was recognised in these studies (when the academic research team read transcripts of the interviews) that some of the interview data lacked depth, due to the interviewer moving on from questions without probing for further information. Further training was offered to help peer researchers gain confidence in this area. There was also a recognised tension between the desire to involve peer researchers in the analysis and ensuring that the analysis was both manageable and robust.

Participatory research design can therefore raise several challenges. Complete Learning Task 3.4 to consider some of these.

LEARNING TASK 3.4 CHALLENGES OF PARTICIPATORY RESEARCH DESIGN

Take time to explore some papers and websites that discuss the challenges associated with designing research in a participatory way.

1 What are the main challenges that you identified?
2 Did any of your sources discuss the inclusion of vulnerable or disadvantaged groups of people as a challenge?
3 Listing the key barriers that you found, now consider how you would remove these barriers to participation.

In completing Learning Task 3.4 it is likely that you identified many challenges in this area. The literature mentions several challenges to the 'purity' of research. Cleaver (2001) argues that a key challenge is ensuring that those involved in research are 'empowered' to make a difference while at the same time ensuring that studies remain academically robust. As Lushey and Munro (2015) report, the validity of findings from research adopting less traditional methods may be questioned and policy makers may be cautious about accepting this evidence, thus limiting its contribution and impact. Finally, partnership working can involve different and competing agendas, different 'languages' and disagreements. Kavanagh and colleagues (2002) outline some further challenges for academics using PAR, which are also common to other kinds of participatory research design:

- it is time consuming and unpredictable;
- it is unlikely to lead to a high production of articles in refereed journals;
- its somewhat 'messy' nature means it is less likely to attract competitive research funding.

....

CASE STUDY PRODUCTIVE DISRUPTION OF A PARTICIPATORY COMMUNITY PHOTO-ELICITATION PROJECT

A participatory research study aimed to explore people's perceptions and experiences of community and 'place' in the semi-rural English village where they lived. The study sought to conduct qualitative research with three community groups, ensuring a mix of ages, gender and social backgrounds: a female choir (eight white British participants aged between 74 and 87 years), a running club (six males, three females, all white British, aged 23–60 years) and a mobile youth project (four white British males aged 13–14 years). The project was designed as a photo-elicitation project where participants were asked to produce 27 images that represented their village – how they saw and experienced their community. The intention was that data generation was shifted from the researcher to the participants, and the photographs produced would stimulate group discussion in the place of an in-depth group interview.

When the cameras were collected and photographs developed, it was seen that members of the female choir had taken only a few images each, while members of the youth group had taken their photographs at the same time, in the same place, and comprised mainly of close-up images of other participants. The researchers were concerned about how useful these images would be in the group interviews. However, the participants went on to adapt the photo-elicitation brief in the following ways:

The female choir participants supplemented their photographs with old photographs, newspaper cuttings, hand-drawn and photocopied maps, and long, written narratives about their perceptions and experiences of place in the village and how these had changed over time.

The young people acknowledged that their photographs did not give a sense of being 'out and about' in the village but asked for a map. The group then spent two hours tracing their movements through the village naming and explaining places where they 'hung out' or those they were scared of or not allowed to go.

The researchers concluded that, although for two groups the approach shifted from photo-elicitation to co-constructed mixed media elicitation, the disruption was not detrimental to the research brief, and that researchers should practise flexibility when conducting participative research, as participants' input can enrich the research in ways unanticipated by the researchers. They reflected that the original research design did not ensure that participants were confident or capable with what they were being asked to do, and building discussion with participants about preferred media for elicitation would be wise.

(Vigurs and Kara 2017)

....

Summary

- Participatory research should ideally involve research participants in all aspects of research design, as this ensures its relevance to, and uptake in, the target population and enhances engagement with effective interventions. This is possible to some extent for all research study designs, not just those labelled as 'participatory'.

- Researchers should be guided by ethical standards and guidance such as the NIHR National Standards for Public Involvement in Research (https://sites.google.com/nihr.ac.uk/pi-standards/home) and be mindful of power imbalances between themselves and research participants and how to manage these, so that research participants are as fully involved as possible, while experiencing no detrimental effects from their involvement.

- Although there are many challenges in participatory research design, with the possibility for potential disruption or 'failure' of the original plan, this need not necessarily be seen as a bad thing, if researchers are prepared to be flexible and responsive to unexpected developments.

Suggestions for further reading

1 Bowling, A. (2014) *Research methods in health: investigating health and health services*, 4th edn, Maidenhead: Open University Press.
   This is an accessible introduction to research, discussing the concepts and practicalities of research methods, specifically focusing on the context of health and health services. This edition contains details on a range of qualitative and quantitative methods, as well as research design.

2 Braun, V. and Clarke, V. (2013) *Successful qualitative research: a practical guide for beginners*, London: Sage.
   A clearly written introductory text book providing detail about all qualitative methods such as discourse analysis, diary research, focus groups, grounded theory, interpretative phenomenological analysis, interviews, online research, pattern-based qualitative analysis, qualitative methods, qualitative reports and more.

3 Peters, D.H., Tran, N.T. and Adam, T. (2013) *Implementation research in health: a practical guide*, Geneva: Alliance for Health Policy and Systems Research/WHO.
   This book gives readers a basic introduction to implementation research, including the concepts and language used, what this approach involves, as well as describing the types of opportunities that such an approach can present.

Questions for reflection

1 Looking at the types of participatory research design and the examples given in this chapter, how distinct are they? How much overlap is there between different designs? Do they all follow a set formula or are they more flexible, guided by a set of principles and to what extent can they be participatory?

2 If the research design is truly participatory, how much does it matter if it doesn't all go to plan (as in the case study presented in this chapter)?

3 How important do you think it is to 'label' your research design, or is it enough to be transparent in reporting your aims, and methods used?

Top tips for practice

1 When working towards designing a participatory study, consider creating a mission statement or a plan of action to support and develop your approach through strategic planning. To be truly participatory the creation of the statement should involve all research partners. Starting the participatory project with a carefully facilitated strategic planning meeting, in which all partners define research goals will enable the team to have a clear plan to work to. The mission statement/project plan can then be collectively reviewed throughout the project and revisited if necessary.

2 Consider the context in which your research design is being created and tailor your approach accordingly. How can you enable people to participate in designing research; for example, in a way that fits with the general principles of participatory research, that will facilitate learning and build capacity, while ensuring that you are working in a culturally sensitive and appropriate way?

3 The National Institute for Health Research in the UK has issued updated guidance on patient and public involvement in research in the form of a series of principles, with questions for researchers to consider whether they have met the principles. Draw on these principles to inform your own practice in relation to research design.

- Inclusive opportunities: offer opportunities that are accessible and that reach people and groups according to research needs.

- Working together: work together in a way that values all contributions, and that builds and sustains mutually respectful and productive relationships.

- Support and learning: offer and promote support and learning opportunities that build confidence and skills for public involvement in research.

- Communications: use plain language for well-timed and relevant communications, as part of involvement plans and activities.

- Impact: seek improvement by identifying and sharing the difference that public involvement makes to research.

- Governance: involve the public in research management, regulation, leadership and decision making.

Further teaching and learning resources to accompany this book can be found at https://bristoluniversitypress.co.uk/creating-participatory-research-website. The companion website includes:

- teaching slides for lecturers
- further information on learning tasks
- lesson activities
- further reading, links to websites and practical resources
- examples from practice
- additional case studies

4

Ethics of participatory research

Key learning outcomes

By the end of this chapter, you should be able to:

- Define the key ethical principles associated with participatory research and understand their importance

- Demonstrate awareness of the principles and values associated with the ethics of undertaking participatory approaches to research

- Identify several challenges in doing participatory approaches to research in an ethical manner

Introduction

This chapter will cover the research ethics process as related specifically to participatory approaches. How can ethics be managed within approaches that have not been tried before, or that are evolving because of the nature of the participatory research process? What ethical dilemmas arise and how can these be managed? This chapter will explore the many complex ethical issues that arise within the practice of participatory research and offer practical advice about how to manage them.

Importance of research ethics

Research ethics and the associated need for scrutiny of proposed research have developed over a number of years, in response to previous historical abuses. Ethics as a term covers a large number of areas related to what is right and wrong.

Within any research study, there is always the potential for abuse to take place, for researchers to misuse power and for participants to be harmed or disrespected. Historically, there have been many unethical research studies that have resulted in harm to people in a range of fields. Some harm has been deliberately inflicted on people, with human subjects used in physically damaging experiments. Other research studies may have resulted in psychological harm. For example, Milgram (1963) conducted a psychological study into obedience. He was interested in exploring ordinary people's responses to obeying instructions, even if this involved harming another individual. In a lab setting, he conducted a series of experiments in which volunteers were asked to 'administer' electric shocks to another person whom they were unable to see but could hear, when they answered questions incorrectly. Each incorrect answer resulted in the voltage associated with the electric shock being increased. The shocks were not real and neither was the hidden individual a genuine participant, but the volunteers were not aware of this. In most cases, volunteers followed the instructions from the source of authority (the man in the lab coat who took charge) to the point of administering a fatal electric shock. Following these experiments Milgram (1963) drew conclusions about the extent to which people will follow instructions from perceived authority. Fascinating results but was this ethical, and what of the potential psychological harm to those who volunteered? Furthermore, research studies can cause harm without ever intending to do so, for example in the case of drug testing. Therefore, research ethics guidelines and review processes are intended to work as a mechanism to prevent harm, and to ensure that research is conducted appropriately and morally.

Principles of research ethics

The literature suggests that there are key principles relating to ethics that should underpin all research projects. Many institutions such as universities and health services also have specific guidelines detailing the principles that researchers are expected to adhere to. To learn more about research ethics principles as they are enshrined within codes of conduct, complete Learning Task 4.1.

LEARNING TASK 4.1 EXPLORING ETHICAL CODES OF CONDUCT

Using the internet to search, find some example ethical codes of conduct for researchers. Here are some suggestions to get you started.

- Economics and Social Research Council
- Social Research Association
- Professional bodies – for example, the College of Occupational Therapists or the Chartered Society of Physiotherapists
- Health Research Authority (UK – NHS)

1 Choose a code of ethics to read in more depth.
2 Are the key ethical principles applicable to participatory research? Are some areas more difficult to apply than others?
3 Is there evidence that the principles have been created in a participatory way?

Now that you have completed Learning Task 4.1, did you consider that ethical research practice in one context may actually be harmful in another (Brunger and

Wall 2016)? Were you able to find any evidence of participation within the codes? Public involvement (participation) in the design of studies prior to ethical review has been described as having the potential to increase the ethical acceptability of research. However, researchers themselves may not see the added value of such participation, and lay people's ethics-related contributions are often excluded from research reports (Staley and Elliot 2017). Do codes of conduct act as barriers to some participatory research approaches, and perhaps limit their scope?

All research projects including those designed to be participatory usually require ethical approval when they are being conducted by university staff and students. Professionals working in health services and associated roles are also expected to seek relevant ethical approval prior to conducting any data collection and then adhere to ethical codes of conduct such as those illustrated in Learning Task 4.1. In general, these codes detail the need to respect the autonomy of those being researched, ensure confidentiality, adhere to the principle of informed consent and ensure that harm to participants is considered and minimised. These standard ethical principles are outlined in Box 4.1.

Box 4.1 Standard research ethics principles

- Protection from harm – harm to both participants and researchers should be considered in each research study. Researchers should either avoid harm or minimise harm if it seems likely. This can be supported by the use of risk assessment processes as well as adherence to health and safety guidelines. Risks can be psychological, social and physical.

- Participant information – full information to all participants should be provided so that they are aware of the project, their role within it, and the expected outcomes from the study. This is always the case unless the research is covert (hidden) from participants who remain unaware that they are being studied.

- Informed consent – participants should be fully aware of the research process and be able to consent freely. This is usually achieved by the use of information sheets and consent forms.

- Anonymity – participants should not be identifiable in any research results. Research results are often in the form of reports, briefings and academic papers so participants can be allocated different names or codes in the presentation of the data. More innovative and creative methods may include photographs, films, poems and plays. Each dissemination format raises different challenges in terms of anonymity.

- Confidentiality – participants should be aware what happens to the data they provide and who will see it when the results are disseminated.

- Right to withdraw – participants need to be made aware that they can change their mind about their involvement, even after participating. Once results are published withdrawal is no longer possible.

- The research should benefit society in some form. How will participants themselves benefit from the research or be able to share in the knowledge that has been generated from the study?

- Care of participants should be ensured within a research culture of respect. Researchers should not exploit participants and they need to protect community values and relationships.

- Secure data storage should be guaranteed, with data having names and other identifying information removed. Electronic data should be stored within password-protected systems or encrypted and paper copies of information should be locked away.

Reading through the contents of Box 4.1, did you consider what these ethical principles actually mean in terms of conducting research? Kara (2018) argues that research ethics processes tend to focus on data gathering in the main, and that approval systems lead researchers to view ethics as a discrete bureaucratic process rather than as a series of principles which need to be applied in a continuous manner. She also points out that there are pressures on Euro–Western researchers from an economic point of view, which makes doing no harm an easier to achieve ethical principle than attempting to achieve social justice through research (Kara 2018). In one of her blog posts, she writes that the system of ethical governance within universities is itself unethical because it has to be complied with rather than questioned. This process-based approach leads researchers into filling in forms about data storage and participant welfare, rather than enabling them to reflect on the realities of ethical practice during fieldwork (Kara 2017). Furthermore, ethical principles and processes tend to be Euro–Western and as a consequence are full of unacknowledged colonial privilege. They have therefore been criticised for: leading to injustices affecting Indigenous populations (Rix et al 2018); applying deficit models that focus on issues and problems rather the than strengths of communities (Garcia et al 2013); and for being limited in terms of focusing on research as a mechanism to tackle structural inequalities (Smith 2013).

Having ethics codes and research principles, even if there are some criticisms of these, can lead to the view that there is a right and wrong way in which to conduct research ethically. However, ethical approaches may need to be adapted for different contexts and participants, and therefore are better understood as a 'line of best fit' (Kara 2018:9). For example, if you are planning to collect data from a vulnerable group of research participants, then special consideration should be paid to their needs within the study in an ethical manner to ensure that they are protected. Vulnerable participants include populations without literacy, people with limited economic resources, individuals without decision-making power with regard to informed consent, young people and those with learning disabilities (Shallwani and Mohammed 2007). This list is not exhaustive, so other population groups can also be considered vulnerable. Given the many criticisms cited in the literature about the limits of standard research ethics policies and procedures, some researchers have focused on developing more specific guidelines for participatory approaches.

How are participatory approaches ethically different from traditional research approaches?

Armstrong et al (2011) conducted a study focusing on the nature and range of ethical issues within community-based participatory research (CBPR) and concluded that there are two ways in which ethics is framed within the literature in relation to CBPR. First, CBPR is discussed as being more ethical than traditional research because traditional scientific approaches have been harmful, exploitive, and damaging to vulnerable groups such as those with disabilities and Indigenous populations. In comparison, CBPR is seen as a more ethical model because it accounts for power, rights and roles for all of those involved and is driven by egalitarian principles based on respect for community members within any research partnerships. Second, CBPR involves complex relationships associated with power and accountability because it is frequently based on a partnership approach, has blurred boundaries between researchers and participants who may coexist within one community, and it may be linked to campaigning.

Given the differences between traditional research approaches and those which use a participatory framework (see Chapter 1 for more on this), some authors argue that different research ethics principles and practices are required. Complete Learning Task 4.2, to help you reflect on ethical issues specifically in relation to participatory approaches.

LEARNING TASK 4.2 ETHICS IN PARTICIPATORY APPROACHES

Each research project that you engage in will raise different ethical challenges irrespective of your approach, method and the context. Therefore, creating participatory research projects will involve ongoing negotiation related to ethical issues. In light of this, consider the following questions.

1 Revisit the standard ethical principles outlined in Box 4.1 and consider which of these should be maintained in participatory research. Are some less relevant than others? Do they all apply?

2 Do you think that there should be additional ethical principles for all partners who are involved in participatory research projects? If so, what areas do these need to cover?

Make some notes of the key points that you considered in relation to these questions.

While you were completing Learning Task 4.2, were you able to identify areas that needed consideration beyond those described within the traditional principles already highlighted earlier in the chapter? Kawulich and Ogletree (2012) discuss the need to go beyond traditional principles and to consider power sharing in order to produce research that is more likely to benefit communities. They also point out that gaining permission can be difficult and time consuming, researchers need to be mindful of community issues, and cultural differences can determine what is seen as data. They conclude that review boards are the beginning point, but that researchers working in a participatory manner within communities need to consider additional ethical principles in their approaches.

Ethical values underpinning participatory research approaches

Banks et al (2013) explore a range of ethical issues experienced by researchers who have been involved in CBPR projects. They explore 'everyday ethics' which is described as, 'the daily practice of negotiating ethical issues and challenges that arise through the life of CBPR projects' (Banks et al 2013:266). This is in recognition of the limitations of ethical review boards' policies and processes, which do not always fit well with participatory approaches. Box 4.2 outlines some additional considerations in relation to ethical participatory research, which are highlighted within the literature.

Box 4.2 Additional ethical considerations in participatory approaches

- Ethical principles underpinning participatory research are broad as they include the actions of those involved, the relationships between people and their interrelated emotions as well as researcher conduct (Banks et al 2013).

- Researchers themselves need to work with sensitivity so that they can identify the ethical issues in each context. For example, it may be inappropriate for local researchers to work on certain types of research projects. Cornwall and Jewkes (1995) provide one such example in Uganda, where non-local people had to be employed to collect data about HIV/AIDS as a mechanism to avoid further stigma within a local community.

- Researchers need to be trustworthy and reliable, so that they do not let partners down. This involves developing relationship-based ethics, generating trust among all of those involved and negotiating power (Banks et al 2013).

- Researchers can 'retreat from the stance of dispassion' (Fine et al 2000:202) as they have to acknowledge the tensions existing between impartial rules (ethics guidelines) and the realities of working for a better world in a participatory manner.

- Researchers should adopt the principles of care and concern within all participatory approaches. This ethical principle is about researchers being obligated to create improvements in the lives of those who participate (Stuart 1998).

- Researchers working in participatory ways need to use reflexivity: they need to think about their positionality in the research process, power, group dynamics, inclusiveness and the needs of lay researchers.

- Maiter et al (2008) suggest that reciprocity is an essential ethical principle for participatory research. They describe this as an ongoing process of exchange to maintain equality between parties. Reciprocity in their view is an approach that can help to resolve ethical problems in participatory approaches.

- Jamshidi et al (2014) note the importance of local scrutiny in CBPR and the need to consider how to implement appropriate principles in practice. They note the importance of developing consensus in relation to expectations, using cooperative agreements and maintaining developed relationships.

- The Centre for Social Justice and Community Action (2012) suggest seven ethical principles for researchers to consider when conducting participatory research.
  1 Mutual respect: for example, accepting diverse perspectives.
  2 Equality and inclusion: encouraging and enabling all to take part.
  3 Democratic participation: communicating in ways that everyone can understand.
  4 Active learning: learning from each other and reflecting throughout the process.
  5 Making a difference: promoting research that makes a difference to communities.
  6 Collective action: working together to promote change.
  7 Personal integrity: participants behave in a reliable, honest and trustworthy fashion.

As Box 4.2 shows, there is widespread discussion of the need for researchers engaged in participatory approaches to consider ethics beyond the scope of the need for approval. The literature also provides insight into some of the ethical dilemmas that arise when using such methods.

Ethical dilemmas and challenges within participatory research

The literature provides a wide range of discussion about the many ethical challenges that emerge within participatory research studies. As researchers we all hold our own opinions, values and beliefs, and these need consideration within all of our studies. Positionality describes the way in which a researcher's position influences a study in a range of ways, including in relation to ethics. Complete Learning Task 4.3 to consider your own positionality in more depth.

LEARNING TASK 4.3 RESEARCH VALUES, POSITIONALITY AND ETHICS
Take some time to reflect on the following questions.

1 Think about your identity – what is your social class position, gender, ethnicity, sexual orientation? Are you marginalised in any way? How might these characteristics and your position in relation to them influence your view of the world?

2 Do you consider yourself to be privileged? How do you decide this and who are you comparing yourself to?

3 How might these influences shape your understanding of ethics within the research process? For example, do you have a status that affords you more power in society (culturally or professionally), and how might this determine your research practice?

Now that you have completed Learning Task 4.3, did you reflect on the ways in which your social world informs your understanding and approach to research ethics? Might this raise some ethical challenges when conducting participatory research? There are many ethical challenges associated with doing participatory research, so Table 4.1 provides a summary of the key areas needing consideration.

Table 4.1 Summary of ethical challenges in participatory research practice

Ethical challenge	Summary
Partnership, collaborations and associated power dynamics	There may be different expectations between community members and professional researchers (Love 2011). Funding bodies usually have requirements too.
	There may be inclusion and exclusion at various points on the research journey (Dodson et al 2007). Debates are still ongoing about who represents the community (Minkler 2004).
	Partnerships are not static, and so evolve over time (Banks et al 2013).
Blurred boundaries	Community members work as researchers, and professional researchers adopt other roles akin to community development workers, which can result in blurred boundaries. Researchers may also work as community advocates, academics and activists (Horn et al 2008).
	Community members may be both researchers and participants (Banks et al 2013). This can lead to insider-outsider tensions.
Community rights	Most ethical codes and approval processes focus on the rights of individuals (e.g. to choose to be involved or to withdraw). However, in participatory approaches the rights of both communities and groups need to be considered (Quigley 2006).
	Controversial topics also raise further issues in relation to community relations, for example, attitudes of disabled people towards assisted suicide (Minkler et al 2002).
Ownership of the findings and dissemination	Partners may well want different things from the findings and there can be challenges in relation to dissemination, e.g. publications and policy impacts are usually more of a concern for academics than community partners (Quigley 2006, Love 2011).
	It is important to be clear about who owns the data or any outputs that are created. Sometimes funders own the data or universities do (Centre for Social Justice and Community Action 2012).

(continued)

70

Table 4.1 Summary of ethical challenges in participatory research practice (continued)

Ethical challenge	Summary
Anonymity, privacy and confidentiality	When research takes place in local contexts where people know each other well, maintaining anonymity may be difficult (Banks et al 2013). In some instances, participants may wish to be identified, e.g. among indigenous populations (Kara 2018).
Institutional ethical review	As discussed earlier in this chapter, many assumptions linked to ethical review requirements do not fit well with participatory approaches (Banks et al 2013). Participatory research approaches deviate from traditional models of research which can lead to some approval systems not being able to account for community risk, participation, resources and power struggles. The ethics forms and systems in place within many settings have not been adapted to accommodate less traditional research approaches (Tamariz et al 2015). Traditional ethical principles such as those espoused by university research ethics committees may not match those of Indigenous communities. Kara (2018) describes Indigenous principles as: 1 relational accountability (research happens in relationships between people); 2 community of knowledge (everyone can contribute to research); 3 reciprocity (mutual exchanges) benefit sharing so that communities gain as much as other partners.
Emotions and wellbeing	Strong feelings may be involved in research using participatory approaches, for researchers and community members alike. Feelings should be discussed as part of reflective practice (reflexivity) and as a tool to understand decision making. Attention should be paid to ensuring all participants are comfortable. Researchers should develop and employ strategies to manage the emotions for all of those involved, including wider community members. Ethical practice also means supporting participants with access to counselling services, if they are needed – this is part of the ethics of good care (Pain et al 2011).

Table 4.1 offers a summary of some of the ethical challenges discussed in the literature but this list is not exhaustive, and many other ethics related issues are also debated. Wilson et al (2018a:20) explored researchers' experiences of conducting participatory research across different national contexts, using social media as a methodological tool. They note 'evidence of enduring impacts on researchers of the "tightrope" they walked in the interests of maintaining research integrity and ethical responsibility'. Long et al (2016) also discuss the need for researchers to consider questions that won't go away in participatory research. They provide a list of questions that are intended to help researchers critically analyse their own ethical stance in relation to their participatory research practices. Illustrative examples of such questions include:

1. What are the implications for participatory research when communities are divided?
2. When researchers wear different hats (for example, organiser, teacher, consultant, funder), what issues does this raise?
3. What are appropriate ways to credit and reward community members who work on research projects?
4. How can research be done so that it promotes lasting benefits for the community?

Kwan and Walsh (2018:383) conducted a narrative review of the literature about CBPR and argued that 'ethical concerns need to be acknowledged, discussed, debated, and addressed within the literature'. They suggest that ignoring the ethical challenges that arise in participatory approaches may result in them being silenced. They also challenge specific participatory research guidelines. For example, they suggest that a rigid focus on equal participation as being ethical fails to recognise any existing inequalities within the community, such as those related to status, education, gender and age. Flicker et al (2007) provide a list of questions to aid reflection by researchers engaged in participatory approaches, suggesting that these types of considerations are not always raised during traditional ethical review processes. They state that there are rarely right or wrong answers to challenging ethical issues, and that reflection is therefore needed throughout the life of any research project. Their questions include the following:

1. How will decisions be made, and what role with community researchers have in decision-making processes?
2. What are the potential risks associated with involvement for communities?
3. How will conflicts of interest be dealt with?
4. Are there mechanisms in place to deal with unflattering research results?

Researchers also need to consider consent in terms of how it will be obtained (once, or in a more negotiated ongoing manner) and in what form (verbal or written). Flicker et al (2007) ask researchers to consider what communal consent looks like, to think about gatekeeper permissions, and the mechanisms that should be put into place to ensure that all participants really understand the risks and benefits of the study, to enable them to give informed consent.

Confidentiality and anonymity also need further consideration in participatory approaches as identities are more likely to be disclosed or inferred within such contexts. Are all participants made aware of any limits to confidentiality? Researchers need to consider issues, such as blurred boundaries in relation to anonymity, being inclusive while protecting participant identity and who will have access to data (Flicker et al 2007).

Attention needs to be afforded to the characteristics of participants, as many CBPR studies engage with vulnerable and disadvantaged populations. As is the case in traditional research approaches, any participatory studies involving children or vulnerable adults need to contain additional ethical assurances and consider a broader range of ethical issues. Some Indigenous communities have also developed their own guides of good practice for researchers, such as the Te Ara Tika, Guidelines for Māori Research Ethics, from New Zealand, and the San Code of Research Ethics from South Africa. Furthermore, there are guidelines for specific populations, such as for researchers working with disabled participants, and for those working with children. When working with children access has to be negotiated at multiple levels with adults who control children's spaces and lives, such as parents and schools. Informed consent should ideally come from the children but debates about the ability of children to fully understand are often highlighted in the literature, and some parents would prefer to give consent on behalf of their children. Other questions raise further ethical debate. For example, should children be rewarded for their contributions in the same way as adults and who should be included and excluded within any participatory approach (Sime 2008)?

The data collection methods that are being used may also generate additional ethical considerations. For example, visual and creative methods can result in limitations to anonymity. Complete Learning Task 4.4, which will encourage you to think about the use of non-traditional methods in an ethical manner.

LEARNING TASK 4.4 EXPLORING THE ETHICAL IMPLICATIONS OF NON-TRADITIONAL METHODS

Much of the ethics literature offers guidance on how to be ethical when using traditional research methods such as questionnaires, interviews and focus groups. However, there are many ways in which researchers can gather data, so:

1 Make a list of all of the non-traditional methods of data collection that you can think of.
2 Pick one of the methods from your list and consider some of the ethical issues that might arise when using this method in practice; for example, are there issues with permissions or anonymity?
3 Think about how you would set about a non-traditional research approach in an ethical manner.

In completing Learning Task 4.4, did you think about gathering data via the internet, or social media? Did you consider using methods that might include photographs and videos? In Learning Task 4.1, you were encouraged to think about codes of ethical conduct, which in the main cover traditional approaches to research. There are now codes available related to visual methods (see https://visualsociology.org/) and guidance for researchers using the internet to gather data (https://aoir.org/), as each of these methods raises different ethical challenges.

Given all of these complexities, Wilson et al (2018a) highlight the need for training and education at all levels for those involved in conducting participatory research as well as those ethically approving proposed projects. They recognise that training cannot resolve all of the ethical issues that arise in practice, but note that a wider understanding of these approaches and a reciprocal learning culture would nevertheless be beneficial. Buchanan et al (2007) also suggest that funders allocate support for pilot projects for at least a two-year period before the actual participatory study commences, to enable partnerships to develop and confidence to grow within host communities. Ethical issues could be identified early on during the pilot phase, and partners would have time to engage in discussion about these with reference to the context of the research project. Table 4.2 provides example case studies of ethics in practice.

Table 4.2 provides two different examples of how ethical issues were debated and to some extent resolved. These examples illustrate how each study is likely to raise different ethical challenges. This range of differences raises questions about how researchers can use participatory research in an ethical manner.

Table 4.2 Ethics in practice

Research study	Ethics in practice
Evaluation of the Inspiring Change project, Manchester Inspiring Change offered a new and innovative approach to supporting those with multiple needs in Manchester, underpinned by multi-agency partnership working and collaboration. Service user views and experiences were at the heart of the evaluation, which used innovative peer-researcher methods (one-to-one interviews) to gather data to understand service user experiences, explore the impacts of the programme and explore how person-centred approaches worked. Service users and peer researchers were both categorised as homeless (Woodall et al 2016).	The evaluation team adhered to standard requirements by gaining approval from the university where researchers worked (Leeds Beckett). They also applied traditional ethical principles in their practice by ensuring informed consent and anonymity. In addition, the evaluation team trained people with lived experience (homeless community members) to become peer researchers. The training provided to the peer researchers focused in detail on ethical principles, staying safe, gaining consent and doing no harm. The research team carefully considered the ways in which taking part may harm the peer researchers and the participants (Woodall et al 2018). This training provided the peer researchers with increased confidence, and raised self-esteem and transferable skills. This is arguably a more ethical approach to research as it has the potential to empower those in receipt of the training (Woodall et al 2016). Peer researchers were all compensated for their time, skills and efforts through shopping vouchers – considered to be good practice in the academic literature (Terry 2016).

(continued)

Table 4.2 Ethics in practice (continued)

Research study	Ethics in practice
Using participatory visual methods in global health research Black et al (2018) reflect on the use of participatory visual methods in health-related research with economically disadvantaged participants located in Vietnam, Kenya, the Philippines and South Africa.	Participatory visual methods such as the creation of films and photovoice encourage research participants to express themselves in ways that are not open to them when traditional methods are used (such as interviews and focus groups), and therefore have been described as more ethical (Wallerstein and Duran 2010). Ethical challenges in relation to the use of visual participatory methods are numerous and contextually specific (Black et al 2018). For example, using photovoice in the Philippines to explore children's views of malaria resulted in changed family dynamics in the homes of participants with researchers debating if this was ethical. While participants should be granted the power to make decisions within participatory visual research, outputs can be personal, intimate and identifiable – at the beginning of a project participants are unlikely to know what the final output will look like so do they fully understand what they are consenting to? Dynamic consent is therefore needed (Black et al 2018). When using photographs, it is ethical to have the full consent of all of those whose pictures have been taken. Therefore local researchers need to be able to communicate the purpose of the study, how it will be disseminated and have consent forms in various languages (Black et al 2018). Approaches that use drama and role-play methods can be made less sensitive and avoid identity issues, via the use of fictional characters. This was particularly important when exploring HIV in Vietnam (Black et al 2018). In some instances, the visual methods were chosen by the researchers, rather than the local community members because of ethical concerns. Ethics here was prioritised at the expense of full participation (Black et al 2018).

How can I use participatory research in an ethical manner?

There are many suggestions in the literature in relation to doing ethical participatory research. Table 4.3 provides an overview of some of these guidelines and recommendations.

Table 4.3 Summary of ethical practice guidelines

Authors	Suggested ethical practice
Wilson et al (2018a, 2018b)	Generate clear statements about expectations from all parties early on in the process to try to address social, cultural and political issues before the data collection starts.
	Provide robust training for all researchers.
	Engage in discussion with official research committees to gain support, and to generate understanding of the nature of ethical issues that participatory research creates.
Long et al (2016)	Start with the questions that will not go away and use these as a discussion point within your research team. This approach will help those involved in the partnership to make decisions, and to promote reflection throughout the process.
Kwan and Walsh (2018)	Understand identities as shifting.
	Employ critical discussion throughout.
	Focus on equity rather than equality.
	Focus on positive uses of power rather than trying to be neutral.
	Include resources for training and competency building.
	Negotiate consent in an ongoing manner.
	Ensure that professional researchers reflect on their own assumptions and practices.
Centre for Social Justice and Community Action (2012)	Prepare and plan – think about who should be involved and what the aims of the study are.
	Doing the research – consider how participants will work together and agree ethical principles. Consider too if other protocols are needed such as for communication. Agree how to treat people and what to do with the data.
	Share and learn from the research – consider analysis, sharing, dissemination formats, making an impact and how to achieve a good ending.

Again, the list provided in Table 4.3 is by no means exhaustive, as there is a vast expanse of literature in this area, but these guidelines are a useful reference point for those engaged in participatory research approaches. Kara (2018:172) makes the case for being ethical in all aspects of the research process, from start to finish and suggests that 'we cannot design a perfectly ethical research project, write a report that accurately represents all the messy particularities of our work or present our findings in a way that meets the needs of every audience member. But this does not absolve us of the responsibility to try to act as ethically as we can.' Therefore, participatory researchers need to act as ethically as they are able to within each study.

••

CASE STUDY ETHICS IN PRACTICE: THE 'BEYOND SABOR' STUDY

Bastida et al (2010) describe a CBPR project that they implemented in the US and highlight the six ethical principles that were of most significance in their study.

Community context
This study took place in the Lower Rio Grande Valley (southern Texas). The area is economically disadvantaged and previous health inequities research has been funded for researchers living hundreds of miles away. These historical studies used a model of temporary employment for researchers who gathered data but did not offer feedback to local residents.

Participatory approach
Beyond Sabor researchers worked closely with community members (advocates and residents) to develop a code of ethics to guide the project, during the pilot phase of the study which lasted for six months.

Ethical principles in practice
1 *Respect* A code of respect was developed between community members and academics. The academic team participated in training focused on respecting the voice of community members, not contradicting them, and building on their comments within the context of the study. The academics also received training on how to avoid conflict, how to stay neutral and the management of bias.
2 *Transparency* Information about the budget was shared with community members, and the research team aimed to be transparent at all times.
3 *Fairness* Team members were trained to explain the study's inclusion and exclusion criteria and to work fairly as a mechanism to build trust with community members.
4 *Informed consent* The researchers in this study included five people who were bilingual, and therefore able to address community members' questions in a variety of languages. Researchers simplified slides, used pictures to convey ideas and repeatedly emphasised the rights of participants.
5 *Reciprocity* The time that participants gave to the research project was recognised as valuable, therefore contributions (for example, travel time) were rewarded.
6 *Equal voice and disclosure* Everyone's ideas were discussed in community meetings; researchers disclosed their own academic interests and the study results were communicated to participants in an understandable and respectful manner.

Lessons
No single set of principles can ensure that researchers avoid ethical issues in their study.

Ethics as a topic should be addressed early in any participatory study to build trust and create positive working relationships with community members. In addition, ethical codes of conduct need to be applied throughout the duration of all participatory projects.

All researchers in any given participatory study should be trained to conduct research with community members in a respectful manner, and to understand that ongoing ethical negotiation is required rather than a one-step process.

•••

Summary

- Traditional ethical guidelines have been criticised by researchers who use participatory approaches. Participatory research approaches should therefore consider additional ethical principles beyond those often specified by official research committees.

- Participatory research projects are diverse, and therefore raise many ethical challenges for researchers and partners engaged with their use. These challenges and appropriate responses are discussed in the literature in depth, and there are many guidelines for researchers to consult.

- Researchers using participatory approaches within their practice are advised to consider contextual factors in relation to each study, and to negotiate ethical parameters and issues with all partners in an ongoing manner throughout the study.

Suggestions for further reading

1 Kara, H. (2018) *Research ethics in the real world. Euro-Western and Indigenous perspectives*, Bristol: Policy Press.
This book is an introduction to the importance of research ethics in social, professional, institutional and political contexts. The author compares Euro-Western research traditions with those of Indigenous community practices to illustrate differences between them and the need for a nuanced approach to ethical practice within different contexts. Ethics throughout each stage of a research project is detailed in a practical and understandable manner. The book also has a useful companion website containing additional materials.

2 Centre for Social Justice and Community Action (2012) *Community-based participatory research: a guide to ethical principles and practice*, Bristol: NCCPE. Case studies, case examples and commentaries Bristol, NCCPE and Durham University. www.publicengagement.ac.uk/sites/default/files/publication/cbpr_cases_booklet_revised_title_from_ben_4.4.13_19.59.pdf
Rather than providing a discussion of ethical principles that are useful for community-based participatory research projects, this document outlines four different case studies

of example research projects and the associated ethical issues within each of them. Interesting commentaries are also included, as well as questions for discussion.

3 Connected Communities (2011) *Community-based participatory research: ethical challenges*, Centre for Social Justice and Community Action, Durham University. https://ahrc.ukri.org/documents/project-reports-and-reviews/connected-communities/community-based-participatory-research-ethical-challenges/
This is a report that discusses ethical issues in participatory approaches drawn from evidence in the literature. While several challenges are noted, the report provides some useful recommendations for those engaged in CBPR.

Questions for reflection

1 How will you adapt your approach to ensure that you are using ethical principles suitable for participatory research in practice? In your view are some of these ethical principles easier to achieve than others, and if so, how might this influence your approach to 'doing' ethics?

2 How will you ensure that you encourage participation among all of those involved in ethical debates and achieve ethical consensus as the project develops? What mechanisms will you need to use to ensure that you are always working ethically?

3 How will you build trust with community members from the start of your research project and maintain it throughout? Are you able to work with partners to develop ethical ground rules as a starting point of the process, and what are the limitations of such an approach?

Top tips for practice

1 Consider the community context in which you are using a participatory approach to research and all who are likely to be involved. Remember to consider all ethical issues in relation to this context. What aspects of the community context need to be given additional consideration in your ethical framework? For example, vulnerabilities, sensitive topics, stigma and community divisions. How do your own personal characteristics compare with community members' and what does this mean in relation to how you all interpret and understand ethics?

2 A training needs analysis is a good way to assess the skills that participants have and the areas for development. Training can be a useful tool in such contexts to start to build relationships, develop a team and enhance participatory practice. All training should cover ethics and ethical issues as applicable to the context in which you are working together, as a mechanism to raise awareness of ethical principles and a way in which

to begin to understand some of the ethical challenges that may arise. As a researcher, consider what training you also need to enhance your ethical practice.

3 Ethics in participatory practice need to be considered as an ongoing area to revisit throughout each stage of the research project. Each project will raise different ethical considerations, so use an interactive approach in which ethics is discussed regularly. In addition, consider using a phased review process when applying for official ethical approval, as this will allow you to seek approval as each stage of the project as it develops. While this may take more time, such an approach allows for negotiation and consensus building among all partners involved in the process.

Further teaching and learning resources to accompany this book can be found at https://bristoluniversitypress.co.uk/creating-participatory-research-website. The companion website includes:

- teaching slides for lecturers
- further information on learning tasks
- lesson activities
- further reading, links to websites and practical resources
- examples from practice
- additional case studies

5

Data collection approaches within participatory research

Key learning outcomes

By the end of this chapter, you should be able to:

- Define and outline the strengths and weaknesses of different data collection methods, define the key data collection methods associated with participatory research, and those that are not generally associated with participatory research

- Demonstrate awareness of the principles and values associated with participatory data collection methods

- Identify several challenges associated with participatory approaches to data collection

Introduction

This chapter outlines a range of methods that can be used within a participatory approach, and provides several examples of these. The chapter includes discussion of traditional qualitative and quantitative approaches to data collection, as well as more creative techniques that lend themselves to participatory approaches. For example, visual, audio, storytelling and photographic approaches within focus group and interview methods are drawn on to show data collection approaches within participatory contexts. Designing questionnaires within participatory approaches is also explored. This chapter emphasises the importance of inclusive practice to ensure that research is accessible for those involved such as community partners.

What is data collection?

Research methods involve: the type of practices or techniques used to collect, process and analyse the data (for example, what kind of survey to use); the sample size and methods of sampling; assignment to experimental or control groups (see Chapter 3); data measurement and tools; and how data will be processed and analysed (see Chapter 8) (Bowling 2014). This chapter covers which data are collected, how data are collected, data measurement and tools. Table 5.1 provides comparative detail of traditional methods compared with participatory approaches.

Table 5.1 Traditional data collection compared with participatory data collection

Aspect of the research process	Traditional data collection	Participatory data collection
Methodology and study design	Quantitative methodology is chosen when research questions are about effectiveness; qualitative when research questions are about beliefs or experiences. Hierarchies of evidence are often used to 'rate' study designs in terms of methodological robustness; these almost all favour quantitative methodology and experimental design.	Either quantitative or qualitative methodology may be chosen, as for traditional research design, but the majority use qualitative methodology. Many studies use multiple and creative approaches to participant engagement and data collection. Traditional evidence hierarchies are not commonly used. Quantitative designs or elements of design are usually observational; often surveys.
Data	Quantitative: data from biological and other direct measurements or observations; statistics from routinely collected data; questionnaire responses scored and converted into a scale. Checklists to assess methodological rigour favour objective, reliable and valid measures, such as results from blood tests. Qualitative: data from documents, observations, interviews and focus groups.	Either qualitative or quantitative data may be used, but qualitative data predominate; other kinds of data are also more likely, such as visual (e.g. photographs, videos, paintings, storyboards, animations), audio (e.g. stories, poems, songs), existing and created objects (e.g. fabric, artefacts, pottery), and performance (e.g. drama, dance). Data collection tools may be adapted to suit the local cultural context.
Data collection methods	A wide range of data collection methods such as observations, direct measurements, validated scales, semi-structured interviews and focus groups may be used.	A wide range of data collection methods may be used, but creative methods such as video or photo diaries, photovoice or photo elicitation, story boards, singing or drama are often used. In community-based research, neighbourhood walks or asset-mapping techniques may be used.
Data collection tools	Quantitative: checklists; questionnaires; tools for taking direct measurements such as blood pressure monitors and weighing scales. Qualitative: interviews and focus groups using voice recorders are the most commonly used methods and tools; field notes; and other observations may be recorded on a checklist.	In participatory research, there may be less of a clear distinction between data, tools and methods for data collection (e.g. video diaries), but creative methods are usually complemented by another method, such as interviews or group discussion in which the participants share their thoughts about what they have produced.

Quantitative data collection

Quantitative methodology, as we saw in Chapter 3, is concerned with measurement of constructs. This means that the data we analyse are in the form of numbers – for example, height, weight, blood pressure and so on. Biological measurements such as these are naturally numeric but sometimes need to be converted into different units – imperial measurements to metric, for instance. Routinely collected data, such as number of visits to hospital or how many people in a GP practice have been diagnosed with asthma, are also often numeric. Some quantitative data are converted to numbers after the data have been collected; for example, in a questionnaire you might be asked to choose a response to a statement which best represents your experience. The statement might be 'I've been feeling optimistic about the future' and the responses that you can choose from might be: 'none of the time', 'rarely', 'some of the time', 'often' or 'all of the time'. Although the responses are in words, each corresponds to a numeric score. The above statement is from the Short Warwick-Edinburgh Mental Wellbeing Scale (Stewart-Brown et al 2009; Haver et al 2015) which, like all validated scales, has a numeric scoring system. If you develop your own questionnaire, you will need to think about what type of data you have – whether it is nominal, ordinal or continuous (Urdarn 2010) – and how to assign numeric scores to each item to prepare the dataset for analysis.

Epidemiological studies, and other quantitative study designs, may draw on routinely collected data such as:

- Health and social care service use
- Public health data (for example, Public Health Dashboard https://healthierlives. phe.org.uk/)
- Local authority-level data (for example, crime statistics)
- Panel surveys (for example, the Community Life Survey www.gov.uk/ government/collections/community-life-survey)
- Census data (www.ukdataservice.ac.uk/get-data/key-data/census-data.aspx)
- Big data (Mooney and Pejaver 2018)

As mentioned in Chapter 3, Bach and colleagues (2017) developed a conceptual framework outlining the potential for participatory approaches to contribute to the following aspects of epidemiological studies: research goal, research question, population, context, data synthesis, research management and dissemination of findings. Their scoping review cites a community driven monitoring study (AirBeat) which aimed to investigate the links between high asthma rates and air pollution in a neighbourhood. The study produced reliable data on the long-term effects of air pollution at the community level. Frequent meetings of researchers and community members enabled planning of subsequent monitoring and communication processes (Loh et al 2002).

Quantitative design for participatory research

As mentioned in Chapter 3, participatory research rarely takes an experimental approach. Instead, observational study designs are often used, such as surveys, which use questionnaires as data collection tools, and epidemiological studies, which use routinely collected data.

Cross-sectional surveys collect data to provide a 'snapshot' of the population to make inferences at one point in time. Cross-sectional surveys may be repeated but respondents to the survey at one point in time are not intentionally sampled again, although a respondent to one administration of the survey could be randomly selected for a subsequent one (Hall and Lavrakas 2008). In other words, repeated cross-sectional surveys provide a series of 'snapshots' of the population, but do not necessarily sample the same people in each one.

Panel surveys do follow up the same cohort of people in the sample through time. An example of a panel survey is the English Longitudinal Study of Ageing (www. elsa–project.ac.uk/, 2002–, n=18,000+), which collects data from people aged 50 years and older, who are re-interviewed every two years. The study collects information on people's physical and mental health, wellbeing, finances, attitudes regarding ageing, and informs policy across all aspects of ageing including health and social care, retirement and pensions policy, and social and civic participation. Younger age groups are replaced or refreshed to retain the panel.

Box 5.1 provides an example of a survey used in a participatory way.

Box 5.1 Healthy Neighborhoods Study

The Healthy Neighborhoods Study involves nine different groups of community members in collaborative research design and data analysis, including developing a survey instrument, as part of a participatory action research (PAR) study in Boston, USA (Binet et al 2019). The study relies on a network of 45 'resident researchers', who are residents of the study communities working in collaboration with academic, non-profit and public agency partners to design the study protocol and data collection tools, collect primary data, analyse primary and secondary data, and act on the data at the local and regional level. Each study community is represented by four or five resident researchers.

The researchers found that, while there was enough existing guidance in the literature on establishing partnerships with community members and local organisations, on training community members in research ethics and study protocol, and even on gathering survey data, there was little on collaborative processes to engage resident researchers in instrument design and data analysis.

As a result, they designed and facilitated their own workshops. These involved considerable time commitment from the resident researchers, with each attending 15 hours of workshops over five sessions.

Two of the workshops were held to facilitate the development of a survey tool. In these workshops, facilitators led resident researchers through activities designed to generate research questions based on the themes identified in the first workshop, and then to develop a tool to collect data. The participants agreed that this would be a questionnaire with one core component common to all nine study communities, to which each community would add its own set of additional measures based on its own priorities.

Quantitative tools for data collection in participatory research

Questionnaires are used to collect quantitative data in surveys. These can be administered in person by researchers using paper copies or handheld computers (for example, household surveys), filled in over the telephone, delivered by post, or done online or via computer applications (apps). Traditional research favours questionnaires that use validated scales to collect data, as the findings can be compared across different studies and populations. In participatory research, questionnaires may still include validated scales, but are more likely to be developed with the target population and contain questions that address issues of importance to them. Existing scales and tools, if used, should be piloted with the local community and may be adapted in terms of:

- The questions asked – what's relevant and meaningful to the participants.
- The language or words used
  - Jargon should be avoided and plain language should be used. The NHS recommends assuming a reading age of nine (the average reading age in the UK), but for some communities with lower literacy or who do not have English as a first language, this should be adapted to a lower reading age.
  - Some words are offensive in some communities but not in others; involvement of community members can prevent offence or omission being caused accidentally.
- The ways that responses are given – for example, piloting a questionnaire with community members – may reveal that use of a visual analogue scale (see Figure 5.1) for pain measurement may be confusing for most, but that use of a smiley face graphic (see Figure 5.2) may lead to a higher response rate with more accurate reporting.
- The mode of delivery – postal questionnaires have a wide range of response rates, with an average response rate of around 50 per cent for community-based surveys.[2] Online surveys, surveys via mobile phone messages and via apps may have a higher or lower response rate, as not everyone has access to or can use computers or mobile phones. The best way to decide on mode of delivery is to ask the potential research participants and community stakeholders.

---

[2] www.customerthermometer.com/customer-surveys/average-survey-response-rate/

Figure 5.1 Example of a visual analogue scale

No pain   Worst pain
                                                        imaginable

Figure 5.2 Example of a smiley face graphic

No pain   Mild pain   Moderate pain   Intense pain   Worst pain
                                                                    imaginable

Source: Adapted from Wong and Baker (1988)

Box 5.2 gives an example from the literature of participatory development of a questionnaire.

Box 5.2 Participatory questionnaire development

Parrado et al (2005) report on participatory survey design with community collaboration, as part of community-based participatory research (CBPR), in a study of gender and HIV risks in Hispanic migrants. A group of researchers and community members who had been working together to design and set up the study continued to meet biweekly to design the survey questionnaire, which was to be delivered face-to-face. It was felt that the questionnaire needed to be non-intimidating yet able to collect complex data that could be analysed statistically.

After discussing a draft section of the questionnaire, the group expressed concern about the wording of several items, and the potential for variation in how people interpreted phrases or questions based on their place of origin (whether they were from different countries or differences between rural and urban dwellers).

In some instances, the wording was changed and in others, alternative words for the same concept were listed in case they were needed. The group fed back that questions about sensitive issues such as drug use and homosexuality were too controversial to be asked, and these were changed to hypothetical scenarios. CBPR members were then trained to conduct the surveys.

The research team reported that using the CBPR members in this way enhanced access to the migrant community and impact of the research, and the combined experienced gained from developing the survey and familiarity with the Hispanic community meant that CBPR members were very knowledgeable about the topics being researched and the information needed.

Complete Learning Task 5.1 to consider how to work with stakeholders and community members in designing questionnaires and surveys.

LEARNING TASK 5.1 PARTICIPATION IN DESIGNING QUESTIONNAIRES

Surveys are the most commonly used quantitative designs in participatory research and questionnaires are the associated data collection tool. Using your searching skills, the internet and other relevant resources such as books and journal articles, find some examples of commonly used questionnaires and consider the following questions in relation to a population or group you are familiar with.

1 Which of these questionnaires would your population or group find it easiest to answer, and which might they have trouble with? Why is this? What are the issues (if any)?
2 Choose one questionnaire – what changes could you make to it that would make it more accessible for your population?
3 Who else would you need to involve in developing a participatory questionnaire for this population group?

Epidemiological data and health impact assessment

An example of how routinely collected data can be used in a way that has practical and direct implications for an area is the health impact assessment. These are not always participatory, but ideally, they should be, as stakeholders and key informants are involved in predicting potential health impacts of interventions, evaluating the importance of impacts and considering alternative options or mitigating factors.

Health impact assessment (HIA) is a way of assessing the health impacts of policies, plans and projects, particularly on vulnerable or disadvantaged groups, in diverse economic sectors using quantitative, qualitative and participatory techniques. It is concerned with improving the health of populations and the reduction of health inequalities. HIA identifies and encourages policies and practices to promote health and wellbeing in a way that is sensitive to local conditions and communities. It is flexible, practical and systematic, using a combination of procedures, methods and tools to identify the likely effects of a proposed policy, programme or project on a population's health and the distribution of those effects across different population sub-groups. HIA then considers what changes are needed to maximise the health benefits and reduce any health risks, with particular emphasis on reducing health inequalities and promoting socially just, evidence-based interventions.[3]

---

[3] www.liverpool.ac.uk/population-health-sciences/departments/public-health-and-policy/research-themes/impact/

The European Portal for Action on Health Inequalities[4] defines HIA as

> a practical tool, which allows for evaluating the health impact of policies, strategies, and initiatives in sectors that indirectly affect health, such as transportation, employment and the environment. The overall goal of HIA is to inform decision-makers of adverse health effects of proposed actions, and support identification of appropriate policy options.

The International Health Impact Assessment Consortium (IMPACT) defines HIA as 'A combination of procedures, methods and tools by which a policy, programme or project may be judged as to its potential effects on the health of a population, and the distribution of those effects within the population.'[5]

The methods for undertaking HIAs are flexible; however, Scott–Samuel et al (2001) suggest the following overview:

- Policy analysis (where appropriate)
- Profiling the areas and communities affected
- Involving stakeholders and key informants in predicting potential health impacts, using a predefined model of health
- Evaluating the importance, scale and likelihood of predicted impacts
- Considering alternative options and making recommendations for action to enhance or mitigate impacts

Qualitative data collection

As we saw in Chapter 3, qualitative methodology is about meaning and interpretation, perceptions and beliefs. It is commonly accepted that data will be in the form of words and not numbers, but as we will see, meaning can be expressed in other ways, whether through objects that have meaning to the research participants, or through creative arts-based media, such as photographs, videos, storyboards, music, poems, drama, dance, or through made objects such as pottery or quilts.

Qualitative design for participatory research

Interviews are one of the most popular and commonly recognised methods of data collection in qualitative research. These can be with individuals or in groups (focus groups) and carried out face-to-face or over the telephone or internet. Social research interviews can be viewed along a continuum, ranging from the formal questionnaire style interview to the open ended, unstructured approach

---

[4] http://health-inequalities.eu/tools/health-impact-assessment/
[5] See note 2.

(Byrne 2004). Generally, interviews fall into three broad categories: structured, semi-structured and unstructured.

Observations or observational methods can be qualitative or quantitative and can add to self-reported data (for example, on people's behaviours), especially if there is a discrepancy between what people say they do and what they actually do. Behaviours can be studied in context, but this can be very time consuming. There are multiple observational research methods, including participant observation, non-participant observation, covert observation and online observation, each of which may be appropriate in certain contexts for answering relevant research questions in these fields (Pope and Allen 2020). However, observational methods cannot necessarily explain why people are behaving in certain ways, and unless you are there all the time you may miss something important.

Ethnography is the study of social interactions, behaviours and perceptions within groups, teams, organisations and communities. It aims to provide rich, holistic insights into people's views and actions, as well as the nature of the location they inhabit, through the collection of detailed observations and interviews (Reeves et al 2008).

Documentary analysis is a systematic procedure to analyse written documents in relation to specific research questions, which uses repeated review, examination and interpretation of the data to gain meaning and empirical knowledge of the construct being studied. Documentary analysis can be a stand-alone study or part of a larger qualitative or mixed methods study (Frey 2018).

Qualitative tools for data collection in participatory research

Interviews, as already mentioned, are one of the most common methods for collecting qualitative data in participatory research. Individual interviews can be most appropriate where there is not an existing group, or where you want people to be able to speak freely about sensitive or controversial issues, or perhaps about their colleagues or other group members. Focus groups can be most appropriate when working with some stakeholder groups who work as a team, or with vulnerable groups in the population who may feel nervous about taking part in a research interview on their own. Interviews or focus groups should ideally be held in a setting that is familiar and feels safe to the research participant. In community-based research, going through 'gatekeepers' to groups can help to identify suitable settings for data collection. Similarly, in participatory research, having community members as part of the study group will enable safe settings to be identified.

Some advantages of interviews or focus groups as a data collection method are: they have potential for depth, richness, or illuminating material in the data; they allow the researcher to access participants' attitudes and values; they offer flexibility and adaptability (the enquiry or focus of enquiry can be modified during the interview if needed); sensitive issues can be raised; this method does not discriminate against those who cannot read or write.

Some potential disadvantages of using interviews or focus groups as a data collection method are: they are time consuming – not only in developing interview schedules and carrying out interviews, but also in transcription of the data for analysis; they require a skilled interviewer; arranging interviews can be difficult and time consuming.

In semi-structured interviews, an interview schedule is used, which guides the researcher in their questions (Box 5.3).

Box 5.3 Tips for designing interview schedules

- Ask clear questions – don't be ambiguous.
- Avoid leading or closed questions (for example, 'I love going to the cinema with my friends, do you?').
- Put yourself in the interviewee's shoes – would you like to be asked those questions?
- Think about how much time you and the participants have available for each interview.
- Use plain language and try to avoid using jargon.
- Think about your opening and closing questions.
- Pilot your interview schedule on willing members of the target population, and get feedback.
- Refine your interview schedule accordingly.

Now complete Learning Task 5.2 to consider how to incorporate participatory research principles into developing interview schedules.

LEARNING TASK 5.2 PARTICIPATION IN DESIGNING INTERVIEW SCHEDULES

Thinking about the research you are planning to do, and the population you are working with, consider the following issues, with reference to research literature and guidance cited here or elsewhere.

1 Which community members do you need to work with to develop your interview schedule? Whose 'insider' knowledge will you need to draw on? Are you already in touch with them or do you need to approach a 'gatekeeper' to introduce you?

2 How will you work with community members to develop an interview schedule that meets everyone's requirements? Are there any potential areas of disagreement that you can see? How will you handle this?

3 Are there any potentially sensitive or controversial questions you need to ask? If so, what groundwork do you need to do first, and what measures might you need to have in place?

Creative methods

Warwick-Booth and Coan (2020) argue that creative research methods are a way to try to address the power imbalance between researchers and participants, as they offer participants a range of options for contributing their experiences in a relaxed atmosphere. Creative methods can make the data collection process more enjoyable and democratic, placing a high value on the stories and feedback of research participants and allowing them to tell their stories in a way that makes most sense to them (Deacon 2000). Halcomb (2016) lists a range of creative approaches in qualitative research, including art, dance, poetry, photography and combinations of these and other approaches. The following sections describe some of the more creative methods and tools for data collection, with examples from research in practice.

Visual methods

Photovoice is a CBPR method that has been used to address many public health and social justice issues. It has been defined as 'a process by which people can identify, represent and enhance their community through a specific photographic technique' (Wang et al 2000:82), and is particularly used to empower vulnerable or stigmatised groups. Typically, participants use photography to capture their personal and community strengths and concerns, engage in critical group discussions about the photographs and their meanings, and disseminate their ideas to their communities in exhibitions of the photographs.

A systematic review of 37 studies using the photovoice method found that the exact methods used were tailored to suit the needs and constraints of each project (Catalani and Minkler 2010), although the review authors also reported a lack of detail about methods, particularly for analysis, in the published literature. Levels of community participation and community impact were also poorly reported. The review found 'increasing' evidence that photovoice can be used as a participatory tool for engaging communities in a CBPR process, and promising evidence that photovoice enables researchers and practitioners to make contact with hard-to-reach communities and engage them in meaningful research.

Ronzi and colleagues (2019) used photovoice to explore households' perceptions of factors influencing the uptake of liquefied petroleum gas (LPG) for cooking in South-West Cameroon, with the aim of advancing the uptake of clean cooking and improving health. Following training in photography and ethics, and an initial focus group, participants photographed subjects that they felt prevented or facilitated LPG uptake in their communities. They shared reflections on their photographs in interviews and group discussions, and then presented their photographs at a public exhibition, which generated discussions with key stakeholders (for example, government ministries) about how to support communities in this transition.

Box 5.4 Example of a photovoice study

In a study of photovoice in women living with HIV/ AIDS in North America, the researchers proposed that photovoice was a way for these affected women to inform health promotion programmes which were designed to affect their lives (Teti et al 2012). The authors report on two studies, which each included three group sessions and an exhibition of the photographs. Group sessions were co-facilitated by an experienced health educator and a researcher. In session 1, the goals and purpose of the project and the ethics of picture taking were reviewed, and the participants were trained in camera use. Participants then took photos, and sessions 2 and 3 were facilitated discussions of their pictures, using the SHOWeD technique (Wang and Redwood-Jones 2001) and including both individual and group discussion:

- What do you <u>S</u>ee here?
- What is <u>H</u>appening?
- How does this relate to <u>O</u>ur lives?
- <u>Wh</u>y does this problem or strength exist?
- What can we <u>D</u>o about it?

During session 3, participants planned a public photo exhibition, and discussed where to hold the exhibition, whom to invite and which pictures to share publicly.

Photo elicitation is using photographs or other visual media in an interview to generate discussion. Different layers of meaning can be discovered as this method can evoke deep emotions, memories and ideas (Harper 2002; Noland 2006; Glaw et al 2017).

Autophotography is asking participants to take photographs of their environment and then using the photographs as data. Glaw et al (2017) state that autophotography is an important tool for building bridges between marginalised groups in research because it does not rely on participants having to speak for themselves. It therefore gives those who may not be fluent in the researcher's first language to express themselves with confidence and clarity, giving them the same opportunities as those who are fluent in the primary language (Noland 2006).

Digital storytelling refers to a two- to five-minute audio-visual clip which combines photographs, voice-over narration and other audio (Lambert 2009). It was originally applied for community development, artistic and therapeutic purposes, and has more recently been adapted as an arts-based research method. A systematic review of 25 studies of digital storytelling in research reported that it was especially appropriate for use with marginalised groups, and was most commonly used in this context, yet surprisingly few research projects used the digital stories generated for knowledge translation. Across research projects, participants reported several benefits of digital storytelling (de Jager et al 2017).

Participatory video aims to support an empowering process, whereby community members engage in iterative cycles of shooting and reviewing videos to create video narratives that communicate what the participants want to communicate, in a manner they feel is appropriate (Kindon 2003:143). It is said that it has the potential to bridge a communication gap between non-literate or less literate groups and decision makers due to its non-written form (Protz 1998; Braden 1999; Suarez et al 2008; Plush 2009).

Arts-based methods

Storyboards Cross and Warwick-Booth (2016) describe using storyboards in focus group discussion with young women to facilitate reflection on three positions – 'where I was' (reflecting on the past), 'where I am now' (reflecting on the present) and 'where I want to be' (aspirations for the future). The participants were each given a large sheet of card that they were invited to divide into three equal sections representing the three positions: past, present and future. A range of materials were provided to create the storyboards (for example pens, pencils, stickers, and magazines/newspapers to cut out words and pictures). Some participants chose to write on their storyboards instead of drawing or sticking images on it. Once everyone had finished, they were invited to talk through their storyboard with the rest of the group. The researchers led the discussion by presenting their own storyboards first. Not every participant wanted to speak about their storyboard but all consented to having them photographed and used as data, and some took them away with them. The authors reflected that the storyboards served as a mechanism for participants to convey complex personal and emotional journeys in a non-threatening way. They were able to draw, write or create images representing experiences or feelings they might otherwise have found hard to describe or share.

Metaphors Cade (1982) noted that using metaphors gives participants the freedom to use their own creativity and experiences in a reflective way. Warwick-Booth and Coan (2020) state that the use of metaphors in qualitative research allows participants to describe one thing (in this case, the way a group works) by using an analogy of another. They outline the use of a cake metaphor (Nind and Vinha 2016) in their focus group discussions with vulnerable women being supported by a third sector organisation. Participants were asked to think about the support service as a cake recipe and represent the essential elements of the service as cake ingredients, as well as those who they felt were non-essential added extras. Pictures of suggested ingredients (such as butter, eggs, sugar, flour), a bowl and utensils were prepared by the researchers, as well as themes relating to different components of the project taken from previous interviews with service users, to be used as prompts if necessary. The activity was used as an icebreaker before the more formal recorded focus group discussion, and the participants engaged with it well. On reflection, the researchers felt that, although the activity worked well, it may have worked even better (with less input required from the researchers) at the end of the focus group discussion, once participants had 'warmed up' and felt more at ease.

Participatory theatre   O'Neill et al (2018) report on a PAR project exploring participatory theatre and walking methods to help understand how migrant families construct their sense of belonging and social participation. The authors argue that both methods create a space for sharing, exploring and documenting processes of belonging and place making. The research aimed to generate new knowledge about the social exclusion experienced by migrant mothers, girls and families with no public financial support. A range of partners were involved in the project, and academics and arts practitioners worked closely with the research participants. The participatory theatre methods used built on Kaptani and Yuval-Davis (2008) guidance:

- Two sessions of Playback Theatre to start workshops. In playback theatre, local and personal stories are seen 'on stage' and thereby given validity. As the authors explain, this method opens a space for the stories to be told, where emotions can be expressed through the narratives and enactments as well as reflection with the facilitators and actors.
- Theatre of the Oppressed (Boal 2000) – based on the principles of collective empowerment and emancipation outlined by Freire (1970), this comprised image theatre and forum theatre:
  Image theatre   Participants create shapes or sculptures with their bodies to express a feeling, issue or scene, without using words.
  Forum theatre   Participants share stores of issues or problems. The group decide on one story they will perform as a short sketch. They show this to other participants, who are invited to intervene by taking the place of the protagonist and suggesting better strategies for changing the course of action.
  Legislative theatre   These activities are taken into other social settings to enact social, legal or policy changes. In this study, theatre produced by the mothers was taken to a policy event where people from policy and practice in migration, families and the arts were invited, and to an event at the House of Commons co-organised with the All Party Parliamentary Group on Migration, as well as other voluntary and community sector organisations and statutory groups.

Participatory mapping

Emmel (2008:1) describes participatory mapping as 'an interactive approach using accessible and free-ranging visual methods in an individual or group interview setting to interrogate qualitative research questions'. He reasons that participatory mapping techniques complement conventional verbal interviews in that the act of drawing enables the participant to focus attention on a feature of the map, and it gives the researcher a record of the map that can be interrogated both during and after its production. The tangible presence of the map allows the researcher and the participant to return to features of the map in present and future interviews to move through description to depiction to theorising the reasons for the ways features have been represented. Mapping can be of a place or of other kinds of knowledge, such as people's bodies or networks of friends or connections. Maps can be drawn with individuals or with groups, but the researcher points out that group maps are best achieved with a homogeneous group, and that the researcher needs to facilitate negotiation among the group members about how the map is drawn. As well as the map, the interview or discussion that takes place during and after its creation should be recorded. Video recording is more useful than audio, as participants may point at features on the map as they are talking.

In O'Neill et al's study (2018) which combined participatory theatre with neighbourhood walks, they cite a tradition of walking in ethnographic, anthropological and sociological research with communities (Lee and Ingold 2006; Pink 2008; Edensor 2010). They argue that walking is an embodied research practice that is sensory and multimodal (O'Neill and Hubbard 2010). In this project, migrant mothers and girls were invited to map their everyday routes and the researchers walked with them either in pairs or collectively.

- Participants were asked to visualise and reflect emotionally and through the senses on their everyday routes (for example, to work, school and so on)
- Participants were asked to draw a favourite walk, marking important landmarks along the way
- Participants walked in pairs in the workshop space, describing their walks to each other
- Participants shared their maps with the group, describing the places and spaces on them
- The group agreed a schedule for the walks, and the routes to take, using the maps
- Walking in groups and pairs
- Walks were discussed in the workshops, photographs and maps were gathered and walks integrated into theatre forms

The researchers reflected that walking and reflecting on the walks with participants helped them to gain a better understanding of the group's experiences of living in London as girls, migrant mothers and mothers with no access to public money.

Complete Learning Task 5.3 to consider how to incorporate creative methods into your research.

LEARNING TASK 5.3 THINKING ABOUT CREATIVE METHODS

Considering your own planned research, take time to think about the following questions.

1 Choose one of the creative methods described above and think about how it could be incorporated into your research study.

2 What would be the benefits of doing this, for researchers, participants and other stakeholders?

3 How feasible and practical would it be to incorporate this creative method?

4 Can you think of any challenges you might face?

Challenges of participatory data collection

Warwick-Booth and Coan (2020) note the importance of timing when using creative methods – both allowing enough time for rapport and trust to be established before data collection and allowing participants space for reflection during the activity.

One of the advantages of participatory research is its potential to be inclusive of disadvantaged or vulnerable groups of people who are often overlooked in traditional research – for example, people with disabilities, people with severe mental illness, sex workers, or people who are homeless. Although the methods outlined in this chapter and others give a framework for researchers to build on, they also need to be open to adapting the methods in response to unexpected developments or feedback from the participants – for instance, they may not feel comfortable being filmed or recorded. In traditional research, this might lead to them being excluded from the study, but in participatory research it is the researchers who must 'go back to the drawing board' and be creative and flexible in offering and co-designing solutions to address power imbalances and enable non-researcher perspectives to be both heard and included.

When reflecting on the usefulness and challenges of participatory theatre and walking methods in PAR, O'Neill et al (2018) noted the following challenges.

- Extra time was needed to build relationships, to take care of participants and each other in the team, especially when working with emotive and sensitive issues.
- Team consideration and reflection on working across boundaries, relationships, power, trust, language and ethics were important.
- PAR can be costly when you take into account staff time, the need to bring in trained arts or theatre specialists to work with the participants and the wish to financially reimburse participants for their time.
- Balancing multiple demands, for example:
  - The wish to create a presentable piece of work within the aims of the PAR.
  - Group building, so that each participant has the opportunity to share their views even if these conflict with those of other participants.
  - The team must be open, transparent, and facilitate sharing of ideas, reflection and communication.

- Ethical issues and challenges, for example:
  - Power relations: it cannot be assumed that all participants hold equal status in co-production of knowledge, as power differentials between researchers and participants may be disguised.
  - It takes a long time, sometimes months, to connect with participants, potential partners and build trust, skills and enthusiasm for collaborative projects.
  - Emotional labour is often involved in this work, from both participants and researchers.
  - Managing expectations: the authors state that researchers, policy makers and practitioners using PAR with marginalised communities need to tread a careful path between generating interest to participate and valuing participants' contributions, without raising false hopes.
  - Clarity over the ethics and principles underpinning the research are needed.

LEARNING TASK 5.4 CHALLENGES OF PARTICIPATORY DATA COLLECTION

1 Building on the potential challenges you identified in Learning Task 5.3, have you now identified any more potential challenges in your own planned research?

2 Take some time now to think about potential solutions to these challenges. How will you identify these? Will you need to test them out with participants? How will you do this? Who will decide which solution to try and which to adopt? How will you manage this decision-making process?

....

CASE STUDY PARTICIPATORY VIDEO TO EMPOWER MARGINALISED GROUPS

A one-year PAR project in Nepal explored participatory video as a supportive development tool to generate local knowledge on impacts and coping strategies, build the capacity to act on this knowledge and advocate for adaptation support from the local to the global level.

The lead researcher in this study was an experienced professional video producer. Their experience suggested that video could be a potential development tool for addressing climate change. The researcher wanted to explore whether participatory video led to local impacts in a more meaningful way than traditional academic studies.

The researcher worked with women and children in Nepal, with the aim that community members would become film makers documenting local climatic impacts, reflecting on their findings, prioritising adaptation needs and making final films for change, to influence decision makers.

Poor women and children were selected as research participants because their marginalised status in Nepal and consequent poverty means they are especially vulnerable to disasters and climate change hazards. The researcher developed a conceptual framework based on Gaventa and Cornwall (2008) in which participatory video was used as a tool for social change, and is defined by awareness/knowledge, capacity for action and people-centred advocacy.

The participatory video research was integrated into the existing structure of the Disaster Risk Reduction for Schools project (DRRS). The researcher trained community members who also worked with DRRS to become participatory video facilitators with the women and child groups, as they were already engaged with them. The methodology was as follows:

- Participatory video workshop – train the trainers.
- Trained participatory video facilitators worked with communities to create key informant groups of women and children.
- Researcher formally hands the project over to the community.
- Climate change education meeting for key informants.
- Community interviews – key informants interview each other on camera using research questions developed in the participatory video workshop.
- Key informants review the videos, discuss problems and impacts, and reflect on what they are learning.
- Storyboard meeting – key informants use their new knowledge to create a drama or documentary on the topic.
- Make film – make a film showing what they have learned and their suggestions for climate change adaptation support.
- Community showing – films are shown to family members and the community. Ideally, combine with climate change films and bring a climate expert to answer questions. Discussion about actions and next steps.
- Show films to decision makers who can address the main issues at local and district levels.
- Show to national and international decision makers.
- Researcher follow-up – a report of the key informant needs as identified through the film-making process and explored further through focus group discussions and informal interviews.

The researcher's role was to facilitate the workshops, formally hand over the research project to the key informant groups in each village, provide ongoing support and advice as needed, and oversee national and international advocacy efforts promoting women's and children's rights for climate change adaptation funding.

An example of a film made as part of this study is a children's drama showing how they were impacted by increased flooding: they cannot access school during the monsoon, or they lose books or drown trying to cross the river. They asked for a bridge over the river to safely reach school. The film was shown to community members who were impacted by the drama, showing the difficult crossing and the trauma faced by a drowning child. Community members and key decision makers agreed to make the bridge their top priority. The bridge was funded.

(Plush 2009)

Summary

- Data collection in participatory research has an emphasis on power and specifically on ways to shift the power imbalance between researchers and participants, and to genuinely empower participants. The ultimate goal is for both researchers and participants to gain something from the process. For participants this may include any or all of the following: new skills and confidence; new connections; development and articulation of a shared vision; advocacy; and impact on local conditions.

- Creative methods are often used in participatory research, on their own or as an adjunct to focus group discussions. These can be particularly helpful when working with marginalised populations, to help build rapport and trust with the researchers and within the group, and to elicit discussion in a non-threatening way.

- Researchers need to be alert to challenges and obstacles that may arise in the process of participatory data collection, and be open and flexible to co-creating feasible and acceptable solutions with the research participants. These considerations need to be carefully balanced with the need to produce robust data.

Suggestions for further reading

1 Denzin, N. and Lincoln, Y. (2011) *The Sage handbook of qualitative research*, Thousand Oaks, CA: Sage.
   This is a comprehensive and detailed book covering all aspects of qualitative research. This is an edited volume, that also discusses issues of social justice in relation to policy change. The book offers critical insight into inequalities, as well as outlining how the practices of qualitative research are important in relation to social change.

2 Green, J. and South, J. (2006) *Evaluation: key concepts for public health practice*, London: Sage.
   This book introduces the reader to evaluation in the context of public health. The book outlines how evaluation can lead to improved health outcomes, as well as providing an introduction to principles, challenges and complexities.

3 Kara, H. (2015) *Creative methods in the social sciences: a practical guide*, Bristol: Policy Press.
   This book discusses four areas of creative research methods: arts-based research, research using technology, mixed-methods research and transformative research frameworks. Written in a practical and easy to read style, the book also has lots of examples of creative approaches.

Questions for reflection

1 Looking at the types of participatory data collection available and the examples given in this chapter, how distinct are they? How might they complement one another? Can you think of any examples of traditional research studies that may have benefited from a more participatory approach?

2 This chapter covers a range of data collection methods but is not exhaustive. Are there any data collection methods that you were expecting to read about that are not here? How can you find out more about these?

3 What are your feelings about participatory data collection methods? How comfortable are you with the balance of power between researchers and participants and the effects this may have on the quality and relevance of the data collected?

Top tips for practice

1 When working towards designing data collection tools in participatory research, think about how you will apply the principles of inclusive practice, fully involving research participants in the process. As for research design, try to build in a carefully facilitated meeting at the start of the project which allows all participants to have a say, and check in with them regularly as the project progresses. Have a look at the NICE guidance on community engagement, particularly the overview of good practice, which applies as much to evaluation of projects as delivery: https://pathways.nice.org.uk/pathways/community-engagement

2 Consider participants' capacity to be involved in data collection, and balance this with the principles of participatory research. Although, in principle, research participants should be fully involved at all stages, in some situations especially in areas of deprivation and when working with vulnerable groups, people have other priorities and, despite the best intentions, may not have the time or the enthusiasm to be fully involved. By all means encourage and support them to be fully involved, while building capacity and confidence, but allow them to take the lead in terms of commitment, and respect their boundaries and decisions.

3 Teti et al (2012) made a number of recommendations for best practice when using photovoice, some of which can also apply to other forms of data collection:

- Consent process – a three-stage consent process was recommended to protect both participants and people in the photographs: project consent; consent for releasing photos for public display; photo release form to include others in photos.

- Release forms – allow participants to practise asking permission and completing the forms, to help them become comfortable with the process.

- Picture-taking plan – discuss photo ethics with participants, including what kinds of pictures they might take.

- Meeting the needs of diverse participants – in this project some participants preferred to be open about their identity as living with HIV/AIDS while some preferred to keep this private. Programme leaders can help participants choose pictures that meet their needs.

- Adequately addressing status disclosure – project leaders should plan for difficult discussions about personal issues such as HIV status disclosure, and remind participants that each person's decision about disclosure is valid.

- Internet photo sharing – project leaders should discuss the challenges that are posed when photos are shared on social media.

- Collaborative exhibit planning – when the issue being explored (for example, HIV) is associated with stigma, and/ or if there are issues of disclosure or non-disclosure of disease status, the authors recommend making the exhibit an optional part of the process, and allowing participants to choose which photos they exhibit, to choose captions for the photos and use pseudonyms if they wish. Collaborative planning means that there may be disagreement about the scope and location of the exhibit. The authors recommend choosing a plan that feels safe for all participants.

- Ongoing support – help participants to access support and referrals that they might need to resolve the problems identified in the project, even when the formal sessions are over.

Further teaching and learning resources to accompany this book can be found at https://bristoluniversitypress.co.uk/creating-participatory-research-website. The companion website includes:

- teaching slides for lecturers
- further information on learning tasks
- lesson activities
- further reading, links to websites and practical resources
- examples from practice
- additional case studies

6

Approaches to analysis

Key learning outcomes

By the end of this chapter, you should be able to:

- Define research analysis and understand why it is so important
- Demonstrate awareness of the principles and values underpinning participatory approaches to analysis
- Identify several types of participatory analysis methods

Introduction

This chapter explores how the analysis of data can be participatory. It outlines how analysis can include participants in a range of ways, offering examples from practice. This chapter links the techniques for data collection to appropriate analysis approaches and offers examples of how these can be conducted in a more participatory manner. Both qualitative and quantitative approaches to participatory analysis are outlined; however, there is limited literature in this area with a lack of examples about participatory quantitative analysis. The chapter discusses how collaboration can work within analysis approaches, as well as issues with this aspect of the research process.

What is data analysis?

Data are the information that researchers collect when they use different research methods. Data come in a range of different formats, such as words from interviews, diaries and observational fieldnotes (qualitative methods), and numbers from measurements, such as surveys and experiments (quantitative). Data can also be in the form of visual images (photographs), film and art. Making sense of data is termed the process of analysis. Data analysis is well described in the academic literature but is not simple in that it can be viewed as a process, and it involves specific procedures and methods, as well as decision making, ideas and the actual handling of the data. There are many different types of data, therefore, and the analysis of data varies significantly. Trained researchers apply one or more analytical procedures or methods on their collected 'raw' data, to interpret and then illustrate what the data are actually saying, usually in response to research questions set prior to data collection. Results are then presented and disseminated (see Chapter 7 for more on this).

Traditional analysis compared with participatory approaches

In traditional approaches to data analysis, academic/professional researchers conduct data analysis and interpret the findings. In comparison, participatory analysis approaches involve community members and/or stakeholders in the interpretation of the findings. Cahill (2007a:306) notes that the forms that participatory analysis takes are largely variable and 'moments of analysis emerged organically at multiple and regular points as part of our reflective praxis rather than being a set "phase" of research'. Table 6.1 provides an overview of the main differences between traditional qualitative and group participatory approaches to analysis by way of an example. Table 6.1 focuses on qualitative analysis; however, community members can also be involved in quantitative analysis, as discussed later on in the chapter.

Nind (2011) suggests that notions of what it means to undertake participatory analysis vary, which is unsurprising given the diversity of approaches that are available to those who are professionally trained researchers. Holland et al (2008:15) also discuss the complexities of what it means to 'do' participatory analysis:

Table 6.1 Overview: differences between traditional qualitative and group participatory analysis approaches

Traditional qualitative analysis	Group participatory analysis
Data management: voice files and/or notes from focus groups, interviews or observations are typed up, or transcripts are created by a member of the research team (usually someone employed in a research role).	Data management: the data are made usable by the group of participatory researchers. This might involve coloured paper, larger font sizes or statement 'strips' of words. In doing this, the group becomes familiar with the data.
Classification: a researcher or in some instances team members code the transcripts or notes. This may involve drawing on emergent codes (those seen in the data) or working to label the data according to predeveloped themes.	Classification: the group organise the data (i.e. the strips of paper) into clusters and then into themes. Theme titles are decided on in the group, by discussing ideas so this is a more emergent way of working.
Interpretation: the researcher and/or other team members develop a hierarchy of themes and sub-themes, linked to each other, to the existing academic literature and to theory.	Interpretation: the group of co-researchers attempt to make sense of the 'whole thing' by discussing the stories and the data.
Reporting the findings: a researcher or team member writes up the data usually in the format of a report.	Reporting the findings: a member of the group writes up the story of the data.

Source: Adapted from Jackson (2008)

It is often claimed that participatory research rarely involves participants beyond the data generation stage and that participants involvement in analysis is minimal. This perhaps reflects a conceptualisation of analysis as a separate, formal stage of the research process, yet in qualitative research analysis is more often conceived of as beginning with the development of the research questions and occurring throughout data generation [...]

This quote points out that in some instances, participatory analysis can have fluid boundaries, and involves dialogue rather than being a distinct method or stage in all cases (Thomas and O'Kane 1998). Complete Learning Task 6.1, which will help you to consider if participatory analysis is appropriate for your project.

LEARNING TASK 6.1 CONSIDERING THE APPLICABILITY OF PARTICIPATORY ANALYSIS

Think about the research project that you are planning to do and consider the following questions.

1 To what extent will the research be participatory in the design and data collection? If the design is participatory does this provide a gateway into more involved and engaged analysis?
2 How can participatory analysis improve the findings of the project? Think about the quality of the results and the use of recommendations as starting points here.
3 Are there likely to be positive outcomes for lay researchers/community members/stakeholders engaged in the analysis?
4 In terms of practical considerations, do you have both the time and budget to be able to 'do' participatory analysis?

In completing Learning Task 6.1, did you think about the principles that might inform your approach to involving lay researchers in your analysis?

What are the principles of participatory analysis?

Israel et al (2008) define the key principles of community-based participatory research (CBPR) (see Chapter 1), which link to the processes associated with data analysis. CBPR involves participation by non-professional researchers, therefore this can and should include the involvement of non-researchers in data analysis. Equality is frequently cited as a value of CBPR, therefore communities and researchers should be equally involved in analysis. Given that participatory approaches to research also involve joint learning, then analysis is an area in which learning and reflection can take place. Israel et al (2008) further argue that CBPR is underpinned by empowerment as a principle, enabling participants to take control of their lives. Involving community members in analysis can enable them to frame the research findings in a way that is suited to their needs and requirements, a starting point for social action. Inclusive and meaningful involvement are also both basic principles of participatory analysis. However, given the debates in the literature, the extent to which these principles can be achieved in relation to analysis is still ongoing.

Spears Johnson et al (2016) examined 25 CBPR projects that had been conducted for the National Institutes of Health and the Centers for Disease Control and Prevention in the US and found that only four of the projects had lay researchers involved in the analysis. This reflects power dynamics and the point that not all research projects can implement CBPR principles in the same way or indeed to the same extent for all aspects of each study (Israel et al 2005a). Spears Johnson et al (2016) therefore state that the scientific community needs to recognise that there is huge variability in the application of CBPR principles, and that each project will need to reflect on how well the ideal can be achieved. Involvement in analysis is clearly an area that needs further assessment in relation to CBPR principles, but many academics argue that it remains an important aspect of the research process in which lay researchers can and should be included.

Why is participatory analysis important?

Nind (2011) discusses how some researchers debate what it means to do participatory research, and questions which aspects of the research process matter the most, noting that far more attention has been paid to involvement in defining the problem, data gathering and dissemination. Participation in data analysis remains a relatively neglected area despite researchers arguing that it produces more authentic knowledge (Grover 2004). Charlton (2000) argues that the politics of inclusion underpinning participatory research are based on the idea that nothing about us should be done without us, therefore participation in analysis is essential. Pankaj et al (2011) discuss how participatory data analysis can be used with stakeholders to present first draft findings for feedback, contextual updates, input and recommendations, as a way to encourage and maintain involvement, identify the most meaningful findings and increase the potential usage of the findings. Box 6.1 illustrates the strengths of participatory analysis approaches.

Box 6.1 Strengths of participatory analysis

- Useful in research projects in which academic researchers do not need/want to dominate.
- Increasing the mix of participants involved in analysis can lead to both richer interpretation of the data as well as learning for all of those involved.
- Participatory analysis is a useful tool for fostering dialogue and reflection between participants, such as community members and academics as well as other stakeholders and professionals.

- Having more people involved increases the capacity of the team to handle data.
- Group participatory analysis is inexpensive, and many approaches are available to community members and organisations.

Source: Adapted from Jackson (2008)

Box 6.1 provides an overview of the positive aspects that are associated with qualitative participatory group analysis, but not all projects gather qualitative data and not all data can be analysed in a group setting.

Research methods and analysis approaches

Each research design (see Chapter 3), and methodological approach (see Chapter 5), will call for a different approach to data analysis given that the form of the data available will vary, as indeed will the purposes of the study, its underpinning research questions/hypotheses and the format of the final findings. Therefore, there is no ideal set of techniques that can be written about here as analysis decisions will change according to the requirements of each project. There are, however, incremental stages involved in the analysis of any data set, therefore when working to ensure participation academics can start by considering the potential involvement of community members at each point of the analysis process. Table 6.2 outlines these stages for both qualitative and quantitative projects.

Table 6.2 Stages in the analysis of data

Qualitative data analysis	Quantitative data analysis
Creswell (1998) outlines five main steps in qualitative analysis:	Again, there are several stages involved in quantitative analysis. Aleman (2017) describes three stages involved for quantitative analysis:
1 Data management – this means creating and organising the data.	1 Data evaluation – this involves reading the data, looking for inaccuracies and outliers and spot checking.
2 Reviewing and familiarisation – this means reading, making notes and defining initial codes.	2 Data cleaning – this is the process of taking often 'messy' data and transforming them into a format that enables analysis.
3 Classification – this describes the coding and the grouping of data.	
4 Interpretation – this refers to developing patterns, meanings and making sense of the findings.	3 Summarising – this involves working with the data to summarise and present the findings. This may involve the use of statistical packages and the generation of descriptive and/or inferential statistics.
5 Representation – this final stage is the point at which the researchers draw conclusions and present the findings (e.g. a report, stories, visual images or a film).	

As Table 6.2 shows, there are several stages of analysis, therefore community researchers can potentially be involved in any of these stages, or indeed all. The level of involvement depends on a range of factors (skills, time, commitment) and the way in which the analysis process is itself viewed by the lead researcher. Holland et al (2008) also point out that what is potentially fascinating to researchers may be dull for lay researchers, or too challenging (on an emotional or intellectual level), meaning that attention should be paid to how participation in analysis can be enacted. Box 6.2 therefore provides an example of how participatory analysis was enacted in a quantitative study. (Examples of qualitative participatory analysis can be found in Table 6.3 on p 110)

Box 6.2 Example of quantitative participatory analysis

Binet et al (2019) were involved in a longitudinal study in Boston, USA, as part of a consortium, which has a network of 45 community researchers, all with varying levels of experience. Resident researchers were paid $15 per hour.

Using a collaborative workshop approach, led by the academics, hypotheses were generated with the resident researchers and community partners. These were used to guide the agenda for later workshops. The analysis workshops introduced community members to the basics of data analysis and generated interpretations of descriptive statistics and outputs drawn from regression models, structural equation models and factor analyses. Academics conducted initial analyses of some of the data prior to delivering the analysis workshops with the resident researchers. For example, the academics designed and conducted an exploratory factor analysis to test a hypothesis generated by the resident researchers. The results of this were then presented to the community researchers for them to discuss, and this was used to inform a decision about how to conduct a confirmatory factor analysis.

This study was a long-term process, taking place over a period of seven months, with resident researchers (n=45) completing a total of 15 hours of workshop time, over five sessions across nine different geographical areas. The resident researchers were involved in the design of the data collection tools (survey) as well as the analysis. Two workshops were specifically focused on data analysis.

All of the workshops were facilitated to include group activities, with guides developed in advance of the meetings; however, the sessions also involved considerable improvisation by the academics in response to community researchers needs, as well as some preliminary analysis of the data set prior to the workshop meetings. Binet et al (2019) also reflected that the processes they used in the workshops varied in effectiveness, and that they missed an opportunity to evaluate the resident researchers' experiences of involvement.

Having considered the example in Box 6.2, complete Learning Task 6.2 to consider how analysis might work for your own participatory research project.

LEARNING TASK 6.2 ANALYSIS IN PRACTICE

You are working on a collaborative research or evaluation project, in which you are planning to involve community members in the analysis stages of the work. You have several community members who have already been involved in the data collection, and some of these are keen to continue working with you. You are planning to run an introductory workshop, to start the analysis process. So, consider the following.

1 Referring to Table 6.2, which stage of the analysis are you planning to open up to participation?
2 How will you effectively facilitate the workshop(s), to ensure that you are listening and using the perspectives that emerge? What will you need to include on the agenda? Will the workshop need to include training?
3 How will you effectively use your time, to try to synthesise the data from all of those involved? For example, might all of those involved need to do some pre-reading/preparation before they come together in the workshop?
4 Given that you are planning to use a group approach to analysis, think about how you can encourage group reflection during the workshop time. Do you need to allow space for discussion about the main findings?
5 Have you considered which aspects of the analysis matter most to the lay researchers, and paid attention to how you can incorporate this into your approach?
6 How can you start to link the analysis workshop to dissemination (see Chapter 7)? Do you need to ask for collective insights into a report plan, and gauge potential involvement in the writing of this?

Context

As previous chapters have pointed out, the methods that are used in each project will vary according to the context in which the project takes place. Analysis approaches are the same in that researchers will need to work with community members and stakeholders in each project context to establish what is possible, feasible and useful with regards to analysis. Table 6.3 provides several examples of participatory approaches to analysis from a range of contexts and illustrates a wide range of qualitative methods that have been used with varying success.

Each of the projects in Table 6.3 used a different model of participation; however, all of the authors cited noted that there were clear challenges associated with trying to do participatory analysis.

Table 6.3 Examples of qualitative participatory analysis in different project contexts

Project	Analysis approach
Researching Our Lives	Early school leavers in Ireland were trained in the voice-centred relational method to enable them to collaboratively analyse interview transcripts. Participants were required to learn about listening to the voice telling the story when they were looking at interview transcripts. They worked on the transcripts in teams and pairs. The teenagers were able to correct inaccuracies, fill in gaps and add to the analysis. They described the process as tedious and time consuming, and according to the professional researcher, tended to forget their own role as story-tellers and participants, instead focusing on other teenagers who were disadvantaged (Byrne et al 2009).
Makes Me Mad	In a participatory action research project, Cahill (2007b) worked with six urban young women of colour. The data were in the form of written contributions (journals) from the young women, who then self-analysed their reflections. This made the coding complex and difficult, and the young women were already being reflexive and analytical in collectively discussing their contributions. There were disagreements, emotions and discussions about representation and misrepresentation. The young women described the analysis as a struggle in their attempts to make the invisible visible, to produce new knowledge.
Patient-User Involvement	Locock et al (2019) aimed to extend patient involvement in research to the process of analysis, attempting to explore what this would bring to studies about young people with depression and people with experiences of stroke. The research team led the interviews and analysed the data, therefore this was not a CBPR project by design. The team then ran two one-day workshops with people who had experience as patients/service users/carers. The training involved content on how to analyse interviews, as well as how the data could be used to improve care. Lay researchers identified the same themes as the professional researchers, as well as some details that had been missed. However, their feedback was that reading large amounts of text was not the most positive use of their time and experience. They recommended that in the future, they could meet with researchers at the start of any analysis to discuss their ideas about what to look out for.

Challenges associated with participatory analysis

Complete Learning Task 6.3 as a starting point to enable you to reflect on some of the challenges that might be encountered in relation to doing participatory analysis.

LEARNING TASK 6.3 CHALLENGES ASSOCIATED WITH PARTICIPATORY ANALYSIS

Using your searching skills, the internet and other relevant resources such as books and journal articles, take time to reflect on the question, 'what are the common challenges associated with doing participatory analysis?'.

1 What are the common barriers that you can identify? Think about practical issues (such as time, money and skills), and more theoretical challenges such as how the principles and values underpinning participatory models of analysis work in practice.

2 Think about your own skills as a researcher and how these relate to your ability to support the use of participatory analysis approaches. Are you able to train community members in appropriate analysis techniques? Do you have the capability to arrange, lead and facilitate group analysis sessions?

3 How can you ensure meaningful involvement in the project that you are planning, and so avoid a tokenistic approach?

Having completed the Learning Task 6.3, you will have discovered that there are well reported barriers to doing participatory analysis. For example, there is a plethora of material available about participatory approaches to research but far less about analysis as a particular component of this process. Therefore, it is not easy to draw on existing frameworks to support this activity given that there are limited examples. Binet et al (2019) found very little practical guidance in the literature (academic and non-academic) for how to facilitate the collaborative analysis of quantitative data with lay researchers and community members who had limited prior experience. There are some examples for qualitative data, and more are being published, but quantitative frameworks are especially lacking.

Hacker (2013) suggests that the roles participants play within participatory analysis will vary according to their expertise, the time available and their level of interest in the project. She suggests that analysing statistical data is better left to academics who have the knowledge, skills and access to software packages, but that the insight of community researchers into any results remains important because they can assign meaning. She suggests that working with qualitative data is usually more approachable for community partners because they listen to others frequently, therefore they can integrate into the processes of qualitative analysis more easily. Nind (2011) makes similar points when she suggests that there are likely to be areas of analysis that remain inaccessible to community members, such as structural equation modelling for quantitative projects and using all of the features of qualitative software packages to do data analysis.

Stoecker (2013) discusses the different ways in which academics and community members deal with analysis, suggesting that community workers are more likely to take action, whereas academics operate much more reflexively, taking time to think about ideas and to discuss them. These differences can pose challenges when academics and community workers are analysing data together. Successful collaborations can arguably overcome these challenges. Jackson (2008) more critically argues that data analysis is one of the key skills held by professional researchers, therefore when academics work with community members in participatory projects, the analysis stage tends to be one of the last areas to be opened up for participation.

Franz (2013) writes about the challenges within participatory analysis when lay researchers are presented with large amounts of raw data, because these are difficult to make sense of. She therefore frames raw data as a barrier to participation in analysis. Some researchers also express concerns that community members involved in analysis will place too much emphasis on their own experiences; however, researchers also bring their own biases and views of what is important (Locock et al 2019).

Cahill (2007b) suggests that participatory analysis challenges researchers' understandings of validity, reliability, rigour and interpretation. She notes the danger in group-work approaches to participatory analysis because she argues that they work to produce shared stories, and to tidy up (and therefore potentially exclude) aspects that do not neatly fit. Holland et al (2008:25) also caution against the assumption that participatory analysis automatically leads to a better end product, and conclude that the strongest evidence is still likely to come from the combination of participatory studies with other methods. Furthermore, each participatory project is likely to use different methods, tools and techniques; therefore, in each instance different technical issues are likely to emerge in relation to conducting participatory analysis (Cahill 2007b). Box 6.3 provides an overview of some of the limitations of participatory analysis.

Box 6.3 Limitations of participatory analysis

- Usually requires an expert researcher/academic to lead the process.
- Expert researcher needs skills to facilitate the process.
- Lay researchers/stakeholders are expected to 'make sense of the data'.
- The process is time consuming, especially if there are large numbers of people/organisations and community members involved. Additional time is likely to be needed to conduct 'deeper' analysis, for example to produce sub-themes in qualitative projects.
- Capacity building may not result from such approaches – can lay researchers manage the analysis process on their own for other projects, if they are involved in just one participatory model?

Source: Adapted from Jackson (2008)

How can I conduct participatory analysis in an inclusive manner?

Stevenson (2014) argues that to be inclusive when doing participatory analysis requires researchers in university-based contexts to reject the idea that only they can understand, build and own theory because co-researchers from other contexts do have the ability to acquire these skills. She also argues that university-based researchers need to be flexible in their approaches, because examples published in the literature are usually not generalisable.

Jackson (2008) notes that professionals and those with experience of research can tend to dominate in any group discussion about analysis, so she argues that if all partners are committed to the principles of inclusion, then they should work together to create a positive and supportive atmosphere as a way to enable participation and ensure that all of those involved listen to each other. Jennings et al (2018) outline the following typology of collaborative data analysis drawn from mental health research, which can be used as a benchmark.

1. *Consultation*   Researchers lead the analysis and present it to lay researchers for comments.
2. *Development*   Lay researchers help to develop a coding framework, which is then used by the researchers to analyse the data.
3. *Application*   The lead researchers develop a coding framework and this is applied by lay researchers.
4. *Development and application*   Lay researchers are given extensive training in data analysis, they are involved for long periods of time, they develop the coding framework and then use it on the data set.

Jennings et al (2018) describe the development and application model as the gold standard of inclusion, but also point out that while the consultation model may seem to be less inclusive, it can be helpful in including community members as a mechanism to challenge the categories of professionals versus community members.

Franz (2013) offers the model of holding a 'data party' as a way to tackle some of the potential barriers to participation. The research team or lead researcher should survey all interested stakeholders such as community members (online or via the phone), to explore which aspects of the research they are most interested in and view as being the most useful to their community. This information can then be used within a 'data party', which is a gathering of people who come together to discuss the findings and their usage. There are several other ways in which participatory analysis can be designed to be more inclusive, so complete Learning Task 6.4 to develop your ideas about inclusivity in relation to analysis.

LEARNING TASK 6.4 INCLUSIVE APPROACHES TO PARTICIPATORY ANALYSIS

Review the discussion points in the section above, and then take some time to reflect on the following questions.

1 How might you create an inclusive atmosphere in your own study to ensure that you are supporting the involvement of co-researchers? Here you need to consider any training requirements that lay researchers might have as well as how you can create collaborative spaces for group analysis (such as a potential data party).

2 Finally, how skilled are you at working flexibly, given that you may not be able to involve all co-researchers in all stages of the analysis? Lay researchers are likely to have a wide variety of skills, as well as numerous other commitments and interests, which will affect their level of activity within the analysis process.

In completing Learning Task 6.4 did you consider the ways in which your own views of the analysis process might frame the level of participation in any given research project? Locock et al (2019) note that in their approach, they found themselves too attached to their own views, processes and concepts, which included the view that close immersion in large amounts of text are needed to do qualitative analysis. Service users working on their study as co-researchers preferred conversational engagement in the analysis process (see Table 6.3). Therefore, to be inclusive, researchers need to consider being creative in supporting involvement, having less of a focus on the process of analysis and instead trying to address power imbalances, to enable non–researcher perspectives to be both heard and included.

CASE STUDY ANALYSIS ALONGSIDE RESEARCHERS WITH DISABILITIES

There is limited literature about involving people with learning disabilities in the analysis of data, and some discussions convey a range of problems with attempts to achieve this (Stalker 1998). For example, Kiernan (1999) states that because the research process requires intellectual skills, co-researchers with learning disabilities are likely to need much more support when compared with other lay researchers. Others write that involving people with learning disabilities in research and analysis creates a burden of support for professional researchers and limits the use of research findings in terms of potential contributions to the evidence base (Walmsley 2004). Not all agree, and some universities involve individuals with learning disabilities in research, though this tends to be limited to gathering feedback on results rather than full involvement in analysis (Yuffrey-Wijne and Butler 2009).

Yuffrey-Wijne and Butler (2009) provide an example of one research analysis experience involving a co-researcher with a learning disability. The co-researcher worked with a university-based staff member (Yuffrey-Wijne). This was a three-year ethnographic study gathering the experiences of 13 people with learning disabilities who also had cancer, mainly using participant observation (over 250 hours in total). Ten of the participants died during the course of the study. Butler (the co-researcher) analysed extensive vignettes (stories) and extracts from fieldnotes using a thematic approach, over a three-month period. His work was then cross-compared with the analysis of Yuffrey-Wijne. Vignettes were also analysed by three additional researchers to reduce bias and increase the credibility of the results. Reflections from Yuffrey-Wijne and Butler (2009) illustrate that both analysts were able to provide emotional support to each other during the process, and following on from some initial support at the start, Butler's contribution was described as invaluable in validating the data analysis. They conclude that it is possible to include people with learning disabilities in analysis but that this does require a level of verbal ability.

Stevenson (2014) also provides an example of participatory analysis alongside co-researchers who have Down Syndrome. In a study developed with young adults (aged 18–25) who had Down Syndrome, interviews were conducted by co-researchers to explore participants' life goals and social connectedness. Seven interviews were conducted, and three co-researchers worked with the lead academic to analyse the data in what she describes as an inclusive and authentic contribution, which included coding transcripts, the basic negotiation of themes and the discussion of observations about the data set. However, Stevenson (2014) does note that her approach is not generalisable, and that participatory analysis with individuals who have learning disabilities is likely to vary hugely.

In conducting participatory analysis, professional researchers also need to be aware that lay researchers with disabilities will need one-to-one support to be able to contribute fully, and this therefore needs to be budgeted for. Academics should also be clear about their expectations of lay researchers in terms of what contribution are they being asked to make.

Summary

- Participatory analysis approaches involve the application of CBPR principles to support non-experts and community researchers in working with professionals to process, interpret and present the results of research. However, lay researchers' involvement in analysis is achieved to a lesser extent than in other areas of participatory research projects, such as data collection.

- Participatory analysis is an underexplored area in the academic literature, especially in relation to the involvement of lay researchers working with quantitative data sets. There are several examples of qualitative participatory approaches to draw on, especially involving group approaches to analysis, but frameworks to inform practice remain limited.

- Participatory analysis can be achieved across a range of contexts and involving a variety of different groups of people. In reality, there are many challenges noted to 'doing' participatory analysis, therefore each project's context and wider factors (for example, lay researcher skills, time, commitment, type of analysis required and budget) will need consideration in each instance.

Suggestions for further reading

1 Binet, A., Gavin, V., Carroll, L. and Arcaya, M. (2019) 'Designing and facilitating collaborative research design and data analysis workshops: lessons learned in the Healthy Neighborhoods Study', *International Journal of Environmental Research and Public Health*, 16(324), doi: 10.3390/ijerph16030324.
This article describes how a consortium of community members, organisations and professionals (both academic and public institutions) worked together in the US to conduct a participatory action research project about neighbourhoods and health. The article provides a clear discussion of the analysis process (quantitative data), and outlines the lessons that the researchers learned.

2 Nind, M. (2011) 'Participatory data analysis: a step too far?', *Qualitative Research*, 11(4): 349–63.
This article discusses participatory data analysis with children and people with learning disabilities, noting the challenges that are involved given that this is an under-explored area. These challenges are outlined, and then some responses to them are provided. Useful for all researchers considering trying to involve lay researchers in the analysis of data, irrespective of the life experiences of community members involved.

3 Public Profit (2019) *Dabbling in the data. A hands-on guide to participatory analysis*, Oakland, CA: Public Profit. www.publicprofit.net/Dabbling-In-The-Data-A-Hands-On-Guide-To-Participatory-Data-Analysis
This is a practical toolkit designed to introduce people to data analysis (both quantitative and qualitative). There are practical worksheets and activities are described in a step-by-step manner to guide facilitators in supporting and training groups of people to learn about analysis. Particularly useful for group-based analysis activities.

Questions for reflection

1 How will you adapt your approach to analysis to ensure that you are being inclusive and working in a participatory way? Think about your own values here and views about analysis – do you see this as something that has to be done by skilled academics or something that can be taught to community members who will bring a different but equally valid perspective to both the process and the findings?

2 In which contexts do you think participatory analysis approaches can be used most effectively? Might some contexts lend themselves more easily to such approaches, and might others be more of a challenge? Reflect on how you can use strategies to manage some of the potential challenges, rather than discounting participation as a result of the barriers that may well emerge.

3 In many research projects, the findings are not always what you or members of your team 'expect', and there may be associated controversy. How might you deal with

controversial or negative research results that participants encounter when they are involved in the analysis of data? Here you will also need to think carefully about working in an ethical way to resolve such situations.

Top tips for practice

1 Jackson (2008) suggest that analysis needs to be broken down for community researchers so that it is more understandable, and can be done in engaging steps with clear instructions provided as this will facilitate participation. In her experience, group work was preferred by co-researchers.

2 Pankaj et al (2011) discuss the importance of planning in terms of time management and budgetary considerations. Participatory analysis is time consuming, often involving preliminary analysis, the communication of some aspects of the findings, arranging meetings and then conducting meetings, all of which may involve intense discussions and challenges for facilitators. It may not be feasible to hold a single meeting in which to conduct analysis, therefore two days can be needed. Day one can be used to review findings, and day two to agree on recommendations. Therefore, you will need to allow time for all elements and budget for room hire, travel expenses and refreshments at the very least.

3 Binet et al (2019) outline the several lessons that they learned about using workshops to facilitate participatory action research processes. They report on the importance of using mechanisms to sustain residents' involvement over the lifetime of the project; the need for researchers to have skills in improvising in response to lay researchers' needs; time to build both consensus and trust; space to discuss power relations and to learn especially in areas where there are tensions; and finally, they note the importance of shared commitment to connecting research to action.

Further teaching and learning resources to accompany this book can be found at https://bristoluniversitypress.co.uk/creating-participatory-research-website. The companion website includes:

- teaching slides for lecturers
- further information on learning tasks
- lesson activities
- further reading, links to websites and practical resources
- examples from practice
- additional case studies

7

Dissemination

Key learning outcomes

By the end of this chapter, you should be able to:

• Define research dissemination and understand why it is so important

• Demonstrate awareness of the principles and values underpinning participatory approaches to dissemination

• Identify several types of participatory dissemination

Introduction

This chapter explores how the dissemination of research findings can include and involve participants and take a more collaborative approach, drawing on practical examples to illustrate successes. This chapter explores a range of dissemination approaches enabling non-academics to be involved, and considers approaches that enable knowledge to be shared more widely. Many forms of knowledge have been excluded from dissemination and there are limitations to some traditional approaches, because of ethical boundaries and the complexities of working with vulnerable and marginalised communities. This chapter therefore considers managing participatory dissemination when using a range of formats and approaches.

What is dissemination?

Research dissemination is a term that is used to describe a process by which investigators communicate the findings from their research projects. There are a range of purposes associated with dissemination, and the particular audience to which the information is directed may influence and determine the dissemination method used. Dissemination can be classified according to its purpose. Myers and Barnes (2004) discuss disseminating for awareness and profile building as part of a marketing approach. They also note that dissemination can be done for understanding, to explain the purpose of certain projects as well as their effectiveness, so that community members know how resources have been used and that interventions are accountable to funders. Finally, they describe dissemination for action, to illustrate evidence that can influence decisions such as the extension of funding or the expansion of programmes. Myers and Barnes (2004) argue that these three goals are not mutually exclusive. While the dissemination of research results can be for different purposes, Chen et al (2010) argue that in academic circles, dissemination is generally viewed in narrow terms and involves peer-reviewed journal publications, excluding study participants and the public in general. However, dissemination can move beyond publication, and be more inclusive which is arguably a more ethical approach (see Chapter 4 for more on ethics).

Traditional dissemination and participatory approaches

The main difference between participatory and traditional approaches to dissemination is in relation to the involvement of community members in the process. Table 7.1 provides an overview of the main differences between traditional and participatory dissemination.

As Table 7.1 illustrates, the communication and dissemination needs of these two groups have been disparate and sometimes at odds (Bodison et al 2015). Timmins (2015) argues that traditional forms of dissemination have value, but they do not always result in enough impact with diverse audiences, thus raising the question, what impact does such dissemination have, if no one is listening? There tend to be long delays in the publication of research findings in the form of journal articles, once research projects have concluded, which is a source of frustration for community members who have been involved as they wish to see impact quickly (Hacker 2013; see also Chapter 10 for more on impact). For many academic researchers, dissemination outside the traditional academic setting may well be unusual territory. Efforts to move dissemination beyond academic involvement only are being made but in some instances the focus of this work also remains narrow; for example, by segmenting the recipients and disseminating the

Table 7.1 Overview: differences between traditional and participatory dissemination approaches

Traditional dissemination	Participatory dissemination
Academics (university staff) disseminate the research findings.	Community members are involved in the dissemination process.
The dissemination is about the needs of the university and the interests of the academics, e.g. it is about submitting a report to the funding agency and producing high-impact journal articles that are of interest to other scholars.	The dissemination is intended to benefit those who have participated and therefore serve the needs of the population under study. Therefore dissemination is about more than just academic texts.
Dissemination is in the format of academic language.	The format of the dissemination is decided by the community members and is intended to be more accessible.

findings solely to professionals such as care providers (Katon et al 2010). Bodison et al (2015) highlight how community participants often complain that research findings are rarely communicated meaningfully back to those who took part, which can contribute to them feeling that their time and effort in participating has been wasted. The principles of community-based participatory research (CBPR) highlight the importance of involving community members in dissemination, but there is limited literature about how to do this in practice and few direct comparisons have been made between traditional approaches and those that use more participatory models (Chen et al 2010). Literature about how to conduct dissemination with Indigenous communities is also underdeveloped (Cooper and Drideger 2018). This is despite increasing recognition of the importance of knowledge utilisation (Vaughn et al 2013) and knowledge translation (Cooper and Drideger 2018). There are a range of approaches to expanding the reach of dissemination within community contexts, as outlined in Table 7.2.

Table 7.2 Labels given to types of dissemination practices

Type of dissemination	Definition
Participatory dissemination	This involves the central inclusion of research participants in dissemination activities of any research project. There are a range of approaches to involving community members in participatory dissemination, which is an umbrella term describing a way of working, rather than a specific model. Participant involvement may include dissemination through a range of techniques such as the use of drama or visual art (Kindon et al 2007).
Community-derived research dissemination/ participant engagement	This involves asking community members what they would like research dissemination to look like and to involve. They do not necessarily participate in the dissemination but they inform the researchers of useful strategies, and what works for their communities (Pufall et al 2011).
Knowledge translation	Knowledge translation is described by the WHO (2019) as an approach that aims to close the 'know–do' gap, which is about using the knowledge gained from research and putting it into practice. Again, this is not necessarily participatory dissemination because translation can be for policy makers and practitioners as well as community members, though participation can be applicable in some models.
Knowledge utilisation	This term is used in a variety of fields, and according to Heinsch et al (2015) it can be a broad umbrella term to describe the ways in which knowledge is being used or it can be used in relation to a specific event. Again, knowledge utilisation is not necessarily participatory in basis, but can be used in such a manner in suitable instances.
Knowledge exchange	This is defined as 'the process by which researchers and decision makers share expertise and knowledge for a specific purpose' (Bowen and Martens 2005:207). Knowledge exchange can be conducted for a range of people, including community members, who can also participate in its design and accompanying activities.

There are a variety of approaches to dissemination, as illustrated in Table 7.2, and there are many ways in which research findings can be used. This chapter is concerned with outlining participatory approaches to dissemination, based on specific principles being used to guide the ways in which research findings are communicated.

What are the principles of participatory dissemination?

Chapter 1 outlined the principles that underpin participatory approaches to research, noting that these involve the collaboration of community members, organisational representatives and researchers. Similarly, participatory dissemination is about collaborative working in combination with 'non-experts', often underpinned by attempts to facilitate social change (Minkler and Wallerstein 2003). Thus, a core principle of participatory dissemination is the involvement of non-experts and community members. The involvement of participants in dissemination offers one way of foregrounding their voices, rather than simply drawing on the authority of the 'expert' researcher (Kindon et al 2007). Therefore, this is about moving beyond simply feeding back any research results to those who have participated, which is considered to be good practice anyway.

Another principle underpinning participatory dissemination is that of ethics. Manzo and Brightbill (2007:39) argue that involving participants in dissemination is a more ethical way of working. Some commentators have argued that academic research is often a conversation of 'us' with 'us' about 'them', and therefore unethically reproduces inequalities (Cahill and Torre 2007). Complete Learning Task 7.1 to explore the ethics associated with participatory dissemination in more detail.

LEARNING TASK 7.1 ETHICS OF INVOLVING PARTICIPANTS IN DISSEMINATION

Refer back to Chapter 4 if you need a reminder about ethical principles associated with research. Now consider dissemination involving participants, and how this might raise additional ethical questions for researchers. Imagine that you have been involved in a study with young patients, exploring their views of the treatment that they received from a healthcare provider. Several of the young people involved as participants are keen to be involved in communicating the research findings alongside you. They have lots of creative ideas that they are keen to try out.

1 What ethical issues might arise in relation to involving young people in dissemination, when they have been participants? Start to reflect on anonymity and confidentiality. Then think about the perceptions that others may hold about young people (for example, professional staff in organisations such as local authorities) as well as how the nature of the topic might influence how it can be disseminated.

> 2 In your view is it 'more' ethical to involve participants in disseminating findings than a researcher using a traditional academic approach, which is researcher-led and has no involvement from participants?

Did you consider the issue of representation during completion of Learning Task 7.1? Cahill and Torre (2007) suggest that when using participatory approaches in research, questions about who represents the community are fundamentally linked to how findings are produced and communicated. In their view, participatory research creates spaces for self-representation and insider knowledge – something that outsiders (that is, academic researchers) do not have.

Participatory dissemination is also about trust building, especially important because CBPR approaches offer an orientation to research with a heavy accent on trust (Minkler and Wallerstein 2003). Knerr et al (2016) argue that not only are research participants beginning to expect to be involved in the creation of strategies for dissemination, but that the successful distribution of research findings informed by the engagement of participants is essential for building and sustaining trusting relationships. They argue that trust building is especially important when working with community members who are experiencing inequalities.

Another principle underpinning participatory approaches is that of ownership. The products of the CBPR process belong to all partners (Goodman et al 2018), therefore their use should be guided by all who have been involved in creating them, to facilitate social change. Mosavel et al (2016) also discuss the importance of accountability in transferring knowledge back to community members to facilitate co-learning.

Thus, participatory research should also be underpinned by the principle of social change, with any findings linked to action, which according to Cahill and Torre (2007) will push researchers into working with new and unfamiliar dissemination approaches, beyond the conventional journal article. Researchers should be challenged to think about reframing social issues in their findings to create action for social change (Cahill and Torre 2007), and community mobilisation in relation to the tackling of the issues under scrutiny, such as health inequalities (Garnett et al 2015). Hacker (2013) similarly notes the importance of disseminating in a way that speaks to advocacy as a starting point to address any issues identified in CBPR projects. She suggests that advocacy is one of the most important aspects of added value that arises from CBPR results, which therefore need to be disseminated quickly.

Why is participatory dissemination important?

Sharing research findings with community members is important for a number of reasons. For example, communicating public health research findings to community members can be part of a broader strategy to implement meaningful change (Cooper and Drideger 2018). Community partners involved in the dissemination of research findings can also promote joint learning, share knowledge, and increase the capacity of researchers to work with the ideas of community members (Komaie et al 2018). Dissemination in such instances can be viewed as a potential agent of social change (Van Blerk and Ansell 2007), and while it may not necessarily result in any recommendations being acted on, such approaches can at least open up conversations and increase understanding. Chen et al (2010) argue that it is a researcher's ethical responsibility to disseminate both with and to those who participated in the research; that it is a valuable activity both intrinsically and more broadly as a mechanism to develop, bolster and maintain relationships between academics and community members; and finally, such involved and co-produced dissemination can play an important role in enabling change and sustaining it, as well as in securing future funding.

How research results are shared is indicative of who the beneficiaries of the research should be (Drake 1997). Sharing with participants can bring benefits to both researchers and participants. Participants are more likely to feel that their contributions are valued, and they may also feed back to the researchers about their experiences of involvement within the study, which can provide valuable learning for researchers. Grieb et al (2015) argue that the power of any knowledge creation emerging from CBPR can only be fully realised when research partners share their findings with others. Ultimately, research is only useful if the findings are disseminated to an audience who can directly benefit (Balandin 2003). Finley (2008) cites the importance of writing up research findings from CBPR without 'othering' the participants, exploiting them or leaving them without voice, suggesting that consideration should be given to empowering community groups to have voice through creative dissemination. Box 7.1 summarises why it is important to share research findings with participants.

Box 7.1 Importance of sharing research findings with participants

1   Community members deserve access to any knowledge that they have created via their involvement in any study.
2   Community dissemination allows for researchers to explore the ways in which the research findings are viewed locally.
3   Community dissemination allows for the implementation of the findings to begin immediately, which is a positive approach to ensure that potential gaps between research and practice are bridged.
4   Fostering dialogue with those affected by the issues being studied can assist in the development of relevant interventions – for example, with the aim of health improvement.

Source: Adapted from McDavitt et al (2016)

Cargo and Mercer (2008) also discuss the importance of the added value that arises from involving non-academics in the dissemination of research findings, for all of those involved. Academic partners are likely to extend the reach of their research, possibly become involved in political advocacy and increase their exposure via media recognition. Non-academic partners gain benefits via the creation of materials that can improve practice (training manuals and handbooks), and higher participation rates from end-user involvement. Furthermore, disseminating beyond academia links with the responsibility of universities to be socially responsible (Macpherson et al 2017).

Context

Cooper and Drideger (2018) point out that the methods used by researchers to return research results to communities will differ according to each project and context. Complete Learning Task 7.2, to reflect more about the importance of the context underpinning participatory dissemination.

LEARNING TASK 7.2 CONTEXT AND PARTICIPATORY DISSEMINATION

1 Using the internet, find an example of a research project that discusses participatory dissemination. Choose carefully as some papers and examples include the term 'participatory dissemination' in the title but have not actually used this approach in line with CBPR principles.

2 Read the article and summarise the main points from it in your own words, making notes as you go along.

3 Now revisit your notes and consider the context in which the dissemination approach was used, paying attention to the participants, the topic, the methods and the findings. In your view, how did the context in your chosen paper influence the dissemination?

In completing Learning Task 7.2 you should have been able to think more about the context in which any participatory dissemination occurs. Did you grasp that researchers will need to work with community members and stakeholders to try to understand their needs as part of their dissemination strategies, in each context that they work in? Mitchell and Staeheli (2005:360) argue that 'what makes research relevant is shaped not only by those involved in the research but the social context in which the research is presented, interpreted and used'.

CBPR teams therefore need to consider the best ways to communicate research products, and information to people (Israel et al 2005b; Banks et al 2013). Drawing on their own experiences in researching with and disseminating within Indigenous communities in Canada, they list seven key questions for researchers to use when they are trying to create dissemination products that are both useful and relevant:

1. Is it possible for community members to easily copy the resource?
2. Is the product moving beyond the need for people to have written literacy skills?
3. Can some of the message be strengths-based and positive (hopeful)?
4. Is the product interactive?
5. Is there acknowledgement of the contributions made by community members?
6. Is there a component that uses active learning beyond engagement with the researchers?
7. Is the product being returned to the community quickly?

Pufall et al (2011) also discuss the need to use culturally relevant, community-driven approaches that can be easily understood by the target audience when disseminating in Innuit communities. They conducted focus group discussions and interviews with community members to establish a dissemination approach and found that formally presenting research findings in a conference style was not popular, with participants instead requesting an open house, which involved researchers inviting community members to their workplace, where they could ask questions. Some community members also suggested that offering food and prizes incentivised community participation. Language considerations were noted as important, and researchers were advised of community members' preferences for visual tools and face-to-face interaction. Knerr et al (2016) in a similar approach, asked participants via focus group discussions about how they were interested in receiving research results and found that community members had distinct preferences according to their previous experiences of research. Those who had been involved in research before requested copies of reports and asked about conference presentations, whereas others emphasised the need for simple information and basic messages.

Several researchers who have used participatory dissemination discuss how they involved the community in their efforts by initially researching what community members wanted from the research. Table 7.3 provides illustrative examples of participatory dissemination across a range of contexts.

Table 7.3 provides some examples of different approaches that have been used in the co-creation of dissemination in a variety of contexts. These are by no means exhaustive, and there are many other examples of creative ways of sharing research findings. For example, dissemination for children has involved school-based workshops, the development of dramas performed by the children to convey key messages and the production of posters by them (Van Blerk and Ansell 2007). Hacker (2013) outlines a range of dissemination methods that can be used to advocate for a community's needs, drawing on her own experience of using CBPR methods. She cites a dissemination plan that included a community forum, meetings with an advocacy group, presentations to local groups, meeting with police, letters to newspapers, blog submissions, abstracts sent to national meetings, press releases and peer-reviewed publications. While some creative approaches to dissemination are not always participatory, it is worth noting that 'producing a range of multimodal outputs can extend both the reach and

Table 7.3 Examples of participatory dissemination in different contexts

Context	Dissemination approach
Petersburg, Virginia (USA) is an area in which the majority of the population are African American and experience health disparities. Working with a local community development organisation, researchers used a range of data collection methods (meetings, focus groups and a survey) to conduct a needs assessment. In collaborating to design the dissemination approach, a youth day was developed to engage young people in working with the findings.	*Event* A youth day was organised in collaboration with local community groups to enable researchers to share the findings with young people, but also to learn their views about how to implement interventions related to the findings. Breakfast was provided and young people were presented the findings using the world café method, whereby they visited four different workstations to discuss themes linked to the CBPR findings. Young people showed medium to high engagement with the activities, and all reported being happy to help their family make healthier choices (Mosavel et al 2019).
Petersburg, Virginia is an area in which the majority of the population are African American and experience health disparities. Following on from a needs assessment (see the discussion in the row above), researchers and community members used an edutainment approach to disseminate research results. Edutainment refers to integrating education with entertainment to facilitate learning.	*Using theatre* An hour-long ethnodrama was created using the title 'Changes and choices: life and death health decisions'. It used stories, songs, drama and poetry to explore healthy eating and physical activity choices. Using a participatory dissemination approach enabled community members to advise about the importance of this work in tackling the barriers to healthy living that had been reported in the research findings. The play also included personal narratives of local wellness ambassadors (who lived in the community under study), and the play development was an iterative process in which community members provided feedback on draft scripts to ensure that the use of language represented the community voice (Mosavel et al 2019).
Researchers in the US were involved in a funded partnership that aimed to tackle youth violence, specifically via the use of CBPR. Researchers negotiated their approach to dissemination with partnership members, alongside conducting consultations with young people in the form of focus group discussions. A youth advisory board was created to steer the process.	*Digital animation* Animated messages were created with support from artists, and were based on the qualitative research findings as well as the wants of the young people engaged in the focus group discussions. The animated messages were linked to evidence-based tips for violence prevention. The animated messages were disseminated at an existing community symposium (held annually), via the creation of a community Facebook page and through local mass media in the form of advertisements (Vaughn et al 2013).

(continued)

Table 7.3 Examples of participatory dissemination in different contexts (continued)

Context	Dissemination approach
Researchers in the US were conducting a study about racial disparities in excess weight in the community of Cambridge. Using a CBPR approach, they worked with an existing community coalition and black families living in the community, to qualitatively explore the topic.	*Presentations* Researchers disseminated information by informally discussing the findings with existing community groups. They tailored each presentation in an age-appropriate way and left space for discussion, feedback and reciprocal learning. They worked with local investigators who were well-respected in the community and paid careful attention to language, for example not using the term 'excess weight'. Strong community interest in the topic was evident, and the researchers suggest that disseminating local health data in such a way can promote community change (Garnet et al 2015).
During 2009–10 researchers conducted focus group discussions with people from First Nation and Métis communities in Manitoba Canada, about their views of public health recommendations. Community members requested dissemination materials to help them to open up conversations with children and elders, who often could not read English.	*Written/text-based* An activity sheet was designed with key health promotion messages on one side, as well as research results on the other. The sheet included a colouring picture with a series of health-related images, designed as a tool to encourage conversation. These sheets were distributed to schools, and three years later in a separate project unprompted positive comments were made about this approach (Cooper and Drideger 2018).

impact of research studies' (Mannay et al 2019:58). Azzarito (2016) created a public photo exhibition, drawing on diary extracts which included photographs following on from a research project that had engaged ethnically diverse young people in expressing their ideas about moving 'in their own worlds'. This creative approach to dissemination was intended to increase the reach of the findings, but this was not participatory. It is also worth noting that there are many challenges to participatory dissemination, so it is to these that we now turn our attention.

Challenges and limitations

Complete Learning Task 7.3 to enable you to think about some of the challenges that you may face when trying to disseminate in a participatory manner.

LEARNING TASK 7.3 CHALLENGES ASSOCIATED WITH
PARTICIPATORY DISSEMINATION

Use the internet, and any other relevant resources that you have (for example, books and articles). Explore the question 'what are the challenges associated with participatory approaches to research dissemination?' Make some notes on the following.

1 What barriers exist in relation to participatory dissemination? (Think about practical issues, principles associated with such a way of working versus the reality of their implementation and competing agendas as starting points.)
2 What problems may arise in relation to the involvement of community members in the processes of dissemination?
3 Who holds the power in any partnership approach to dissemination, in your view?

Having completed Learning Task 7.3 you will now have an idea that there is evidence discussing several challenges to the use of participatory dissemination. Delafield et al (2016) argue that although dissemination is valued by many researchers who use participatory approaches, substantial barriers remain in terms of how it is conducted. Chen et al (2010) discuss the time and resource constraints often linked to research projects that employ participatory methods to work with underserved communities. They also highlight the differential needs and goals of the stakeholders involved in the process as a challenge. For example, dissemination beyond publication does not contribute to professional advancement in academic contexts. Furthermore, translating research findings into simple language, or different formats for lay members may be limited by the funding available or the consideration of this as additional work from researchers.

Macpherson et al (2017) highlight the need for attention to be paid to the logistical issues that arise when using participatory dissemination approaches. They also discuss the issue of time, and the need to recognise that there is never enough of it when working in such a way. Navigating expectations is also an area that warrants further attention, as expectations of partners may not relate to what happens in reality. They also discuss different cultures of language as a challenge: people from different backgrounds and experiences speak differently and view concepts in a variety of ways. Finally, an area that they suggest has been paid little attention to in the wider literature is about the importance of basics, when working in participatory ways. Food, water and transport all need attention; basic administration and logistical issues are fundamental. 'Satisfying people's basic needs are crucial to meaningful collaborative research activity' (Macpherson et al 2017:310).

How can I disseminate participatory research in an inclusive manner?

Bodison et al (2015:817) state that it is essential for all of those involved in CBPR to understand their varying needs and wants with regard to dissemination, which should involve early planning and decision making to lead to 'a clear vision of the end product at the outset, and can contribute most advantageously to decisions regarding what information will be shared, at what time, and in a format that is relevant and of value to all partners and their constituents'. They suggest a range of approaches including using traditional and social media outlets, developing community specific dissemination plans and conducting community–partner research conferences. Now complete Learning Task 7.4 to reflect on doing dissemination in a participatory manner.

LEARNING TASK 7.4 DOING DISSEMINATION

1 Use the internet to access articles and resources (websites and blogs) that can help to think about 'doing dissemination' in a participatory way.
2 Make a list of top tips about the following.
   • The needs of different audiences (language, literacy, age, culture)
   • Formats that you can use to disseminate findings and how these can facilitate participation for all who wish to be involved
   • Levels of involvement for all who have been involved
   • Participant roles, skills and levels of confidence

As you will have seen from completing Learning Task 7.4, there are some useful tips for those wishing to disseminate research in a participatory manner. McDavitt et al (2016) also offer a number of recommendations for those who are planning a community dissemination phase, which are summarised in Table 7.4.

Goodman et al (2018) pose a series of questions that are intended to support the value of the products of CBPR belonging to all partners. First, they ask if there is a plan for developing and disseminating research products that are useful, creative

Table 7.4 A community engagement approach to dissemination

Strand of work	Practical tips
Planning the dissemination	• Dissemination needs to be noted in the project aims and included in any funding proposals. This fosters responsibility and enables the costs of staff time to be covered for the dissemination component of the project. • Researchers should develop a plan with the support and involvement of community members. This will need to be flexible, and it may well evolve as the study develops. • Researchers should present findings at existing meetings and groups where people meet regularly, rather than planning anything specific.
Reaching out to community partners	• Have a single point of contact for community members such as a named researcher, as this will make it easier for them to contact the team. • Draw on established relationships via existing partnerships and existing community gatekeepers to enable and facilitate engagement. • Conduct 'pre-meetings' with gatekeepers to explore the relevance of the research for both professionals and service users.
Tailoring content	• Work with community members to select the findings that are of most interest and use. • Content will need to be tailored for different audiences – for example, professionals versus community members.
Sharing findings	• Presentations should be interactive and ideally involve co-facilitation with community members. • Researchers should express why the research personally matters to them, to clarify the motives of the team in studying this area. • Researchers should receive criticism without being defensive and confrontational, to enable community members to comment.
Deepening trust	• Follow-up – researchers should meet service providers and community partners to explore future work (this may be further research, implementation of findings, as well as building new partnerships). • Researchers should also work with service providers and provide brief reports or tailored analyses to enable them to also learn from and use the findings.

Source: Adapted from McDavitt et al (2016)

and have meaning. They also noted that planning dissemination should be at the heart of all CBPR projects from the beginning. Second, they ask CBPR teams to consider how to handle findings that could be misinterpreted or considered harmful. Some communities can be subject to oppression (racism by way of an example), and so research findings in such contexts can require careful framing. Third, they ask who is responsible for authorship and dissemination, suggesting that all of those involved should have the opportunity to co-author work. Consideration of who is best positioned to manage the responsibility of specific types of dissemination is also important. Fourth, CBPR stakeholders need to pay attention to the types of products that will be useful and influential, thinking about the needs of multiple audiences, such as community members, funders and policy makers. Wilkins (2011) suggests that creating a plan for conflict resolution is important, and that discussions with community members need to account for considering if there should be restrictions on the dissemination of findings that might cause harm, on the management of data that is negative or that may feed into stereotypes. Cahill and Torre (2007) also note the need to consider who is made vulnerable through the research findings, and associated protections that may be needed beyond anonymity for communities who are affected by injustices. Finally, Trinidad et al (2015:1549) note the importance of a dialogical approach when disseminating to community members, suggesting that 'the dialogical approach recognises expertise on both sides of the communication, envisions an opportunity for both parties to learn from each other, and posits that information shared between partners can change the direction of the conversation'.

· ·

CASE STUDY CO-PRODUCING NON-TRADITIONAL RESEARCH OUTPUTS

Co-production was discussed throughout Chapter 2 as being unlike traditional research approaches in principle and practice, therefore its potential to create different (non-academic) findings is also acknowledged, with these described as being more relevant and accessible for community members. Kyneswood (2018) offers one example of a non-traditional research output from a co-produced research project called Imagine. Imagine was about historical regeneration in one northern UK community. One component of the research project involved interviewing former residents from the community as well as professionals who worked there. The data from these interviews revealed that the area had a poor reputation. Researchers then applied community development principles when working with current residents to discuss what they wanted to see as an output from the research project. Researchers and community members co-produced a photographic exhibition as one output from the project, and this was used as a way to try to challenge the stigma associated with the poor reputation of the area.

Chiles et al (2019) similarly discuss how they worked with residents living on a UK housing estate, when they were conducting research that focused on the future of living in that area. The researchers used events, workshops and interviews as ways to gather people's views about the future. The result of this research was the production of a film, shown in a local museum.

The use of non-traditional or more creative methods within co-production also lends itself to the production of research outputs that move away from text-based formats. Banks et al (2019) discuss how using art, poems, literary texts and oral histories as data-gathering approaches leads to a variety of research products. Furthermore, Pain et al (2015) outline the many impacts that can result from co-produced research, in their call for universities to broaden out the way in which they conceptualise impact. They describe the creation of a play about austerity that was developed through co-production, as well as impacts such as learning, capacity building (in organisations as well as communities), and institutional or policy change. In their description of several common impacts of co-produced research they highlight a variety of changes brought about by the research process in the form of staff changing the ways in which they worked as well as increased confidence for those who participated.

Dissemination from co-produced research therefore needs to be seen as mutual (for researchers and participants) and linked to the ethics of sharing, therefore it is not something that can always be planned. Changes that arise from co-producing research are then more likely to create impact beyond just the academic dissemination of results.

• •

Summary

- Participatory dissemination approaches are labelled in a variety of ways, but in keeping with the principles of CBPR they involve non-experts and community members within the planning and communication of the research results.

- Participatory dissemination is governed by a range of principles including involvement, ethics, representation, trust building, ownership (of products) and a commitment to advocacy and social change. However, this is not without challenges.

- The contexts in which participatory dissemination takes place in are varied in terms of location, the roles that community members adopt and the nature of the outputs that are created. Context is an important factor that needs consideration in relation to research dissemination.

Suggestions for further reading

1 CARE (Community Alliance for Research and Engagement) (No date) *Beyond scientific publication: strategies for disseminating research findings*, Yale Center for Clinical Investigation. https://ictr.wisc.edu/documents/beyond-scientific-publication-strategies-for-disseminating-research-findings/
The dissemination of research findings to participating individuals and partners is an important principle of community-based research. This resource offers information on developing a dissemination plan and general writing guidelines. Examples of dissemination outlets include media coverage, press releases, research summary documents, flyers, brochures, policy briefs, letter of thanks, events and community meetings. Examples of dissemination documents are also provided.

2 Hacker, K. (2013) *Community-based participatory research*, London: Sage.
This book gives the reader a basic introduction to participatory research by describing how an individual researcher can understand CBPR, and then apply this to using such an approach. There are practical steps and a range of examples, with dissemination discussed at various points but mostly in chapter 5, which considers how to translate research into practice.

3 Mosavel, M., Winship, J., Ferrel, D. and Larose, J.G. (2019) 'Data dissemination in CBPR: accountability and responsiveness', *Collaborations: A Journal of Community-Based Research and Practice* 2(1): 1–11.

This article outlines the importance of participatory dissemination linked to CBPR. The authors describe two different strategies that they used to disseminate findings from CBPR projects, discussing the processes associated with their work as a bi-directional transfer of knowledge. The article also offers some practical suggestions associated with the learning gained by the researchers.

Questions for reflection

1 How will you adapt your approach to dissemination to ensure that you are using the principles noted in the literature? How might the need to consider trust building, ethics, representation, ownership and social change influence your approach?

2 In which contexts do you think participatory dissemination approaches can be used most effectively? Might some contexts lend themselves more easily to such approaches, and might some be more of a challenge?

3 In many research projects, the findings are not always what is expected, and there may be associated controversy. How might you deal with controversial or indeed negative research results while respecting community members contributions and investments in the CBPR process?

Top tips for practice

1 Most academic researchers are expected to publish in academic journals as a critical part of career advancement. Marry this requirement with CBPR values, by working to publish in such spaces with partners and community members, writing about the process (as well as the findings), and considering other types of publications such as manuscripts and theoretical pieces of work (Goodman et al 2018).

2 Build dissemination into any CBPR projects from the outset, to facilitate ongoing discussion and compromises about it with community members and partners. If possible, include a budget allocation for dissemination in any funding applications, and construct this to include more than just academic costs (for example, public events and more creative/artistic products) to support the wishes of community members.

3 Think about the strategies that you can use to facilitate research in ways that actively encourage the involvement of community members as co-creators. For example, should your approach involve the use of a steering group that includes community members (see McDavitt et al 2016)? You may also consider using a community advisory board.

Your strategy should support dissemination as an engaged process involving community members (Mosavel et al 2016).

Further teaching and learning resources to accompany this book can be found at https://bristoluniversitypress.co.uk/creating-participatory-research-website. The companion website includes:

- teaching slides for lecturers
- further information on learning tasks
- lesson activities
- further reading, links to websites and practical resources
- examples from practice
- additional case studies

PART III

Reality

8

Realities of applying participatory approaches

Key learning outcomes

By the end of this chapter, you should be able to:

- Understand the realities associated with community-based participatory research in practice
- Recognise the challenges associated with this approach
- Understand how to minimise risk and overcome some of the difficulties identified by practitioners

Introduction

In previous chapters you have learnt about the meaning of community-based participatory research (CBPR), why it is important and what value it can bring to all involved. In this chapter we will consider what CBPR looks like in practice, and where things don't always go to plan. In addition to being a more just and empowering way to go about research, CBPR can also be an enjoyable roller-coaster of unpredictability – or alternatively, a nightmare of unforeseen problems cropping up throughout! Researchers have to embrace the unknown, think on their feet and be ready for anything. This chapter will therefore introduce the realities of participatory research in practice and offer readers potential solutions to some of the frequently encountered challenges.

What are the core principles that make research participatory?

In Chapter 1, we provided a summary of the central tenets of participatory research (Strand et al 2003). Let's now look at how they play out in the field.

1. Community members conduct research (alone or with the support of the academic community). 'The researched' are actively involved in all of the research process

Real-life scenarios

Community members consider it unethical to be involved in data collection
In a participatory research project on breast cancer care, working groups were made up of patients, volunteers, nurses, doctors and researchers (Bourke 2009). The patients were very concerned about the confidentiality of people's responses in the research and therefore felt it was not appropriate for patients or healthcare professionals to be involved in collecting or collating data. They chose a questionnaire to collect data to allow anonymity – a data collection method not usually used in participatory research (see Chapter 5 for more on methods), but the decision to use it and the design were very much in keeping with participatory philosophy.

Community members don't want to be involved!
In the CBPR breast cancer care project mentioned above, having decided on the data collection method, the working groups and steering committee established the overall question themes but requested that the researcher designed the questionnaire. Some cited time as an issue but 'most were not interested in learning research design, preferring the researcher to draft questions' (Bourke 2009:460–1). That is not to say the community members did not contribute through feedback resulting in a useful questionnaire that had accessible language for patients.

Limited resources make participation a privilege not everyone can afford
Many of the populations that researchers wish to engage in CBPR are marginalised and have limited resources, so their priorities will revolve around covering the basic necessities of life for themselves and their families; CBPR cannot be a priority and they may not have any capacity to engage at all (Sushama et al 2018).

In participatory research carried out in the slums of Bangalore, India, it was especially apparent that the participants had very limited resources, specifically time, money and energy: 'In a community characterised by transience, uncertainty and insecurity, time is money. The morning routine in a slum household is packed and tailored to best navigate the chaos emerging from an attempt to juggle multiple roles and responsibilities within a limited time frame' (Sushama et al 2018). Contributing to CBPR in this context can have detrimental consequences for families on very low incomes, so from a research perspective is therefore unethical, and from a purely practical viewpoint not conducive to the smooth running of the project.

People don't have time

When the community members taking part in the participatory research are volunteers, they may not have the time to be involved in every aspect of the research (Clark 2008), but academic researchers often find they are eager to see findings straight away, perhaps having unrealistic expectations about how long research processes take: 'When the questionnaires were returned, committee members were keen to access results quickly but were clear that they did not want to be involved in collating the information, partly due to confidentiality reasons and partly due to time as they were all volunteers' (Bourke 2009:461). Managing expectations (of both academics and community members) is vital to reduce frustrations.

Relationships need time and space to grow

Building relationships with the community takes time and establishing positive links is just the beginning; it does not mean that data collection can begin straight away (Castleden et al 2012) but university timelines do not necessarily take that into account. When faced with questions about outputs from CBPR, one researcher's light-hearted reply to the university was that "I spent the first year drinking tea" (Castleden et al 2012:168). Pressure to deliver to deadlines from funders, managers or supervisors can make it difficult to invest the required time into relationships, but it is time well spent (see Chapter 9 for more on developing partnerships). This is especially challenging for student research projects, which tend to be of short duration.

Complete Learning Task 8.1 and consider how the context of academia in itself can be a challenge to successful CBPR.

LEARNING TASK 8.1 CHALLENGE OF ACADEMIC DEMANDS

Is CBPR possible when academics/students have obligations to undertake research in a particular timeframe and to formally disseminate it?

1 Can you find an example of a funder's requirements for academic researchers?
2 How can community members' needs be incorporated into the academic demands?
3 Consider the ethics of pushing to do research with people who are struggling to get by versus not including them at all. How can a balance be reached?

Having completed Learning Task 8.1, you will have had time to reflect on the importance of different priorities, and there are many other areas of challenge that also need consideration in relation to the realities of participatory research.

People don't have the necessary skills – for example, report writing
If research is to be truly participatory, community members should have the opportunity to contribute to all stages of the process. This can be challenging when certain aspects of the work require particular skills, as illustrated in Chapter 6 on analysis. Researchers can find it very time consuming when working with others on report writing: 'This was a lengthy process, in part because report writing was a foreign process of information recording' (Bourke 2009:463).

Formal academic writing style is not very appealing to many people outside the discipline, so it is useful to consider how best to share findings to make them accessible to everyone (see Chapter 7 on dissemination). When community members have no interest in working on academic reports, they generally leave this to the academic partners, putting a lot of trust in their interpretation without reviewing it. Academic partners have a responsibility to engage with the community in an appropriate way when 'giving the knowledge back' so that it is accessible and clear (Koster et al 2012).

It is understandable that formal academic jargon is off-putting, but for participation to be meaningful, the research would benefit from findings being discussed and confirmed with the community. This can be achieved by different means – for example, community meetings where results are shared (Castleden et al 2012).

Koster et al (2012) warn against a patronising attitude from academics about 'the validity of the participation and value of the final product' when it comes to co-writing reports and articles. They stress that there are a variety of ways that community members can contribute to the writing process and be recognised as co-authors. Complete Learning Task 8.2, which will help you to think about how to manage the challenges of inclusion in relation to report writing and analysis.

LEARNING TASK 8.2 INCLUSION AND REPORT WRITING

How can community members be included in report writing and analysis, especially in cases where there is a lack of interest, time and/or formal skills associated with this part of the work?

Consider the following suggestions that are discussed in the literature and make a note of the advantages and disadvantages that you may encounter with each of these approaches.

1 Workshops – for example, to provide training
2 Changing the format – for example, summarising in plain English; using community languages
3 Creative ways of sharing information – for example, infographics, more visual approaches

Learning Task 8.2 should have helped you to consider potential solutions to the issue of inclusion, and the success of these is likely to depend on the context in which you are working. Researchers should also recognise that context in the form of historical relationships and experiences can have a significant impact on CBPR in the present.

People come with 'baggage'

University researchers may be ignorant of historical relationships and tensions between individuals, particularly in small communities. It is likely that community researchers will have better relationships with some fellow residents as opposed to others. Various issues can be found in the literature arising from past conflicts; for example, in one case where research was poorly received by some community members, it transpired that they were relatives of a community researcher's ex-partner (Castleden et al 2012).

2. The research is intended to help improve issues within the community and is usually linked to social change and social justice, so is more likely to serve the needs of the local community

Real-life scenarios

The truth hurts!

Findings from research are not always positive, indeed it would be difficult to find a research report credible where everything went perfectly, and no challenges or setbacks were encountered. Some of the most important learning comes from identifying things that are not working so well and possibly how to improve them. This can put community researchers in a difficult position, however, if they have to share negative findings with their community: 'the difficultly the Indigenous researcher had in sharing negative comments about the club; she felt enormous pressure from her own community to write a report that gained the club's approval and resigned before the report was finalised' (Bourke 2009:463).

The community is not one big, happy family

Whether we are working with communities of practice or defined by geography, they are not homogeneous groups: prejudices and conflicts exist. Researchers may experience problematic attitudes from community members about others based on race, religion or other characteristics. In the following example, the researcher had to use her judgement about how best to manage the situation:

> While members from NESB [non-English-speaking backgrounds] were encouraged, the group was less open to participation by

Aboriginal people [...] racist comments continued. An Aboriginal member was not able to be recruited and the researcher was not sure that the group was a safe environment for a consumer who was Aboriginal. (Bourke 2009:464)

In Chapter 7, we saw how participatory research can serve to sometimes further exclude or frame communities in stereotypical ways and how researchers can deal with this. When community researchers only represent a select, potentially elite group, inequalities in the community can be reproduced in the research through legitimising knowledge of more powerful community members (Mey and van Hoven 2019).

Communities are not constant, and research cannot include everyone
Community members may not be able to contribute for the length of the project as life gets in the way. Deciding on the number of participants initially can be challenging; there needs to be enough buy-in from the community for it to be meaningful, but if a university researcher is responsible for training/supporting/facilitating the work, keeping numbers manageable is an important consideration. In a participatory research project on organisational change on an industrial site in Australia, there was only one professional researcher who had to balance the limits on his time with the potential benefits of a larger group of participants: 're-focusing the study on additional people with their added diversity would not necessarily aid the research process nor be practically achievable, given that he was the sole investigator' (Sense 2006:9).

This can be difficult to manage when, in principle, there is an open invitation for community members to participate, and selecting a limited number to take part means decisions are made about who is representing the community – who should make these decisions and how? In practice, researchers are rarely overwhelmed by interest and this would probably be viewed as a desirable problem to have.

Findings are difficult to translate into policy to effect change
Although CBPR research findings can be used by the community in a range of ways to produce changes, when it comes to influencing policy, qualitative participatory evidence is often difficult to use (Mey and van Hoven 2019). Researchers with expertise in this area are needed to guide the research process if influencing local or national policy is a goal of the work.

3. The community member is the expert and the community own the research

There are many implications of giving full ownership of research to communities and all parties need to be clear on where they stand on this.

Real-life scenarios

The community group do not want the data to be published

Giving control of the data to the community means that if they do not want it to be published then they have the final say (Castleden et al 2012), which can be a source of anxiety for academics who have obligations to disseminate their work and have tangible outputs, such as publications (see Chapter 10 for discussion about impact). A memorandum of understanding (MoU) and other contracts are usually only guidelines open to interpretation, so clear and constant communication is always necessary. In the next section, we will look at what an MoU is and how they can support research partnerships.

In one draft report evaluating a community programme, community leaders wanted negative findings to be removed and believed the community ownership of the data stated in the MoU gave them the power to make that decision. In this case, a compromise was reached where new evidence countering negative findings was included and some problematic findings were rephrased rather than omitted (Castleden et al 2012).

It can be difficult for community members to reconcile their identities as being part of the group as well as researchers

A project in the Netherlands on the early identification of frailty in older people living independently in the community involved community members as co-researchers. The co-researchers often offered advice to interviewees about problems they were experiencing, which the academic researchers worried would bias the findings. This issue was discussed in a 'reflection meeting' where community researchers learnt about why advising people during interviews could have an impact on the research and the academics understood more about the co-researchers' perspectives. The compromise reached was that the co-researchers could provide support and advice after the interviews but not during (Bindels et al 2013).

What's in it for me?

It is important to design research that addresses community priorities as opposed to academic preferences for research topics. Community members, as the experts, may wish to focus on social issues or those relating to finances or infrastructure (Sushama et al 2018). CBPR is a process of compromise and balancing the interests of everyone involved, where good communication is vital if community members are going to want to be on board (Sushama et al 2018). Managing expectations should be an ongoing concern throughout projects, particularly regarding what changes can realistically be expected by the community as a result of the research (see further discussion of this in Chapter 10). It is unethical to promise the world and then fail to deliver (Mey and van Hoven 2019).

Table 8.1 provides several examples of principles versus reality; however, these are not exhaustive. Table 8.2 (p 149) offers a detailed case study of the challenges associated with a specific CBPR project, and notes the strategies used to overcome them.

Table 8.1 Summary of the principles of participatory research, alongside a comparison of real-life experiences

Tenets of participatory research	Real life
1 Community members conduct research (alone or with the support of the academic community).	Community members may not *want* to conduct research.
	They may consider it unethical to be researching their own community and feel uncomfortable handling personal data from people they know.
	In communities where resources are scarce, conducting research is a luxury they cannot afford and is not a priority.
2 The research is intended to help improve issues within the community and is usually linked to social change, and social justice, so is more likely to serve the needs of the local community. It can also serve academic needs at the same time.	Are those involved from the community representative of the whole?
	It is not possible to work with everyone in the community, so whose voice is being heard and who is being excluded? Conflict between community members needs to be acknowledged and addressed.
	What happens when the community do not like the findings?
	It can be difficult to influence policy using participatory research findings.
3 The community member is the expert and owns the research.	Ownership of the research should be determined from the outset.
	What happens when the needs/wishes of the community researchers are in conflict with academic requirements? Funding requirements may oblige academics to produce outputs on completion of participatory research projects. How can this be managed? What if the community members do not want the data to be used in this way?
	How can the research be owned by the community if the academic partners have the final say in how it is used and shared?

Source: Strand et al (2003: chapter 1)

Potential solutions to the challenges of CBPR

Research projects are generally more successful when time is invested in the preparation stages. This is even more critical for CBPR where planning also takes into account what form the partnership work will take and the aims that set out what different stakeholders will bring to the research and what they will take away. Many of the potential difficulties in CBPR can be anticipated at the beginning and there are several actions that can be taken to minimise conflict at a later date. One option is to develop a memorandum of understanding.

What is a memorandum of understanding and why is it useful?

A memorandum of understanding (MoU) is a document to be shared with all stakeholders to provide clarity to partners and the opportunity for scrutiny. It can also be a means of providing stability – for example, should a staff member leave, because there is a formal written record of rights and responsibilities. It is not legally binding but it is a 'statement of serious intent – agreed voluntarily by equal partners – of the commitment, resources and other considerations that each of the parties will bring. It has moral force, but does not create legal obligations' (Gov.uk 2019). A guide to writing an MoU can be found on the UK government's website (Gov.uk 2019).

In Bourke's (2009) project with Indigenous communities, it was decided to produce an MoU at the outset to explicitly state the terms of the research. The MoU took over a year to develop, through work with researchers at the university and a number of Indigenous community members. The document defined the way the research would be conducted, stipulating that the research design and implementation would be overseen and approved by Aboriginal leaders and that community members would be involved in collecting and analysing data. It also guaranteed ownership of the data to the community (Bourke 2009).

Despite not being legally binding, an MoU is still a formal document and has to adhere to a lot internal rules and regulations at the academic institution concerned. Another way of preparing for a CBPR partnership is by following suggested guidelines to create a community impact statement (Box 8.1).

Box 8.1 Developing a community impact statement: a participatory 'prenup'

A Healthy Housing Collaborative in Minnesota, USA, developed a community impact statement (CIS) based on the learning from two CBPR projects. They compare the CIS to a pre-nuptial agreement, whereby each partner brings significant resources to the 'marriage'.

They attribute the success of participatory research to having clearly defined relationships, benefits and assets as much as having the right people and motivations. A community activist and an academic researcher who were involved in the projects documented the research process and produced the following guidelines to be a 'prenup' for future CBRP projects.

Laying the foundations
• Members of the research project from all sides should reflect on their histories, what they have in common, what differences there are, and what relevant assets they bring to the project.

• Practical considerations such as where and when to meet should be discussed and 'ground rules' for meetings agreed by the stakeholders.

Establishing relationships
• Before the research begins, partners should agree how decisions will be made in meetings, who will attend the meetings and who will not.
• It is important to recognise differences in culture and potential biases, and to be frank about what each party wants/expects to gain from taking part. This is a good time to address power imbalances and consider how they will affect the relationship, including the preparatory discussions to establish the project processes.
• Training in good communication and resolving conflict may be useful.

Carrying out the research
• The benefits and risks to the community and the academic institution should be transparent.
• Funding sources should be identified, and decisions made about how the money will be managed; for example, will the academic institution apply for and hold it?
• In UK universities, research will always be reviewed by an ethics board. Depending on the institution or research area, this board may not have an understanding of CBPR so researchers should submit robust justifications for this way of working and expect to submit amendments for ethical approval as the work evolves.
• The format and frequency of reports should be agreed at this stage, as well as an overall timeline. It is beneficial to include additional time for building relationships.

Evaluation and dissemination
• The partners will decide how to evaluate the project and process, and where and how to disseminate the findings of the research and evaluation.
• Plans should be made about how the research will be completed, with exit strategies in place.
• Finally, the completion of the work should be celebrated, and recognition given to the input from everyone who has been involved.

Source: Adapted from Gust and Jordan (2007)

Having considered ways of planning projects to prevent or minimise difficulties, let's now look at how problems were dealt with in a specific CBPR collaboration and the learning that came from it. Table 8.2 summarises some of the key problems and solutions implemented, or suggested for future work, from projects involving a collaboration between Boston universities and community partners focusing on public housing and asthma.

Table 8.2 introduces some of the difficulties associated with partnership working and some potential solutions. Community-campus partnerships are explored in more depth in the next chapter.

Table 8.2 Learning from CBPR project collaborations between Boston universities and community partners

Problem	Solution
Building equitable partnerships • Distribution of funds • Significant differences in existing resources • Imbalance of power, with the academic institution being in control of the project	The Asthma Center on Community Environment and Social Stress (ACCESS) project involved one research proposal but 'two separate applications and two separate grant awards, however funded as a partnership'. This meant that the community partner received direct funding independent of the academic institution, which helped to address the power imbalance existing in projects where the university holds the purse strings.
Stereotypes • Academics doubting the capabilities of community members • Distrust towards academics and their motivations	Stakeholders in participatory research should be open about preconceptions and concerns. Building in regular meetings and opportunities for dialogue where partners can build up trusting relationships are essential (see Chapter 9 on community-campus partnerships). Academics need to be willing to yield some control to give community members the chance to step up to the challenges presented.
Culture clashes and structure • Attitudes to research and how it is carried out • Traditional structure of one PI (principal investigator) as the leader with the final say	CBPR benefits from having a number of co-investigators who bring a range of assets to the research. Having one academic who oversees the process does not promote collaboration. Choosing a PI with strengths in applied research and good community connections (as opposed to a traditional academic CV) would be positive. Sharing PI responsibilities between academic and community partners will encourage teamwork and sharing of power.
Balancing scientific enquiry and community needs • Community objections to the funding being used for research rather than service delivery • No direct benefits to the community although potential for future impact	Academics wanted a control group in the research design; community members objected to some people being excluded from the benefits of the intervention. Compromise led to a longitudinal study with intense data collection. Public health research can sometimes be more theoretical and focused on a greater good, whereas community partners are advocating for the people in their community and want to see direct and immediate impact on their lives. As with all challenges, open and frank discussions from the outset are required to ensure everyone has realistic expectations. Conflict cannot, and should not, be avoided – it is part of a healthy relationship.

Source: Freeman et al (2006)

Challenges to creating equal partnerships

Academics often design a research project first and then look to recruit community members to take part (Freeman et al 2006). This is not necessarily down to arrogance about knowing what is best for the community or a lack of will to work with a range of stakeholders, but is often related to funding application processes and in-house ethics review boards (Kindon et al 2007). Another issue with this is that funding comes with strings attached (Freeman et al 2006), regarding what outputs are required and ownership of the data.

Stereotypes can also be an issue, with academics having preconceptions about the ability and capacity of community members to be involved and also community members being suspicious about the motives of the academics, believing them to be out of touch and out for themselves (Freeman et al 2006).

This can lead to academics being reluctant to share control and community members being reluctant to take part. Openly acknowledging biases and concerns from the start can help to build solid foundations for a successful project. Box 8.2 provides reflection about stereotypes of academics and community members drawn from our own experiences.

Box 8.2 Stereotypes: academics in their ivory towers

What do people outside academia really think of academics and students? Do you have your own prejudices about lecturers or researchers you have encountered?

Leeds Beckett University offers course taster sessions for members of the community, generally from groups underrepresented in higher education, to come onto campus and see what it would be like to be a student.

The most common feedback from visitors we had in the early days was surprise that the lecturers and researchers they met were actually 'really normal'; they were expecting unapproachable people who would look down on them. Such perceptions may act as a barrier to participatory research getting off the ground.

Participants of the outreach programme also had prejudices about each other, which dissipated after spending more time together (the group participated in a two-hour session once a week for six weeks). Janice (a black African woman seeking asylum in the UK) shared how her preconceptions about some teenage boys with piercings changed as she got to know them:

> 'I was touched by the humility of those guys. One with rings and his friends (sorry I forget their names) – first impression [you] would think they are rough (at least that what society has taught some of us), but lo and behold! Complete opposite.

> 'I was getting on the bus the other time and one of them from the back seat shouted "Hi Janice!" It just blessed and humbled me, I felt like hugging him.'

Academic context

The context in which CBPR is conducted (the importance of which has already been highlighted in several chapters of this book) affects to what extent a project can be fully participatory, and therefore the realities associated with context need careful consideration. We have seen in this chapter that the context of community members' lives will dictate if they can be involved and to what degree. Let's now turn to the academic context to consider the institution and researchers.

Ethical obstacles

The strict processes in universities require ethical approval for any data collection in the community, understandably, but the nature of CBPR means that researchers need to get university clearance to carry out work without knowing what direction it is going to take, which can be complicated (Castleden et al 2012). This can exclude people external to the university in the initial research design stages.

Apart from the practicalities of official ethical approval, researchers will frequently face ethical dilemmas in their day-to-day work, some of which are difficult to anticipate in advance. One question that thought can be given to (although decisions made in theory can be difficult to maintain in practice) is how much do researchers give of themselves (Koster et al 2012)? In developing relationships with different groups, their cultural frameworks may include interaction outside the research project and an expectation from participants of openness about personal lives, not formal, professional relationships. There is often debate in qualitative research about how much researchers should contribute of their own experiences, with feminist methodologies justifying more open, personal approaches to reduce power imbalances. In recognition that participants are being asked to share deeply personal information with strangers, it only seems fair that researchers reciprocate to some degree to build trust (Acker et al 1983), while taking care not to exploit participants or expose themselves to emotional dangers in the process.

In qualitative research out in the field, it is always important to complete a risk analysis before starting the data collection. CBPR often means working in a wide range of community settings and during anti-social hours; these may range from a draughty church hall on a Tuesday evening to a local pub on a Saturday afternoon. There will often be members of the wider community using the spaces, and researchers need to be open about who they are and what is happening, but also need to be aware of how best to ensure their own and the community participants' safety. If threats come from within the research group, then prior training in mediation or conflict management can be put to use (Kindon et al 2007). Protocols should be in place for other dangers, and where possible, risks should be minimised by following good practice, such as meeting in public spaces, walking in well-lit areas at night and following lone worker guidelines. Complete Learning Task 8.3 to consider how researchers can conduct CBPR safely.

Researchers who embrace participatory methods often do so in order to work with marginalised communities, to improve their situation and perhaps reduce the stigma they face in wider society. They can be quite protective of participants, but such positive bias can lead to us to overlook potential dangers that arise from the difficult and chaotic circumstances of some participants' lives (Adams and Moore 2007).

Adams and Moore (2007) explain that areas of research which do not appear sensitive on the surface, such as air quality, could unearth emotions from unforeseen association leading to unpredictable responses. They also draw attention to the fact that although researchers go through thorough checks to safeguard children in research, it cannot be ignored that children themselves could pose a threat of violence to the adults.

A local ethics coordinator for Leeds Beckett University commented "I also think that ethics in university contexts tends to consider risk to participants more than to us."

Table 8.3 provides some general examples of dangers in the field for researchers. In Learning Task 8.4, consider some more specific situations and what you would do in each case.

Having completed Learning Task 8.4, you will have discovered that there is no single correct answer when it comes to working with people and the complexities

Table 8.3 Examples of dangers in the field

Danger	Measures taken to reduce threat
Physical – threat or abuse from participants, researchers or strangers	Thorough risk analysis should be carried out before working off campus, particularly for out-of-office hours and lone working.
	Researchers should remove themselves from situations if they feel unsafe and check in with a designated contact.
Emotional – from threat or actual violence or from information disclosed	Professional supervision in the workplace to discuss any sensitive and distressing topics that have arisen is advised.
	A team approach means one person does not have to deal with all of the emotional burden of a project.
Ethical – resulting in mental or physical harm	A thorough ethical review and approval from the university ethics committee prior to commencing the work.
	Researchers should prepare a list of places of support to signpost people for issues that may arise in the course of the research.
Professional – threat connected to the researcher's role or positionality	Researchers should follow university guidelines and report any issues to line managers as soon as they occur.
	Well-documented, regular meetings and correspondence can provide a paper trail so researchers can demonstrate why and how decisions were taken.

Source: Adapted from Lee-Treweek and Linkogle (2000)

of community. Researchers can prepare for common eventualities and have to deal with others as they come up.

In the examples featured in this chapter, we have heard from academics about how they have approached CBPR and tackled common challenges. In the name of being inclusive and participatory, it is only fair we include an account from a community member's perspective. In the case study below, David talks about his experiences of being a volunteer in participatory projects.

••

CASE STUDY A VOLUNTEER'S EXPERIENCE OF CBPR

In David's experience, health-related research projects tend to be made up of team members whom he categorises as 'clinical', 'academic' or 'PPI' (patient and public involvement). He has found the 'work' is usually done by the first two groups; members of the third group (if it exists at all) are invited to meetings and asked if there is anything 'from the PPI perspective' after the fact. Despite this approach, "the final write-up will proudly proclaim that full consultation was maintained and a dedicated PPI team involved at all stages".

This can leave the community contributors feeling frustrated at the tokenistic nature of the process, which is more about ticking boxes than genuine involvement. David cites a UK public participation charity (Involve 2019) definition of public involvement in research as "research being carried out 'with' or 'by' members of the public rather than 'to', 'about' or 'for' them" and believes the reality usually falls short of this. In one NIHR (National Institute for Health Research) project he was involved in, he was disappointed to be invited to only three meetings over a two-and-a-half year period. He does not feel this position has given him a voice or has used the skills he brings.

David recommends establishing in the planning stages what characteristics/skills the project requires from the non-clinical, non-academic team members. Targeted recruitment can then take place and relevant training offered. He believes that having trained people from the community as full project team members with an equal stake would mean that "there is thus no need for a 'patient and public involvement group' any more than there is a need for a 'clinical group' or an 'academic group'". Apart from enriching the researcher pool, such a move would also limit opportunities for tokenism and elitism (such as "lay people wouldn't understand the jargon/process/implications").

People do not fall into neat categories with black-and-white definitions of who they are. David identifies as a patient/service user and a member of the public. He has postgraduate qualifications but has never worked at a university, so he is not an academic. He has worked in the NHS but not as a clinician. The boundaries between clinician, academic and service user/community member are not fixed, and many people identify as more than one – but participatory approaches are often keen to put people in boxes to meet criteria for the work.

> 'There is a danger that we define ourselves by social categories (such as occupation and educational status) and as a result we could find within the project that we have three categories – academic, clinical and PPI.' (David)

Summary

- By taking time before the research begins to establish what the rights and responsibilities of the different parties are, problems can be avoided or minimised later. It may not be realistic for research to be carried out and owned completely by the community, but to what extent this will be the case can be discussed at the beginning.

- Flexibility and compromise will be needed throughout the project and the academic partner will not necessarily get the outcome they desired. It is important to manage expectations from all parties throughout.

- Researchers should always be aware of the context they are working in, both from a point of view of understanding the demands of the participants' lives outside the project, and in making sure community members and academics are safe and risk is minimised.

Suggestions for further reading

1 Gust, S. and Jordan, C. (2007) 'The community impact statement: a prenuptial agreement for community-campus partnerships', *Journal of Higher Education Outreach and Engagement*, 11(2): 155–69.

As a result of work on two CBPR projects, a community impact statement was created. This paper suggests that agreements must be developed before partnership work starts because such statements provide the process for community-university partnerships.

2 Castleden, H., Morgan, V. and Lamb, C. (2012) '"I spent the first year drinking tea": exploring Canadian university researchers' perspectives on community-based participatory research involving Indigenous peoples', *The Canadian Geographer/Le Géographe canadien*, 56(2): 160–79.

This article discusses the findings of an exploratory qualitative case study based on semi-structured interviews with Canadian geographers and social scientists working in university contexts using CBPR. The paper notes several tensions for university-based researchers in relation to CBPR theory and practice.

3 Involve.org.uk: 'We believe that people should be at the heart of decision-making.'
This is a charity website that describes the importance of involving people in decision making, drawing on examples and offering advice and tips.

Questions for reflection

1 What is the best way of preparing for a CBPR project? Would an MoU or 'prenup' be necessary? Is it better to have something in writing or is an oral agreement enough? Does it also depend on the community partners, their level of literacy and attitudes to formal paperwork?

2 What can researchers do to ensure community members participate meaningfully when they have so many other demands on their time and more urgent priorities such as providing for their families?

3 How can researchers safeguard themselves and participants from potential dangers? What would good practice look like in risk assessment?

Top tips for practice

1 Take time to lay the foundations and make an agreement outlining what involvement will mean for all parties. Investing time to develop relationships before beginning the research will help build trust so that problems can be dealt with in more open and healthy ways.

2 Be flexible and expect the unexpected. Sometimes life gets in the way and unforeseen challenges come up. The flip side of this is that unexpected benefits and positive outcomes are also frequently part of this work. Researchers need to be open to changes of plans, times, places and, often, participants.

3 Record the ups and downs of the project. As a researcher you can develop professional and personal skills (problem solving, communication skills, creative thinking, planning and organisational skills) greatly through this type of work – and the best learning experience comes from when things haven't gone to plan.

Further teaching and learning resources to accompany this book can be found at https://bristoluniversitypress.co.uk/creating-participatory-research-website. The companion website includes:

- teaching slides for lecturers
- further information on learning tasks
- lesson activities
- further reading, links to websites and practical resources
- examples from practice
- additional case studies

9

Community-campus partnerships

Key learning outcomes

By the end of this chapter, you will:

- Understand what a community-campus partnership is

- Understand what value community-campus partnerships can have in dealing with common challenges of undertaking participatory research as well as their contributions to educational institutions and the wider community

- Recognise successful factors as well as the limitations of community-campus partnerships

Introduction

The chapter begins by describing what a community-campus partnership (CCP) is and some background to the initiative before then exploring what this approach brings to community-based participatory research (CBPR) and how it can counter common challenges, as well as considering some limitations. Key features required for a successful CCP are summarised. The chapter will look at specific examples of CBPR undertaken in the context of a CCP and ends with a case study of a CCP developed at a university in the UK.

Origins of CCPs

John Dewey's work in the US in the early 20th century contributed greatly to both the development of participatory action research and CCPs. His work centred on democracy and civic responsibility, and encouraged the practice of 'co-operative inquiry' – learning that involved the students across all social groups and abilities, which underpins the participatory research approach (Coghlan and Brydon-Miller 2014). For Dewey, education was crucial to developing a 'neighbourly community' and civic responsibility was an important aspect of university education (Coghlan and Brydon-Miller 2014).

Dewey theorised learning as a social process of participation where education must involve working together as a community at class or school level to gain knowledge and understanding (Westbrook 1992), which the CCP model expands to include the wider community outside the classroom. This valued participation is the basis of democracy where people are fully engaged in civil life (Westbrook 1992). When working with groups across a neighbourhood or city, this participation can promote knowledge exchange, inclusion and the levelling out of power imbalances.

In the US, the importance of CCPs to teaching, research and practice was increasingly recognised in the 1990s, with financial support for their development coming from the Department of Housing and Urban Development and non-governmental organisations such as the Kellogg Commission and the Carnegie Foundation (Johnson Butterfield and Soska 2004). This led to many US universities being able to offer undergraduate courses that had civic responsibility at their centre (Hart et al 2007:10).

The focus was frequently on enhancing student learning through providing additional community healthcare support – for example, free clinics for deprived neighbourhoods (Greenberg et al 2003). The intention was to provide direct benefit to all parties as community members received healthcare and students had valuable learning opportunities (Seifer 1998). CCPs look different in different contexts depending on the needs of the community and the specialisms of the educational institution, but there are a number of key components that they share. Complete Learning Task 9.1 to explore these components in further detail.

LEARNING TASK 9.1 KEY COMPONENTS OF CCPs

1 Use the internet to explore CCPs (a simple Google search will bring up plenty of results).

2 Select an example guide to CCPs and then read the information, making notes on the key components.

3 To what extent did the guide that you selected discuss research? Reflect on how the components of CCPs link to participatory research.

While you were completing the first Learning Task 9.1, did you find literature and guides mostly from the US? There are few developed CCPs in the UK, although many universities have strong links to their communities despite not using CCP models. Courses related to health and wellbeing work closely with the surrounding community as students undertake placements during their studies (for example, nursing or dietetics), but CCPs can involve a wider range of partners, including the third sector, as opposed to solely clinical settings. This can give students valuable experience of working with marginalised groups.

CCPs bring the philosophy of participatory research to partnerships in general in order to work towards the greater good without exploiting those outside the institution. Community groups do not want to be the subjects of research, which is done at the convenience of researchers and is dependent on university timelines;

they want an equal stake in directing it and tackling issues in real time (Baum 2000). Having a direct route into the university allows community members to communicate their research needs and to be involved from the very beginning.

Examples of how CCPs enable participatory research are illustrated in Table 9.1.

Table 9.1 shows that CCPs work in a variety of ways to support communities, which includes bridging the gap between traditional and participatory methods of research.

Table 9.1 Role of CCPs in enabling participatory research

Traditional research	Participatory research	Role of CCP
Academics (university staff) conduct research.	Community members conduct research (alone or with the support of the academic community).	Brokering the relationships so community members can connect with relevant academics.
The research is about the needs of the university and the interests of the academics; for example, it is about contributing to a particular topic area.	The research is intended to help improve issues within the community and is usually linked to social change and social justice, so is more likely to serve the needs of the local community. It can also serve academic needs at the same time.	CCPs are a channel through which the community voice can be heard so the research needs of the community are known. Academics can also approach appropriate community partners with suggestions for research.
The academic is the expert and the university or research organisation 'owns' the research.	The community member is the expert and owns the research.	CCPs facilitate mutually beneficial collaborations with an emphasis on valuing experts by experience and academic knowledge equally.

Source: Adapted from Strand et al (2003) and University of Delaware (2016)

Principles of CCPs

The organisation Community–Campus Partnerships for Health (CCPH), which promotes CBPR, has formulated a list of 'Principles of Good Community–Campus Partnerships' (Blumenthal 2011). The following principles drawn from CCPH (Box 9.1) are intended to be used as a starting point to develop more customised principles, rather than a rigid set of rules.

Box 9.1 Key principles of CCPs

The partnership:

1   Forms to serve a specific purpose and may take on new goals over time
2   Members have shared objectives and values

3   Is based on trust and respect

4   Is asset based but also builds capacity for all involved

5   Shares resources and power

6   Requires clear and regular communication and a common language

7   Shares decision making and the development of processes, involving all partners

8   Continues to develop and improve through feedback from all stakeholders

9   Benefits all partners involved

10 Does not have to be permanent, and an exit strategy should be planned

11 Considers the nature of the environment/context in its design, evaluation and sustainability

12 Values community and academic knowledge and experience equally

Source: Adapted from CCPH (2019)

Using the guiding principles set out above, we now consider how CCPs can support and contribute to participatory approaches in research.

1. Having a *specific purpose* is useful for building the momentum of partnerships but has led to exploitation in the past when the purpose was dictated by academic interests. Stakeholders in CCPs view the partnerships as ongoing relationships that are the foundations for the research and knowledge exchange that benefits the community partners, not simply a means of preparing for a project the university wishes to initiate (Thompson et al 2003). As Baum (2000) discusses, it takes a long time to build trust and understanding between different partners, so a model of creating a partnership on demand for a specific goal is perhaps not the most effective way to work. A CCP could be established for a more general purpose rather than a specific project – for example, to improve community health. Therefore, CCPs support CBPR by enabling a more community-driven research agenda.

2. *Shared objectives and values* For a CCP to succeed, it must have 'a clearly articulated and mutually agreed-on mission' (Hubbell and Burman 2006:522), which forms the basis for collaborations that can then put their energy into developing creative and ambitious ways to move forwards (Askew 2001). This gives the work focus and ensures buy-in from the different stakeholders. Authenticity come from the 'mutual respect of values, strategies, and actions' (Ahmed and Palermo 2010:1383) and a CCP cannot be considered to be inclusive and participatory if the objectives and values are dictated by one party.

    For some, the CCP is a vehicle through which community members and academics can work together to set the research agenda (Suarez–Balcazar et al 2005), whereas others put the emphasis on the community defining the needs and priorities (Wolff and Maurana 2001). When the objectives are generated in the community setting, there is more ownership, making joint projects more likely to succeed (Wolff and Maurana 2001).

3. *Trust* Many researchers now wish to work in more participatory ways with communities. However, the reality of financial and time constraints (as discussed in Chapter 8) means that a lot of researchers do not build longer-term relationships with participants or include them in other aspects of the research process such as analysis or dissemination (see Chapter 7 for more on dissemination). Participants often provide the required data for the project and hear no more about it (Blumenthal 2011). This is unethical from the researchers' point of view (see Chapter 4 for more on ethics) and can lead to resentment and distrust of academics from the researched population, especially 'fashionable' populations who are over-researched (Clark 2008). A better approach is to have a regular familiar face from the university in community areas and at events; a named contact who can chase up, update and pass on information, someone who can serve as a trusted link between the two worlds. Ostrander (2004) describes a 'critical bridge person' at the academic institution who has strong links with the community. This needs to be a designated role that exists to maintain partnerships, follow up on links and networking, and to match community groups to the appropriate academics. As has been discussed earlier in Chapter 1, there is no specific model for a participatory research approach but CCPs can provide a foundation for CBPR by managing issues of trust, power and language before research begins.

4. *Asset-based approaches* were detailed in Chapter 1 (see Box 1.1). CCPs can work with community members to explore the skills they bring to a research project, such as local knowledge about key issues and community needs, so that the focus moves away from that of a deficit approach identifying problems, and instead highlights the knowledge and potential already present, where 'the glass is half-full rather than half-empty' (Foot and Hopkins 2010:6). Asset mapping at the start of a research project can be used as the foundation to develop a project and to frame it in a way that has more relevance to community members; one such mapping technique is 'head, hands and heart', which works with participants to identify their knowledge (head), skills (hands) and passions (heart) (Rippon and Hopkins 2015). One of the main criticisms of universities working in community settings as a charitable or altruistic gesture is that the focus is generally on deficits as opposed to the strengths of the population in receipt of the help (Morton 1995). A CCP aims to change this dynamic.

    In addition to recognising the existing strengths of the community members, part of the civic responsibility (Coghlan and Brydon-Miller 2014) of the CCP is to build the capacity of those involved. The CCP should ideally support community groups to develop their leadership and organising skills, enabling them to continue the work even if the university withdraws from the partnership (Wolff and Maurana 2001).

5. *Sharing power* is a crucial element of a CCP model, meaning universities make decisions with community partners and *share resources*; this is integral to a successful partnership (Ostrander 2004). CCPs are a way of sharing power and control of research, making researchers accountable to the community they are working with. This can serve as a starting point for challenging the systems and traditions within universities and in overcoming mistrust in any community fearful of exploitation or misrepresentation (Merzel et al 2007). At the same time, the idea is not to reverse the power imbalance by inviting the community partners to take control of the university's research and teaching (Hart and Wolff 2006). The sharing of resources is a question of justice, demonstrating the equal status of all partners (Bringle and Hatcher 2002).

6. *Language and communication* Even when the common language is technically English, it can be used very differently depending on the sector, with higher education, statutory services and the non-profit and private sectors often using distinct terminology and abbreviations. Overcoming these differences is vital to enable a partnership to explicitly set out priorities and shared values (Askew 2001). Academics are often accused of speaking a different language – indeed, between disciplines as well as compared with groups external to the university. Establishing new relationships for every research project means that this period of learning about the terminology and jargon of each group can take up valuable time. Even with existing partnerships, this area requires ongoing attention and reflection as researchers can easily slip back into exclusionary language. Academic language can be off-putting so the words used to discuss research should be carefully considered at an early stage (Hart and Wolff 2006).

7. *Shares decision making* Cherry and Shefner (2004) believe that CCP work should follow feminist principles, which means adapting meeting structures, locations and language to create a space conducive to shared decision making. This can be a particularly challenging aspect of partnerships for universities, and the extent to which the academic institution can or will do this will have a great influence over the success of the initiative (Ostrander 2004). Effort should be made to include even the 'weakest' partners in the decision-making process (Strier 2010). As we have seen in other chapters of this book, inclusivity is central to CBPR.

8. *Continues to develop and improve through feedback from all stakeholders* Ongoing development of partnerships includes encouraging reflexivity from those involved (Strier 2010). In the initial stages, CCPs can provide a structure for partnerships that already exist and then support them to evolve together

over time with the designated CCP workers facilitating input from everyone (Hart and Wolff 2006).

9. *Benefits all partners involved* Partnership working provides benefits for teaching, student experience and research at universities (Hart et al 2007), and allows community groups to have an influence on the education of future professionals, particularly in healthcare (Carney et al 2011). Student projects provide extra capacity for non-profit groups with limited resources and can lead to tangible outputs that have a positive impact on the health and social needs of the community members being supported (Carney et al 2011).

It is important that the partnerships benefit all parties, that there is equal respect for all partners, that sustainability is promoted and that the portrayal of academics as saviours is avoided (Hart and Wolff 2006). Mutual benefit is important in tackling power imbalances, as work carried out as a charitable gesture generally sees the 'provider' holding all the power over the resources and how the work is done (Morton 1995). Partnership success can be measured by the extent to which all parties reap benefits from their involvement (Suarez-Balcazar et al 2005). Successful CCPs can lead to benefits for the university and the community members/groups involved (Ilustre et al 2012), as Table 9.2 illustrates.

10. *Does not have to be permanent*, although from our work, we believe that the CCP demonstrates an ongoing commitment from institutions of higher education to their surrounding community as part of their civic responsibility. Different partnerships and projects within a CCP may have different lifespans but the overarching structure can offer long-term advantages to the university and community partners. There should be no pressure for the partnership to be permanent if it has reached a natural conclusion, but without longer-term relationships it can be difficult for researchers to grasp the breadth of community members' knowledge, particularly regarding the environmental and social dynamics in their local area (London et al 2011). It is helpful to have a planned exit strategy for projects of fixed duration and this can contribute to maintaining positive relationships.

11. *Context* In the current climate of austerity measures and limited funding, *sustainability* is a great challenge. It is usually assumed that ongoing relationships are successful ones, but it is also important to avoid either party becoming dependent or being exploited (Bringle and Hatcher 2002), which is also central to the values of CBPR. Consistency can be developed and supported within a broader framework of obligation. (Complete Learning Task 9.2 to explore the concept of obligation in more depth.) The design must be relevant and appropriate for those involved and have realistic goals. Equally, the evaluation of projects should be fitting to the context and not involve adding unnecessary burden to any party; ideally it can be incorporated into the project.

12. *Respecting community knowledge* Hart and Wolff (2006) describe the University of Brighton's efforts to avoid a 'patronising charity ethos' by valuing community knowledge and challenging power imbalances. It is also important that all of the partners' contributions are regularly acknowledged so that they feel valued (Askew 2001). CCPs offer a means of providing structure (Hart and Wolff 2006) and consistency to existing partnerships, as well as being a point of contact for potential partners to initiate interaction. As seen in Table 9.1, traditionally, research was carried out by 'experts' from universities in their own interests (Strand et al 2003) who often ceased contact with participants once their involvement in data collection came to an end (Danley 2018). Even when using CBPR approaches, it can be difficult to maintain contact and involvement over long periods, but a CCP model can help to support and maintain links to community knowledge or serve as a point of contact for community members.

Now complete Learning Task 9.2 to explore how the principles underpinning CCPs can work in university contexts.

LEARNING TASK 9.2 CIVIC UNIVERSITIES: DO INSTITUTIONS HAVE AN OBLIGATION TO THE CITIZENS OF THEIR CITY, BEYOND THE STUDENTS?

Think of your own current or previous learning institution. How much interaction is/was there with the community surrounding it?

Use the internet and any other relevant resources that you have (for example, books and articles).

Discuss with your classmates: do educational institutions have an obligation to the citizens of their city, beyond the students? Make some notes on the following.

1 What benefits could collaboration with the community have for students, teaching and research staff?
2 What benefits could collaboration with universities/colleges have for community groups and charities?
3 How could partnerships between the university and local organisations be established and maintained?

Having completed this learning task, you will have debated these questions and thought of some of the benefits of these partnerships for all parties. Table 9.2 provides an overview of benefits for both universities and communities.

Table 9.2 Mutually beneficial partnerships

For the university	For the community
Widening participation: a diverse student body to reflect the community the university serves	Access to education and training, raising aspirations
Enhancing student experience	Informing student learning to serve different communities better
Access to community knowledge	Access to academic knowledge
Research opportunities	Research opportunities: co-producing research agendas
Ethical access to research participants	Informing research priorities
Research impact	Evidence-led service development
Volunteering and placement opportunities	Increased capacity through access to staff/ student support
Meeting corporate social responsibilities	Working towards shared goals, greater sustainability
Addressing the power imbalance, a less exploitative model of working	Increasing control and power in the hands of the community

Source: Adapted from Coan and Witty (2016)

Brokering

There are many academics and community members who are willing and able to engage in partnership work, with CCPs providing a valuable brokering/ matchmaking service to match groups whose interests are aligned (Wenger 1998). The CCP staff can provide a point of contact for community groups and academics, and develop positive connections through providing a route into the university (NFHEPG 2005). Now complete Learning Task 9.3 to explore relationship brokering in more depth.

LEARNING TASK 9.3 BROKERING RELATIONSHIPS

Research two charities in your local areas that serve different communities (for example, a charity supporting homeless people and one supporting people with learning disabilities).

1 What are the priorities for each charity?
2 What research needs do they have?

Look at the website of your institution/a university nearest to the charities.

1 What specialist research areas does the institution have?
2 Is there a research group that would match the needs of the charity?

Outline the research potential and the benefits of working together for one of the charities and a department/research group at the university.

In your view, how could challenges be minimised/overcome?

In completing Learning Task 9.3, you will have been able to see many overlapping areas of interest between community charities and local institutions, which is one potential function of CCPs. CCPs also provide several other opportunities. For example, they provide space for academics and community partners to mix, both on and off campus, helping to build relationships and develop a mutual understanding of needs and interests (Hart and Wolff 2006). They can also increase flexibility between collaborators, particularly for those accustomed to the rather rigid systems in universities, who are then able to work differently with diverse community groups (Askew 2001).

Challenges of CCPs

Chapter 1 states that partnerships are important when working to deliver participatory research because they support 'equitable co-ownership and co-decision making' (Macaulay 2017). This approach to research therefore requires successful partnerships in which willing participants, internally and externally, commit to working together (Hart and Wolff 2006). However, the literature on partnerships offers analysis of the many challenges involved with such ways of working. Complete Learning Task 9.4, which will help you to think about partnerships in further detail. You may have some examples from Chapter 8, which discusses CBPR in practice.

LEARNING TASK 9.4 WHAT ARE THE POTENTIAL CHALLENGES OF THIS WORK?

1 Take some time to reflect on partnership work between universities and community groups in the context of participatory research. What obstacles might researchers face? What difficulties could arise from the perspectives of the community group?

2 Use the internet or other resources (books and journal articles) to find examples of challenges. Are there particular topics of research that would be more suitable for this type of work?

3 Do you have examples of working with people at university or elsewhere where there have been breakdowns in communication or different expectations?

4 In your view, how could challenges be minimised/overcome?

What key learning did you take from completing Learning Task 9.4? There are many challenges related to issues of power and resource inequalities, language differences and the attitudes of different partners. Research findings show that the construction of partnerships is highly affected by the perceptions of members, power relations, institutional contexts, group affiliations, societal views of social problems and role conflicts. Strier (2010) recommends nurturing solidarity and reducing tensions by developing a culture founded on reflexivity. The literature tells us that it is important to approach partnership work with realistic expectations (as discussed in Chapter 8), and the difficulties encountered can actually be a means of strengthening the partnership and realising maximum potential (London et al 2011). Literature on CCPs documents a range of challenges that have been reported in partnership working:

- A lack of clarity of boundaries of the projects and partnership as well as different aims can lead to tensions (Barnes et al 2009).

- Achieving a balance of power can be difficult, and prejudices, as well as mistrust, can linger on all sides. Partnerships have to tackle these attitudes, while recognising that inequality of power and resources is one of the most difficult aspects of this work. Challenges remain in terms of how to engage those furthest from formal education in a truly reciprocal way (Northmore and Hart 2011). The difference in social, economic and political power between universities and community organisations working with marginalised groups can be a great source of tension if not addressed in the early stages of partnership (London et al 2011) and throughout the relationship. Even when the academic collaborators are open to relinquishing some control, this can be difficult if community partners do not want to take on this responsibility or have very limited time to commit to this (O'Connell 2005).

- Historical issues need recognition. There can be difficulties building trust in marginalised communities, particularly in instances where community members have not seen any direct benefits from research conducted in the past. The involvement of trusted local organisations can help to engage community members, but this takes time and does not necessarily fit in with timeframes for funded research (Teufel-Shone et al 2018). Interaction with research may have been negative for community groups and individuals, leading to resistance as a result of previous projects being irrelevant at best and exploitative at worst (London et al 2011). Skilled staff members can work towards overcoming these issues, but if the hostility is deeply embedded then it may not be possible to work collaboratively.

- Conflicting priorities are also reported in the literature. University priorities such as academic publication, funder contracts and public recognition associated with specific publicity may well conflict with the needs of the community; 'community groups do not want to be research guinea pigs, and they do not want to wait for action' (Baum 2000:242). Therefore, CCPs should not be created for a specific participatory research project; rather, there needs to be an ongoing investment in relationship development and trust building. There may also be difficulties defining what the data are and to what extent the dissemination of joint work should and can include identified individuals (see Chapter 7 for more on this).

- Ways of working may well differ substantially. Universities generally have very different timeframes for work compared with those of community organisations, the former working to longer-term outputs, such as journal papers, and the latter frequently needing immediate answers and evidence for imminent funding bids (Soska and Butterfield 2012). As mentioned earlier, language can be a barrier to collaboration and voices of smaller groups can be lost in larger forums (Soska and Butterfield 2012).

- Time can be a significant challenge. Universities need to have a consistent offer taking into account turnover of staff and students. There also needs to be a considerable investment of time in the partnership to build trust and to cultivate relationships as a mechanism to work towards common aims (such as a participatory research project). It is important not to underestimate the time it takes to build relationships that can then work towards common goals (Baum 2000).

- Funding is often an issue, particularly if programmes are terminated when grants come to an end (Suarez-Balcazar et al 2005). Funding periods are often felt to be unrealistic given the time required to build relationships and effect real change in a community, making sustainability difficult (Wolff and Maurana 2001).

- Furthermore, many research projects have specific funder requirements, which can serve to limit opportunities for participatory research, though not in all contexts; some funding is especially designed to encourage participatory research and learning in this area (Tendulkar et al 2011).

- Representation can be an issue. There is the question of who represents the community when only a select number of partners collaborate; for example, a homeless charity does not represent all homeless people. There is also the risk that researchers choose the path of least resistance and work with the usual suspects or those who are easier to work with for whatever reason (O'Connell 2005). Researchers should continue to expand their network of partners to ensure that they are fairly representing the diverse interests and views of the population (O'Connell 2005). Including diverse participants who bring different perspectives and skills strengthens the partnership's ability to find solutions to the challenges communities face (Schulz et al 2003).

Despite the challenges, CCPs have a huge potential to benefit universities and community groups. We now turn to some examples of successful CCPs in practice and their use of CBPR.

CCPs and CBPR in practice

There are many successful examples of how CCPs have enabled and supported participatory approaches to research. Table 9.3 provides an illustrative example from the US.

Table 9.3 CCPs and the promotion of CBPR in practice

CCP	In the US, the Center for American Indian Resilience and the National Institute on Minority Health and Health Disparities funded a CCP support programme.
CBPR approach	The programme was intended to overcome some of the difficulties of building trust in marginalised communities. It provided funding of $5,000 to $10,000 to allow partnerships between academics, community and statutory groups to develop; the money could be used for travel, community-based projects and general meeting administration costs but not to undertake research.
	The programme provided facilitation, training and administrative support to give partners the environment to identify community priorities and design projects to best meet the community's needs. Most importantly, the funding gave the partnerships time to become established without the pressure of deadlines and research outputs and laid solid foundations for CBPR to follow. This sense of shared purpose can be difficult to attain in CBPR.

Added value: CCPs in relation to CBPR

CCPs can and do support participatory approaches to community research. However, they also offer broader potential beyond the scope of 'just' CBPR. CCPs can add value to research, teaching and student experience as well as developing skills and assets in the community. They can contribute to supporting the types of research which value participant contributions and aim not to exploit people, though such approaches are not necessarily participatory. CCPs can utilise student projects to meet the needs of third-sector groups with everything from physiotherapy to marketing. CCPs can also offer a way for research students to work with community partners to contribute to research and evaluation priorities in the absence of funding, while providing students with real-world experience. Finally, student placements can be supported via CCPs; for example, in the fields of nursing, occupational therapy, physiotherapy and dietetics, as there are many learning opportunities available outside clinical settings.

CCPs take the blurred boundaries between academic researchers and community members using CBPR approaches a step further by bringing groups together in ongoing partnerships, not just for the purposes of one project. The ethics surrounding this, as discussed in Chapter 4, are complex and need particular consideration. The lack of definition in terms of roles here can be seen as a strength of partnerships, rather than an ethical concern, where principal investigators can be from both academic and community organisations (Teufel-Shone et al 2018). Blurred boundaries can also serve to enable academics to recognise that they are part of a wider community beyond their institutional margins, although as discussed in the limitations section there needs to be acknowledgement of particular tensions associated with this.

University ethics committees and their decisions about who is included or excluded in research projects sit inside the university and therefore can reinforce power imbalances. However, longer-standing relationships through CCPs can consider such power dynamics, work to understand the expectations of all partners and support more equal involvement during the research process before any data collection starts. The ingredients of a successful CCP, outlined in this chapter, also underpin ethical relationships. In a strong partnership where communication is good, the objectives are clear, and the members trust and respect each other; there can be transparent reflections on ethical considerations and any issues that arise can be resolved.

There is also a lot of learning that can be derived from CCPs and associated CBPR, with several examples included in Box 9.2.

Box 9.2 CCP projects and associated learning

Healthier Homes Partnership (USA)

- Partners: a healthy housing charity, a lay health education programme, and academics in anthropology at the university.
- Project: to educate people about how to make homes healthier. Community health representatives were trained to carry out home assessments to measure the environmental and structural safety of homes, which the academic partner expanded to incorporate cultural aspects of health and wellbeing that community members felt were important to a healthy home.
- Benefits of partnership funding: partners took time to agree on the priorities of the project, based on the need in the community and skills of those involved. The funding allowed regular meetings, training sessions and the development of materials.
- The community organisation moved from practical home maintenance advice to supporting the community to build resilience and other features of emotional wellbeing. This was a difficult transition at times, but managed through the trust built with the academics.
- Outcomes: there was an exchange of knowledge on the practical and cultural information connected to healthy homes, and the approach then used CBPR to include the tenants more in developing the project.

Source: Teufel-Shone et al (2018)

• •

CASE STUDY LEEDS BECKETT–ST GEORGE'S CRYPT PARTNERSHIP

Leeds Beckett University has almost 30,000 students and 3,000 members of staff, and offers a wide range of degree courses, many with a focus on health (for example, nursing, physiotherapy). The university has a long history of working in partnership with community and non-profit groups across the region, and developed a CCP called CommUNIty to support this work.

St George's Crypt is a homeless centre in Leeds which has been supporting homeless and vulnerable people since 1930. In addition to providing a safe place to sleep and hot meals, the charity offers a range of health and wellbeing services including a leg ulcer clinic, physiotherapy, and eye health and dental clinics.

The partnership between Leeds Beckett and St George's Crypt has focused on finding ways of working that can improve the health of the population that St George's Crypt serves. The partnership has produced benefits for both the charity and the university through volunteering and placement opportunities, which not only enhance the student experience and enable students to develop academic, employment-related and personal skills but also contribute to the centre's work.

The CCP with Leeds Beckett University has supported collaboration to promote learning, teaching, research and develop the work the charity does to support homeless people in Leeds though the following:

- Student projects (for example, business, occupational therapy)
- Student placements (for example, occupational therapy, physiotherapy)
- Research and evaluations (for example, a council-funded project on vulnerable populations)
- Knowledge exchange (for example, professors in men's health and nutrition have delivered training at the Crypt and a worker from the centre has delivered training to students)
- Joint funding bids
- Staff volunteering

Through the partnership, community knowledge represented by the workers and volunteers at the Crypt is put on an equal footing with academic knowledge. Through having a positive relationship with the centre, academic staff members can become familiar faces, thereby encouraging service users to contribute knowledge and ideas. Fully participatory research is difficult with transient populations who are highly vulnerable, but this way of working lays the best foundations to work towards that level of participation.

• •

Summary

- CCPs are a way of building long-lasting relationships with community organisations, allowing community members to influence education and research, potentially through CBPR.

- CCPs can reduce the risk of exploiting populations by promoting ongoing collaboration, which benefits both academic and community partners.

- Specific roles responsible for leading partnerships allow the relationships to build over time and not be lost when individuals leave an organisation. Communication, using appropriate language, is key to developing partnerships.

Suggestions for further reading

1 Hart, A., Maddison, E. and Wolff, D. (2007) *Community-university partnerships in practice*, Leicester: National Institute of Adult Continuing Education.
   This book describes university and community relationships, offering a new model of working based on mutuality, reciprocity, shared risk and genuine exchange. The chapters are co-written by community partners and researchers and cover theoretical and practical issues.

2 Ostrander, S. (2004) 'Democracy, civic participation, and the university: a comparative study of civic engagement on five campuses', *Nonprofit and Voluntary Sector Quarterly*, 33(1): 74–93.
   This article presents the findings from a comparative study of civic engagement on five campuses discussing engagement, projects and organisational structures. The article provides a map of changing relationships in conclusion.

3 Rippon S. and Hopkins, T. (2015) *Head, hands and heart: asset-based approaches in health care*, London: Health Foundation.
   This is a report providing a review of asset-based approaches for improving health and wellbeing, including the challenges associated with these. The title is based on a well-known asset-mapping technique: What knowledge do you have? ('head'); What skills do you have? ('hands'); What are you passionate about? ('heart').

Questions for reflection

1 What do CCPs bring to participatory research?

2 What difference would an initiative of this kind make to your educational or work experience?

3 What are the most important factors to consider when setting up a CCP?

Top tips for practice

1 Have a critical bridge person: having designated contacts at the university facilitates communication with external partners and they have a key role in organising and mediating. This can help to maintain the momentum in partnerships and support participatory research projects.

2 Work on communication: academic language and jargon can alienate people. The words used both in spoken and written communication should be carefully considered. Processes for shared decision making and conflict resolution should be put in place at the start.

3 Use the key principles: follow existing guidelines about how to ensure CCPs are successful in practice (see Box 9.1). For example, ensure that the partnership is mutually beneficial, values community and academic knowledge equally, and works to build trust. Make sure that commitments are realistic and deliverable.

Further teaching and learning resources to accompany this book can be found at https://bristoluniversitypress.co.uk/creating-participatory-research-website. The companion website includes:

- teaching slides for lecturers
- further information on learning tasks
- lesson activities
- further reading, links to websites and practical resources
- examples from practice
- additional case studies

10

The impact of participatory research

Key learning outcomes

By the end of this chapter, you should be able to:

- Define research impact and understand why it is so important

- Demonstrate awareness of the principles and values underpinning participatory approaches to impact

- Identify several levels of impact associated with the use of participatory methods

Introduction

This chapter outlines the context of participatory research within the person/participants life and the impact of taking part, for example, in terms of skill building and empowerment. The chapter also explores the impact on the practitioner and the ways in which such approaches contribute to academic learning and knowledge. Given our expertise in relation to public health, we illustrate the links between participatory research approaches and wellbeing for those involved on a personal level as well as more broadly in relation to the impact on specific communities by drawing on the voice of participants to show the outcomes from their point of view, in their own words.

What is impact?

In recent years research impact has become increasingly important in academia, especially in the UK, because of the Research Excellence Framework (REF); however, debates are ongoing about what impact is, and what it means. ESRC (2020a) describe academic impact as the contribution that excellent research makes to understandings as well as the advancement of science, method, theory and application. Impact can also include the development of policy, practice and services, reframing policy debates conceptually and building capacity (either technically or through the enhancement of personal skills). Impact at both the economic and societal level are also discussed by funders, with increased public involvement in research being described as a mechanism underpinning impact for social benefit (HEFCE 2016). Knowledge exchange (see Chapter 7 on dissemination) is seen as the enabling mechanism that allows researchers and research users to share ideas, experiences and skills (ESRC 2020a). However, definitions of traditional impact have received criticism for not being broad enough to capture the legacies of participatory research approaches. Stern (2016) in reviewing the UK REF argues that impact needs to be linked to bodies of work and collaborative activities so that the more nuanced and creative outcomes that emerge are better understood.

Traditional research impact compared with participatory approaches

Table 10.1 provides an overview of the main differences between traditional and participatory research approaches in terms of the impacts that they can have.

Table 10.1 illustrates several differences between traditional and participatory impacts. Some commentators criticise the current measures of impact used in academia, as these are seen as too narrow in relation to many possibilities linked to participatory approaches. Darby (2017) argues that the current impact agenda needs to accommodate values to better understand the contributions that emerge from research in all forms across all disciplines, because it assumes that research will produce results that others will react to rather than supporting research that is itself reactive. Pain et al (2015) outline the many impacts that can result from co-produced research, in their call for universities to broaden out the way in which they conceptualise impact. Flyvberg (2001) similarly points out the need to negotiate values and power relations within the impact agenda.

Table 10.1 Overview: differences between traditional and participatory research impacts

Traditional research	Participatory research
Impact is a linear process, happening at the end of a study as a result of the findings (Pain et al 2015).	Change may occur throughout the research process, at the individual and organisational level irrespective of the findings produced (Banks et al 2017).
Impact is seen as a pathway and is demonstrated via case studies. Analysis of the REF 2014 impact case studies found that the highest ranked impact areas included influencing government policy, technology commercialisation and parliamentary scrutiny (Grant and Hinrichs 2015).	Impact is about process, as much as a pathway (Springett 2017). Many impacts that emerge from co-produced research do not follow the standard routes that are used to assess academics (Pain et al 2015). Research may have unintended impacts on the lives of those involved in the projects, and these are difficult to anticipate (Evans 2016).
Impact is important for academic institutions in terms of publications (Darby 2017).	Participatory research values emergent needs and learning processes as much as final products such as publications (Darby 2017).

What are the principles of participatory research in relation to impact?

Throughout the earlier chapters in this book, the importance of principles and values that underpin participatory research have been discussed. Israel et al (2008) note several principles of participatory research that are clearly linked to the impact that it intends to produce, including joint learning and local capacity building as well as systems development, enabling participants to take control of their lives and encouraging action as well as research. A key principle underpinning participatory approaches to impact is the achievement of social change for people and communities, as well as outcomes that address specific organisational or community needs (Minkler and Wallerstein 2008). While there are a range of definitions of participatory research impacts, Selener (1997) notes three common principles that tend to be seen across such approaches:

1. Valuing knowledge that is useful in solving specific practical problems
2. Valuing attempts to implement changes within the research setting
3. Valuing the participation of the intended research beneficiaries

By engaging all stakeholders in the research process participatory models of research arguably do not leave to chance the usefulness of any outcomes (Hills and Mullett 2000), as discussed in Chapter 7 which examines the importance of dissemination. Evans (2016) describes the importance of achieving impact beyond the academy in her own work, and notes the significance of the ethic of care that should underpin participatory approaches as well as critical reflexivity in relation to understanding the power dynamics that shape research as a process. Attempting to rebalance power dynamics remains central to participatory research because knowledge is not neutral, and those holding more power tend to be heard (Springett 2017). Darby (2017) makes similar points when she states that transformations through participatory research processes occur because of reciprocal relationships and underpinning ethics of care, which lead to meaningful impact. Having considered all of these principles, complete Learning Task 10.1 to explore the notion of impact in more depth.

> **LEARNING TASK 10.1** EXPLORING DEFINITIONS OF IMPACT
> Using the internet, search for and find the Economic and Social Research Council web-pages that discuss research impact (https://esrc.ukri.org/research/impact-toolkit/what-is-impact). Locate the page that discusses 'what is impact?'
>
> 1 Explore the content of this page and make notes on the different types of impact that are listed.
> 2 Can you identify the areas of impact that align to the principles of participatory research approaches?

3 Is there any advice that is applicable and useful in relation to your own participatory practice? For example, which factors align with co-produced/ CBPR approaches?

In completing Learning Task 10.1, did you consider why research impact is important, and for whom it may be important?

Why is research impact important?

There are a range of benefits associated with participatory research in the literature. These include skills development (Green et al 2000), the development of social relationships (Sclove et al 1998), positive local outcomes, increased local knowledge (Ayers 1987) as well as strengthened local networks and empowerment at the individual level (Greve 1975), all resulting from impact. Box 10.1 provides some example impacts that have been discussed in the literature as emerging from participatory research approaches.

Box 10.1 What does participatory impact look like?

- The development of skills, confidence and employability among community members involved in the process (Green et al 2000; Pain et al 2015).
- The increased involvement of vulnerable, underserved and minority community members in the research process (Israel et al 2010).
- Those involved gaining specialised knowledge (Whitmore 2001).
- Research questions becoming more relevant for communities being studied (Wimpenny 2013).
- The development of new social relationships, trust and social efficacy (Sclove et al 1998). Jagosh et al (2015) report that trust is an outcome resulting from CBPR activities.
- Individual and community empowerment (Papineau and Kiely 1996; Whitmore 2001).
- Increased acceptance and use of the research findings (Ayers 1987; Jagosh et al 2012). Darby (2017:235) notes 'the importance of empowering, collaborative processes to creating ownership of impact may be the most over-looked [...] aspect of co-produced research'.
- Facilitation of change within programmes, services and communities. For example, health improvements and improved resources and/or infrastructure (Israel et al 1998).
- The development of social capital in the form of strengthened social networks (Greve 1975; Warwick-Booth 2008) and improved partnerships.
- Increased capacity at the individual and community level (Kramer et al 2012).

Box 10.1 provides some illustrative examples of impacts from participatory research. However, as meaningful participatory processes tend to occur over long time periods, many impacts (both intended and unintended) may not be fully recognised

(Springett 2017). Pain et al (2015) also note that co-produced research leads to a range of impacts, at a number of levels. Banks et al (2017) offer a conceptual framework to illustrate these different types of impact as listed in Table 10.2.

Table 10.2 Types of impact resulting from participatory research

Type of impact	Description
Participatory impact	Changes in the thinking, emotions and practices of those involved in participatory research. Examples include the development of research skills and new understandings as well as increased confidence and empowerment. These changes are associated with the processes of participatory research.
Collaborative impact	These changes are associated with the use of research findings produced within participatory research projects. Changes may be at the level of individuals, organisations and communities (skills, culture, policy) and result from the use of the findings in a collaborative manner.
Collective Impact	This type of change is about the creation of strategy which aims to achieve a specific change based on the research; for example, several organisations working together in partnership to tackle complex, wicked health problems such as health inequalities.

Source: Adapted from Banks et al (2017)

Trickett and Beehler (2017) use the term 'ripple effects' to describe the multiple types of impact created by participatory research. They argue that these ripple effects occur at different levels including individual, interpersonal, organisational and community and that they may be both positive and negative as well as unforeseeable. Jagosh et al (2015) similarly note three types of ripple effects as impacts from participatory research following on from their interviews with community members and researchers working together in long-term partnerships to deliver CBPR. These are summarised in Box 10.2.

Box 10.2 Partnership impacts resulting from CBPR

Jagosh et al (2015) used a realist evaluation methodology to document the impacts emerging from CBPR partnerships. Collecting qualitative data from members of 11 partnerships (n=24 participants), they found that impacts were evident in three areas:

• sustaining collaborative efforts toward health improvement
• generating spin-off projects
• achieving systemic transformations.

Following on from successful research activity, partnerships reported creating new, often unanticipated projects and activities. For example, one partnership discussed success in raising awareness of female reproductive cancers, then went on to work with men in the community at their request. Spin-off activities were evident for academic partners too, in the form of redeveloped university curricula that included taught content about CBPR.

Systemic changes included cultural changes (breaking taboos and stigma linked to specific diseases), the implementation of new policies and improved health service provision. Systemic transformation was also seen within community groups who realised self-empowerment, with one group gaining control of the community hospital.

Jagosh et al (2015) conclude that CBPR partnerships have many significant impacts, but these are often unforeseeable at the outset.

Fenge et al (2018) use the concept of 'long-tail' impact, borrowing the term from the field of statistics in which it means a large number of occurrences far from the central distribution. Similarly Greenhalgh et al (2016) write about the importance of exploring public engagement activities that lead to less directly attributable impacts from research, suggesting that narratives from those involved offer insights into this area (see the case study at the end of the chapter). Pain et al (2015) describe the creation of a play about austerity that was developed through co-production, as well as impacts such as learning, capacity building (in organisations as well as communities), and institutional or policy change. In their description of several common impacts from co-produced research, they highlight a variety of changes brought about by the research process in the form of staff changing the ways in which they worked as well as increased confidence for those who participated. Fenge et al (2018:52) state that 'impact is not always a moment in the sun – an explosion of scientific breakthrough on the public scene – then yesterday's news'. Table 10.3 illustrates the commonly discussed areas in the literature in which impacts emerge as a result of participatory research.

Table 10.3 Example levels of impacts

Level of impact	Example
Individual community researchers	Improved confidence and self-esteem for co-researchers/service users/patients, all associated with the transformational power of learning (Cook et al 2017).
	Warwick-Booth (2007) reports a range of outcomes for community members. Personal-level impacts include research expertise, improved analytical skills, time-management skills, leadership and negotiation skills, and some data-inputting skills (depending on the level of involvement in the empirical work). Volunteers can also develop contracting and management skills.
	CBPR can lead to community changes such as improved social capital in the form of networks and trust (Warwick-Booth 2008), which serve to enhance social cohesion and support improved wellbeing (Hilger-Kolb et al 2019). Mohatt and Beehler (2018) also used CBPR specifically to enhance military family wellbeing.

(continued)

Table 10.3 Example levels of impacts (continued)

Level of impact	Example
Professionals	Professionals can develop and learn research skills including methodological expertise and analytical skills (Warwick-Booth 2007).
	Building networks and developing ongoing relationships as well as transformational learning for service providers are further documented impacts for professionals (Cook et al 2017).
	Interprofessional learning, professional development, empowerment and the creation of new communities of practice can emerge as impacts for professionals when they engage in participatory health research (Ramgard et al 2017).
	Academics can also develop skills and learn from their involvement in participatory research. Banks et al (2017) highlight improvements in their own communication skills and abilities to strategically campaign.
	Jorian and Nicolazzo (2017) discuss the importance of developing professional communities of practice through CBPR, which lead to social change.
	Jagosh et al (2015) also discuss the impact of strengthened partnerships with more sustainable relationships as an impact.
Community	Trickett and Beehler (2017:533) suggest that using the tool of community asset mapping can illustrate the 'changes in mapped local assets, relationships among those assets, or how a new asset map might emerge as a function of the participatory project'. They also suggest that linking networks and changed power dynamics can occur over time within communities.
	Wright et al (2018) point out that participatory health research results in impacts on change processes (for example, in the form of improved service delivery), benefiting communities.
	Hacker (2013) notes a host of benefits (therefore impact) to the community including resources, skills, respect and knowledge.
	Israel et al (2010) highlight the importance of CBPR in tackling health disparities as an outcome associated with capacity building and advocacy skills within community contexts.
	Dias et al (2018) describe a participatory health research project on HIV, that resulted in the development of effective community-oriented health actions and policies focused on prevention. This reduced HIV transmission, improved access to healthcare for sex workers and men who have sex with men – system-level impact changes.

The literature says very little about the potentially negative impacts that can emerge from participatory research, but Trickett and Beehler (2017) suggest that there is always the potential for such approaches to increase rather than decrease inequalities because emancipatory goals may be inadvertently subverted if projects do not tackle power imbalances and associated inequalities. Complete Learning Task 10.2 to learn more about how to map impacts from participatory research approaches.

> **LEARNING TASK 10.2** MAPPING ALTERNATIVE IMPACT
>
> 1 Use the internet to find the following report: Pain, R., Askins, K., Banks, S. et al (2015) *Mapping alternative impact. Alternative approaches to impact from co-produced research*, Centre for Social Justice and Community Action, Durham University.
> 2 Read through the findings section of the report and make some notes about the key points which are detailed under 14 headings.
> 3 How do these points help you to develop your understanding and approach to impact?

In completing Learning Task 10.2, did you consider the importance of context in the way that impact can be mapped?

Context and impact

Throughout the chapters in this book, we have discussed the importance of context in relation to participatory research. Context remains important in relation to the impacts that can be achieved. Jagosh et al (2015:2) report that participatory research works differently according to context, therefore 'a community partnership that achieves "success" in one setting may "fail" or only partially succeed in another setting, because the mechanisms for success are triggered to different degrees in different contexts'. According to MacLeod and Emejulu (2014), negative consequences are often contextual because communities that have more assets are relatively advantaged at the start. Table 10.4 provides three detailed examples of research impact in differing contexts, to illustrate differing impacts.

Table 10.4 Examples of participatory impact in different contexts

Context	Research impact
Debt on Teesside in the UK	This was a partnership between a community organisation working to tackle poverty, a national campaign organisation and a university. The research was co-designed by all three partners to explore and alleviate the high levels of debt documented in one local area. Twenty-four households took part as research participants, 16 of whom also participated in mentoring sessions.
	Banks et al (2017) detail the positive impacts that they recorded as emerging from the Debt on Teesside project but note that a fuller impact assessment would have also included a focus on negative impacts. The positive impacts included household members having better understanding of money management, changed attitudes and improved confidence. Professionals outlined their own increased confidence, changed views of community members (more holistic understandings) and transformed practices.

(continued)

Table 10.4 Examples of participatory impact in different contexts (continued)

Context	Research impact
Debt on Teesside in the UK (continued)	The authors also discuss the collective impact achieved through the involvement of all partners in this research. Collaborative impacts in this context included reform of rent-to-own companies, based on a voluntary code of practice that was developed, and an affordability campaign through which lenders were encouraged to check if borrowers could afford loans. The focusing on these issues to achieve change, was taken as a measure of collaborative impact by Banks et al (2017).
CBPR to address diabetes and obesity in the US	Hillstrom et al (2014) discuss a CBPR approach that was used in South and East Los Angeles to understand and address diabetes and obesity. The impact from this approach was clear: capacity building demonstrated through the participation of community members in the project, the inclusion of community members' ideas to garner additional funding, and pride among participants.
	Hillstrom et al (2014) also report that while they did not offer formal leadership training, several community members took on leadership roles, generated ideas and implemented interventions. These roles emerged through participatory processes. The researchers leading the project drew on local knowledge from community members to enable them to link into existing local structures such as informal community groups and churches. The CBPR used a process model of 'asking why' to promote solutions, resulting in the creation of farmers' markets in local neighbourhoods.
	A small amount of funding was secured to support this project; however, when this was stopped community members were negatively affected as they were left leaderless and without voice.
Participatory research about the needs and experiences of older LGBT (lesbian, gay, bi-sexual and trans) people	Fenge et al (2018: 47) conducted a participatory research project with older lesbians and gay men called the Gay and Grey project. The study aimed to explore the experiences and needs of community members using volunteers to both undertake and disseminate the findings.
	The impact from the study is described as including the use of new methods to engage seldom heard voices within the research process, and the development of learning tools drawn from the research findings to change 'hearts and minds' as a form of social impact. The methods of diversity learning tool was a deck of cards, which provided tasks to support reflections on policies and practices with regard to older LGBT people. These were launched alongside the screening of a film at an engagement event, then followed up with a two-day training event (masterclass), as well as an additional train the trainers event.
	Fenge et al (2018) discuss the social impact that emerged from this project as the promotion of inclusive health and social care practice for older LGBT community members, noting the importance of using participatory workshops in discussing the findings and creating a sustainable response, as well as working with professional champions in other organisations to take forward such work.

Darby (2017:235) notes the importance of context-related impact, because of the real-life applicability of the research findings co-created with community members. Springett (2017) also points out that impact happens in an environment with ripples potentially occurring across individual, community and policy contexts. However, others offer more criticality about context and suggest that wider contexts are limiting participatory impact, because global structures including universities are underpinned by private interests in which research has become a market good, to be bought and sold, rather than a public good (Picciotto 2015). Therefore, the broader environment can serve to limit social justice goals (Springett 2017). This is one of many challenges associated with achieving impact.

Challenges associated with achieving participatory research impact

Complete Learning Task 10.3 as a starting point to enable you to reflect on some of the challenges that might be encountered in relation to impacts that emerge from participatory research.

LEARNING TASK 10.3 CHALLENGES ASSOCIATED WITH IMPACT

Using your searching skills, the internet and other relevant resources such as books and journal articles, take time to reflect on the question, 'what are the common challenges associated with defining and measuring impact from participatory research studies?'

1 Are there any common barriers that you can identify? Think about practical issues (such as time, money and skills), as well as contextual issues (role conflicts and competing demands).
2 Think about your own skills and the time that you can commit to impact in relation to any given project that you have in mind/have completed. Are there any areas where there are overlapping impact interests for all of those involved?
3 How can you ensure meaningful impact that meets your own needs, as well as those of community members?

Having completed Learning Task 10.3, you will have discovered that there is much discussion about impact emerging from participatory research. The REF framework which guides academic practice has been described as undermining the collaborative research impacts that arise from co-production approaches (Darby 2017). Impact is of course linked to dissemination, and as Chapter 7 discussed there tend to be long delays in the publication of research findings in the form of journal articles, once research projects have concluded, which is a source of frustration for community members who have been involved as they wish to see impact quickly (Hacker 2013). In addition, there is often the need to move away from traditional academic approaches to dissemination to ensure community-level impacts. The use of non-traditional or more creative methods within co-production also lends itself to the production of research outputs that move away from text-based formats.

Pain (2014) argues that impact is frequently reflective of masculinist values associated with knowledge and power, in the sense that it prioritises reach, significance and large-scale interventions rather than small-scale, relational outcomes that are associated with many transformational research projects. The impact framework therefore needs to move beyond encouraging researchers to define impact only in big ways such as policy and practice changes (ESRC 2020a) because this approach overemphasises the authority of academic knowledge, rather than supporting research that is reactive and responsive (Darby 2017).

No research design with finite time, money and human resources can examine all of the possible relationships between activities, outcomes and contexts in a community (Gambone 1998). Facer and Enright (2016) argue that there is often a discrepancy between the formal allocation of budgeted time for such research, and the experience of actually doing participatory research, which can mean less time for considering impacts, particularly those that emerge post-project. Pain (2014) writes about the need for slower longer-term engagement in relation to both research approaches and impact, to achieve and capture meaningful social change. However, Evans (2016:217) writes that '[e]ngaging in longer term action research conflicted with my academic role in the neoliberal academy at the time, since I was under pressure to produce peer-reviewed journal articles and submit a large scale research council grant to meet probationary targets in order to gain tenure.' Tensions that emerge between academic environments and participatory research, which is underpinned by ethical values and co-production approaches, remain a challenge (Williams 2012). Chapter 8 offers a more detailed exploration of the realities associated with participatory research.

Springett (2017) argues that principles such as social justice and social action may not directly link to outcomes, which can lead to negative experiences for participants. Hayes and Tanner (2015) write about active participatory dissemination as an important element of participatory research. Evans (2016) however, discusses how from her own experiences of using active dissemination, community members were brought closer to the emotional burden associated with research having impact, and some experienced struggles in coming to terms with the resulting lack of service development in their area.

Evidencing the impacts from participatory research is also a challenge. Hayes and Tanner (2015) note that participatory projects can lead to tangible change at the local level, but Evans (2016) argues that it is much more difficult to achieve and evidence impact at a regional, national or global scale. Despite documenting many positive impacts from a participatory health-related research project in Sweden, Ramgard et al (2017) argue that their research was not able to change structural system-level issues, reflecting the challenges associated with achieving wider impact from action research. Jagosh et al (2015), in evaluating impacts associated with CBPR partnerships, note that they were unable to draw conclusions about partnerships that broke up or were not working or did not operate inclusively.

Inclusive impact

Chapter 1 discussed inclusive research, highlighting Nind's (2017) suggestions that the question of what matters most in inclusive approaches really depends on the standpoint of the people involved and their views. Therefore, community members' standpoints and views require consideration in relation to the impacts associated with CBPR. Complete Learning Task 10.4 to consider how you can work inclusively towards achieving impact within participatory research.

LEARNING TASK 10.4 TRANSLATING RESEARCH INTO IMPACT
INCLUSIVELY

Hacker (2013) notes that CBPR should focus on local actions and sustainable change, not just for research purposes and academics but also for local impact at the level of the community. Take time to reflect on the following questions to develop your own inclusive approach.

1 What impacts do community members want to see? Some of these may not be considered as traditionally legitimate research outcomes but may well be important in relation to sustainable community change.
2 As a researcher are you able to continue to work with community members even after the loss of research funding? Given that impact from CBPR is not linear and can ripple over long time periods, this is an important consideration.
3 How can you ensure clear and transparent communication about difficult issues such as impact, sustainability and funding to build and maintain trust?

Jagosh et al (2015) discuss the importance of trust as a mechanism to support successful and inclusive CBPR partnerships, and to achieve collective but inclusive impact. Kania and Kramer (2011) point out that in terms of solving social problems, collective success can be achieved if five conditions are in place. First, a common agenda is required, based on a shared vision for change, mutual understandings of the problem and a joint approach. Second, they suggest the use of shared measurement systems to map and report on success. Third, mutually reinforcing activities are the basis for success, so diverse stakeholders need to work together inclusively but through coordinated, skills-based efforts. Fourth, continuous communication is needed between all involved to ensure that trust is built and maintained, which often takes several years. Finally, backbone support is highlighted as an important condition, and refers to the need for supportive infrastructure because this work takes time and not all of those involved will have this (for example, small not-for-profit organisations).

• •

CASE STUDY THE VOICE OF IMPACT

This chapter has highlighted the importance of including community members in defining and achieving impact. Several publications highlight impacts associated with participatory research in the voice of the community members who have been involved, pointing out the importance of inclusion within participatory research for marginalised community members. Strang et al (2019:402) offer this illustrative quotation:

> As a member of the autistic and transgender communities, I have first-hand experience being excluded from the important conversations that affect my life. Community research partnerships are a first step to addressing this disparity and ensuring that autistic gender-diverse people have control over the research agenda.

Fraser (2018:216) conducted action research with Aboriginal peoples and reflected on the pressure that community members felt in terms of trying to achieve change, and in being looked at through the lens of an outsider as a result of their participation. This led to her reflecting on her own role and behaviour as an academic, as well as reconsidering her understanding of impact. She wrote in her research log:

> This project is not about observing communities change, it is about experiencing change in our own lives, living our values in every relationship, being conscious of decisions and to be there for each other. This changed a lot of things for me. It made me more conscious of myself, of my actions.

Kendall et al (2013:266) point out the need to recognise unexpected forms of knowledge, and the importance of stories when working with marginalised communities because these are valuable in themselves. Researchers need to allow for shifts in power to fully appreciate the stories of others and to see the stories as a form of impact. An Indigenous participant, in reflecting on the power of her telling her story by being involved in CBPR stated:

> 'I'd have to say I didn't realise how much it would change my perception of myself and I didn't think it would have any impact on anyone. My story is so very similar to many others ... but I hope those who come after me don't have so much of a struggle as I did ... I hope they don't have to work so hard to get recognition of their stories. Someone will eventually get the understanding that they need to listen ...'

• •

Summary

- The impacts that emerge from participatory approaches can be diverse, and do not always align with those described in traditional academic environments. Impacts are underpinned by the principles of effecting change and transformation, learning and capacity building.

- Impacts resulting from participatory research are varied and occur at several levels. There are also many labels used to describe these impacts. While there are many challenges noted in the literature about how to achieve and document impact, many positive impacts are being documented. The literature offers less discussion in relation to negative impacts.

- The contexts in which participatory impacts emerge are varied. Context is an important factor that needs consideration in relation to research legacy and the types of impact that can be achieved.

Suggestions for further reading

1 Pain, R., Askins, K., Banks, S., et al (2015) *Mapping alternative impact. Alternative approaches to impact from co-produced research*, Centre for Social Justice and Community Action, Durham University.
   This brief report describes the limitations of current understandings of impact and offers several recommendations for changes that can/will better support co-produced research. The authors describe the importance of the value-added approach in understanding impact from participatory research, ending with recommendations for how universities can support participatory models of research.

2 Jagosh, J., Bush, P.L., Salsberg, J. et al (2015) 'A realist evaluation of community-based participatory research: partnership synergy, trust building and related ripple effects' *BMC Public Health*, 15: 725, doi: 10.1186/s12889-015-1949-1
   This paper summarises a realist evaluation of community-based research partnerships, detailing a range of outcomes from such work as well as the importance of trust as a mechanism of success in addressing public health problems. Realist evaluation is also outlined as a useful approach in assessing the complex outcomes associated with participatory research partnerships.

3 Israel, B.A., Coombe, C.M., Cheezum et al (2010) 'Community-based participatory research: a capacity-building approach for policy advocacy aimed at eliminating health disparities', *American Journal of Public Health*, 100(11): 2094–102.
   This paper describes CBPR as a tool to support advocacy and policy changes, particularly in relation to health disparities. The authors argue that the information gathered via CBPR is of critical importance for policy developments based on community needs and issues. The role of CBPR partnerships in effecting health-related change is also discussed.

Questions for reflection

1 Facer and Enright (2016) highlight the importance of reframing impact to understand what counts as a positive legacy from academic-community partnerships. How will you define and frame impact in your participatory project, and to what extent will the views of community members be taken into consideration?

2 ESRC (2020b) suggests that you need to reflect on the scope of the legacy that you want from the collaboration, and lists several questions to be considered including:

- What products/outputs can be produced?
- How is the project adding value in the form of learning and capacity building, and is it contributing to more positive emotions?
- Have new networks and relationships developed?
- Have new ideas emerged?
- How has the project contributed to the research landscape?

3 Jorian and Nicolazzo (2017) contend that power needs to be continuously reflected on in collaborative research projects. How is power invisible in impact processes? How can power be acknowledged and discussed ethically with reference to impact?

Top tips for practice

1 Explore examples of impact that have been documented by other participatory researchers from a range of contexts. Those delivering in practice have shared their experiences and learning as well as offering examples of impact. Use these as a starting point to inform your own approach to thinking about impact.

2 Facer and Enright (2016) describe multiple legacies including the creation of new products, networks and relationships, the development of new theories and ideas, the strengthening of institutions and, most importantly, embodied impact (skills, knowledge and understanding for community members). Be flexible and creative in how you define impact and legacy but ensure that you try to capture and/or measure several of these areas, while balancing both professional and community needs. Hillstrom et al (2014) suggest using a research tool during and after the project as a mechanism to understand the contributions that the project made. Jagosh et al (2015) suggest using realist evaluation to assess CBPR.

3 Springett (2017) suggests that impact can be demonstrated in participatory health research by researchers being more explicit about the importance of learning in these models, and by challenging the dominant academic values that determine impact because of the need to speak truth to power. Jorian and Nicolazzo (2017) suggest that liberation as an impact should be explicitly written into research projects when studies are concerned with voice and transformation.

Further teaching and learning resources to accompany this book can be found at https://bristoluniversitypress.co.uk/creating-participatory-research-website. The companion website includes:

- teaching slides for lecturers
- further information on learning tasks
- lesson activities
- further reading, links to websites and practical resources
- examples from practice
- additional case studies

Postscript

COVID-19 and remote participation

The COVID-19 pandemic began just after completion of this introductory text to participatory research. It has caused major disruption to people's lives and society as a whole, with many previously face-to-face activities moving online, from schooling to healthcare appointments. What does this new remote way of working mean for participatory research, which is founded on personal relationships and building trust in the community?

There is, of course, no simple answer and we are still in the process of finding our feet in the 'new normal' but here are some reflections on how to conduct participatory research safely and remotely.

In well-established partnerships, meetings could move online and in some cases, they were able to use strong community connections to investigate the impact of the pandemic. In California, a pre-existing participatory research partnership moved their steering group meetings online and wanted to investigate the impact COVID-19 was having on their target population and any mitigating factors (Nguyen et al 2020). The researchers highlighted the four main reasons that they could respond rapidly in this context: the existing network; a steering committee experienced in collaborating on research; the trusting relationships between academics and community members; institutional support of participatory research. It can, however, be difficult to build or maintain rapport when groups are not meeting in person, a lot of non-verbal communication is lost and participants can feel disconnected which affects the relationships; this could be mitigated by occasional physical meetings if it is safe to do so (Tamí-Maury et al 2017).

On the positive side, virtual communication can be more convenient and accessed using relatively cheap mobile devices, even when participants are in different geographic locations (Tamí-Maury et al 2017). The internet as a research tool can offer 'almost unlimited opportunities for individuals finding, participating in and/or creating distributed problem-solving groups' where discussions between communities of interest can build trust and establish shared practices (Glassman 2019).

There are initial costs in supplying appropriate devices and paying for internet connection, but after this the most commonly used platforms are free and connecting virtually reduces travel costs (Tamí-Maury et al 2017).

The number of adults who use the internet has been increasing year on year, but in 2018, 10 per cent of adults in the UK (5.3 million) either had never used the internet or had not used it in the past three months (ONS 2019). Internet non-users are often people over 65, with disabilities and/or economically inactive adults of working age (ONS 2019). When planning remote participatory research, it is important to take into account how digital exclusion affects the participants and either support people to use the internet and technology (providing access to Wi-Fi and appropriate devices and training on how to use them) or find alternatives that they are comfortable with.

Methods

There are a range of methods researchers can use to connect and collect data online, we will now explore some of the most accessible options. Whichever methods are chosen, researchers and community members leading the work should send out instructions in advance about the platform being used and general etiquette (for example, regarding whether cameras or microphones are on and how the meeting will be structured), to promote smoother sessions (Lobe et al 2020).

- Interviews
  Virtual one-to-one interviews can be conducted in much the same way as face-to-face interviews and offer increased flexibility and the comfort of doing them from home (see Table P1, p 194, for examples of online platforms). Some ethical considerations are discussed later in this section. For focus group discussions that may work with up to ten people face-to-face, it is recommended to reduce the number to a maximum of five or six online (Lobe et al 2020).
  Epistolary interviews (Debenham 2001) are a variation on the interview format in which the two people take turns to ask and respond to questions over a period of days, weeks or longer as would happen with exchanges via letters. It can be done by email, messaging apps, or even using audio or video messages, and brings a flexibility to the process (overcoming technical and timing challenges) as well as time for reflection on questions and answers (Lupton 2020). Respondents reply at their convenience and interviewers can be conducting more than one interview at a time.

- Photo/video/voice elicitation
  Using a Smartphone to take photos, record videos or make voice memos about the topic being researched can provide a wealth of data that can be shared online (Lupton 2020). Questions or prompts can be agreed in virtual meetings of the CBPR project-steering groups or wider involvement through other online forums (Lupton 2020).

- Diaries/journaling
  Diaries or journals can add rich data to other methods or be used as prompts for further discussion. They can be a way of staying in touch with participants during periods where it isn't possible to meet, although some participants can find keeping a regular diary a burden on top of other commitments. Another option would be for the diary to be more visual; for example, taking a photo each day/week. It is useful to pilot an approach before adopting it across a project (Lupton 2020).

- Facebook groups
  Facebook groups can be a flexible and convenient way of staying in touch for participatory research groups. It is a format that is used by many people in their personal lives so they often feel comfortable with it and regular users of Facebook will see updates in the group, which can reduce attrition.

Ethics

The ethics of remote research need careful consideration. During the pandemic there are the additional concerns of the stress and changes of circumstances (for example, loss of employment, increased caring roles) that people are experiencing (Lupton 2020). Many ethical considerations are the same as face-to-face work, but particular attention should be paid to how to guarantee anonymity, and assessing the risks and benefits for participants (Lobe et al 2020).

In remote participation, the researcher has less control over the setting and cannot be sure who else is present in the participants' environment, which could compromise their safety or the confidentiality of the subject matter. On the other hand, in some cases, taking part in remote research can be a positive experience giving participants meaningful occupation to distract them from the difficult situation (Lupton 2020).

Kara (2020) argues that if the piece of research is not essential during a 'global collective trauma' then it is unethical to proceed. If it can be justified then the methods should be chosen that cause the minimum burden on participants (and researchers must also recognise their own vulnerabilities and stress in the context of a pandemic) who will in many cases be under increased pressure in other areas of their lives (Kara 2020).

Some key concerns are privacy, confidentiality, security of the platform, and inequalities in access to appropriate devices and the internet. Participants will need a device such as a laptop, tablet or smartphone, a stable internet connection and some digital skills. They also need to have a quiet, safe place from where to connect (Lobe et al 2020).

Recording meetings and discussions becomes easier and the data are easy to access with accurate records of date and time (Tamí-Maury et al 2017), but when making recordings, researchers should check where the recording is stored (locally or in the cloud), selecting local storage if possible, and should also confirm whether it is shared with all of the participants. Where it is not appropriate for all of the participants to hold the recording, it should also be stressed that they must not record on any personal devices; this can be more difficult to enforce than in physical meetings (Lobe et al 2020).

As in face-to-face work, it is important to discuss ownership of data and have strict consent procedures. Online work can in some ways be more anonymous; for example, if using an email address/username that doesn't include the participant's real name, but it also can be more identifiable if videocalls are used and recorded (Tamí-Maury et al 2017).

Table P1 Platform characteristics

	Video	Audio only	Chat function	Screen sharing	Video recording	Requires participants download application	Requires participants to have an account to attend	Appropriate for low-level digital skills participants	Lags in live feed	HIPAA compliant	Payment scheme
Zoom	✓	✓	✓	✓	✓	✓	✗	✓	✗	✓	Basic free for 40 min, longer fee based $
Webex	✓	✓	✓	✓	✓	✓	✗	✓	✗	✓	Basic free, other plans fee based $
Skype	✓	✓	✓	✓	✓	✓	✓	✓	✓	✗	Free for web
GoToMeeting	✓	✓	✓	✓	✓	✓	✗	✓	✗	✓	Fee based $
Jitsi Meet	✓	✓	✓	✓	✓	✗	✗	✓	✓		Free
AnyMeeting	✓	✓	✓	✓	✓	✗	✗	✓	✗	✓	Starter free, other plans fee based $
Adobe Connect	✓	✓	✓	✓	✓	✓	✓	✗	✗	Upon request	Fee based $$
Telemedicine apps	✓	✓	✓	✓	some	All but Doxy.me	All but Doxy.me	✓	✗	✓	Varies but most are fee based

Source: Lobe et al (2020:3)

For researchers working in Europe, all of the large companies who offer the main software options are GDPR compliant; for example, Apple, Facebook, Google, Microsoft and Zoom (Lobe et al 2020).

Table P1 shows a comparison of virtual platforms and the features they offer. Zoom has been used extensively during 2020 to connect work colleagues, classes and friends, and has the benefit that participants do not need an account.

Suggestions for further reading

1 Ahlin, T. and Fangfang, L. (2019) 'From field sites to field events: creating the field with information and communication technologies (ICTs)', *Medicine, Anthropology and Theory*, 6(2): 1–24.

2 Boase, J. and Humphreys, L. (2018) 'Mobile methods: explorations, innovations, and reflections', *Mobile Media & Communication*, 6(2): 153–62. https://doi.org/10.1177/2050157918764215

3 Copes, H., Tchoula, W., Brookman, F. and Ragland, J. (2018) 'Photo-elicitation interviews with vulnerable populations: practical and ethical considerations', *Deviant Behavior*, 39(4): 475–94.

4 Debenham, M. (2007) 'Epistolary interviews on-line: a novel addition to the researcher's palette', TechDis Website Resource, www.researchgate.net/publication/294718847_Epistolary_Interviews_On-line_A_Novel_Addition_to_the_Researcher's_Palate/citation/download

Glossary

Academia   This term refers to environments that are concerned with research, scholarship and learning. University institutions are synonymous with the term academia.

Action research   Action research is about creating strategies to address and improve specific issues and using action to develop services and organisations (Danley and Langer 1999).

Autophotography   Autophotography is asking participants to take photographs of their environment and then using the photographs as data.

Case-control study   A case-control study is a type of observational study in which two existing research groups differing in outcome are identified and compared on the basis of some supposed causal attribute.

Cohort study   Cohort studies recruit and follow up one large group of people over a number of years or decades to determine whether there is an association between exposure to potential risk or protective factors and development or prevention of an illness.

Co-inquiry   A collaborative form of inquiry is about all of those involved in a research project engaging together in democratic dialogue as co-researchers and as co-subjects (Heron, 1996).

Collaborative impact   Banks et al (2017) describe this as changes that are associated with the use of research findings produced within participatory research projects. Changes may be at the level of individuals, organisations and communities (skills, culture, policy) and result from the use of the findings in a collaborative manner.

Collaborative inquiry   DeLuca et al (2017:67) describe collaborative inquiry as engaging 'teachers as learners within their own teaching contexts with the aim of transforming teachers' conceptions of professional learning and promoting enhanced pedagogical effectiveness'.

Collective impact   Banks et al (2017) outline this as including the creation of strategy that aims to achieve a specific change based on the research; for example, several organisations working together in partnership to tackle complex, wicked health problems such as health inequalities.

Community-based research   Community-based research is defined as a collaboration between community groups and researchers for the purpose of creating new knowledge or trying to understand a community issue in order to bring about change. The topic or issue is generated by the community and community members participate in all aspects of the research process (Hills and Mullett 2000).

Community-based participatory research (CBPR) Community-based participatory research involves partnerships between academic researchers, communities and services, usually with the aim of identifying community needs and working together to develop interventions and programmes to address them (Minkler 2010).

Community-campus partnerships (CCPs) Community-campus partnerships are not-for-profit groups/organisations that promote social justice. There are several in the US focusing specifically on health equity. CCPs are usually made up of members from communities, community organisations and academic institutions such as universities. Chapter 9 specifically discusses CCPs.

Context We use the term 'context' throughout this book to refer to the circumstances that influence, support and/or limit the success of participatory research. These circumstances are variable and can include area-based influences, community dynamics, funding, partnership circumstances and the skills of those involved.

Co-production 'Co-producing a research project is an approach in which researchers, practitioners and the public work together, sharing power and responsibility from the start to the end of the project, including the generation of knowledge.' (Involve 2018:4)

Data analysis This term describes the process of analysing the data collected as part of any study. It can involve a range of activities depending on the data collected. The process involves highlighting useful information, interpreting results and offering conclusions. Nind (2011) suggests that notions of what it means to do participatory analysis vary, which is unsurprising given the diversity of approaches that are available to those who are professionally trained researchers.

Data collection This refers to the overall approach used by researchers to gather information for a research study.

Developmental evaluation Developmental evaluation is a kind of formative evaluation whereby the evaluation is ongoing and the evaluators are embedded within the project as members of the team (Patton, 2010; Simister, 2017)

Digital storytelling Digital storytelling refers to a two- to five-minute audio-visual clip that combines photographs, voice-over narration and other audio.

Dissemination Research dissemination is a term that is used to describe a process by which investigators communicate the findings from their research projects. There are a range of purposes associated with dissemination, and the particular audience to which the information is directed may influence and determine the dissemination method used. Participatory dissemination involves the inclusion of research participants in the dissemination activities of any research project.

Empowerment This is difficult to define as it is used in many ways in the literature. In the context of participatory research, it is taken to mean the process by which people are able to identify their needs and then take action in order to meet them, through their engagement in the research process.

Epistemology   This term is commonly used in relation to research and refers to the theory of knowledge. Epistemology is important in research because researchers draw on different epistemologies to understand and explore the social world. Epistemologically, participatory research is consistent with constructivist and critical theory paradigms which understand knowledge as socially created (Israel et al 1998). Multiple, socially constructed realities exist, which are influenced by social, historical and cultural contexts. Therefore, participatory approaches to research acknowledge the value of multiple ways of knowing and, more significantly, recognise the value of knowledge contributed by community members (Hills and Mullett 2000).

Ethics   The term 'ethics' refers to principles that are used to guide behaviour and action. Participatory research is described as a more ethical approach because it accounts for power, rights and roles for all of those involved and is driven by egalitarian principles based on respect for community members within any research partnerships. More generally, in relation to research, there are specific codes of ethical conduct that researchers are required to follow, and ethical approval is also a requirement.

Ethnography   Ethnography is the study of social interactions, behaviours and perceptions within groups, teams, organisations and communities. It aims to provide rich, holistic insights into people's views and actions, as well as the nature of the location they inhabit, through the collection of detailed observations and interviews (Reeves et al 2008).

Experimental studies   In experimental studies, there is intervention and manipulation under tightly defined or controlled conditions. If the researcher assigns people to groups receiving different interventions then this is an experimental study.

Formative evaluation   In a formative evaluation, assessment and feedback is given before an intervention is rolled out or scaled up; often used in feasibility or pilot studies of new interventions that need testing and refining.

Health disparities/inequalities/inequities   These terms are used to describe population differences in health outcomes, disease and life expectancy, related to policy environments and the many broad influences called the social determinants of health.

Health impact assessment (HIA)   Health impact assessment is a way of assessing the health impacts of policies, plans and projects, particularly on vulnerable or disadvantaged groups, in diverse economic sectors using quantitative, qualitative and participatory techniques. It is concerned with improving the health of populations and the reduction of health inequalities.

Impact   ESRC (2020a) describes academic impact as the contribution that excellent research makes to understandings as well as to the advancement of science, method, theory and application. Impact can also include the development of policy, practice and services, reframing policy debates conceptually and building capacity.

Implementation research The scientific study of the processes used in the implementation of initiatives as well as the contextual factors that affect these processes (Peters et al 2013).

Inclusive research The term 'inclusive research' is used when doing research with people with learning disabilities (Nind 2017). Walmsley and Johnson (2003:10) define this as an approach that 'involves people who may otherwise be seen as subjects for the research as instigators of ideas, research designers, interviewers, data analysts, authors, disseminators and users'.

Interpretivism/interpretivist Interpretivism is concerned with understanding the world from subjective experiences of individuals. It is associated with qualitative methodologies, and links to participatory research in that such approaches tend to see the researcher and the participant as being interactively linked (Israel et al 1998). Participatory research approaches encourage the knower to participate in the known and to generate evidence in many ways (Hills and Mullett 2000).

Involvement Involvement is about participating in something – in this instance, research. Participatory research emphasises the participation and involvement of non-academic researchers in the process of creating knowledge (Israel et al 1998). However, there is no specific 'type' or model for involvement in participatory research.

Knowledge democracy Hall et al (2015:26) define this term as 'expertise residing in the world of practice, beyond academia'.

Knowledge exchange This is defined as 'the process by which researchers and decision makers share expertise and knowledge for a specific purpose' (Bowen and Martens 2005:207). Knowledge exchange can be conducted for a range of people, including community members, who can also participate in its design and accompanying activities.

Knowledge translation WHO (2019) describe knowledge translation as an approach that aims to close the 'know-do' gap, which is about using the knowledge gained from research and putting it into practice. Again, this is not necessarily participatory dissemination as translation can be for policy makers and practitioners as well as community members, although participation can be applicable in some models.

Knowledge utilisation This is a broad umbrella term used to describe the ways in which knowledge is being used, or it can be used in relation to a specific event. Again, knowledge utilisation is not necessarily participatory in basis, but can be used in such a manner in suitable instances.

Lay researchers The term 'lay researcher' is used to describe a community member who becomes involved in a research study more actively than as a respondent or participant. For example, a health service user collecting data by interviewing other service users, is a lay researcher. Other terms are used in the literature to describe this role, including 'co-researcher' and 'community researcher'.

Literature   This is the published material forming a body of knowledge, discussion, debate and critique within all academic fields. Academic literature is based on research and has usually been through a peer-review process, in which other experts in the field review it. There is a large body of literature about participatory approaches to research.

Memorandum of understanding (MoU)   This refers to an agreement, usually between two organisations, about working together. It is a form of a contract to support partnership work, as it details the scope of the partnership focus. It can be seen as a useful tool to support organisations working together generally, as well as more specifically, in relation to enabling participatory research.

Methodology   This term refers to a system of methods that are used to research a topic and or research problem. Methodologies are therefore different approaches to research developed within a particular paradigm. There are two commonly referred to methodologies in research: quantitative and qualitative.

Mixed methods research   Mixed methods research is a purposeful approach whereby the investigators collect and analyse both qualitative and quantitative data within the same study, drawing on the potential strengths of both methodologies.

Model   A model is a system or a structure often used in academic terms to try to explain and understand the social world. There is no single model of participatory research.

Natural experiments   Natural experiments are a kind of non-randomised study where allocation into groups is not controlled by the researchers but by exposure to the intervention or control conditions. This exposure could be determined by nature (for example, a natural disaster) or by policy changes, and the researchers have no control over the exposure.

Ontology   This term refers to the nature of knowledge, and what it is. In ontological terms, participatory research arguably adopts a position influenced by politics. Participatory research can be used as a mechanism to search for meanings that have traditionally been excluded and often attempt to neutralise power differentials, to enable participants' views to be heard (Stringer 1996). The inquirer and the participant are connected in such a way that the findings are inseparable from their relationship (Guba and Lincoln 1989).

Outcomes   Outcomes as a term refers to results and consequences, and they are also related to impact (see earlier definition). The literature highlights many positive outcomes that are seen to result from participatory research, including health improvements and skills development (see Chapters 1 and 10 for more on this).

Outlier   In quantitative research, an outlier is a term used to describe a statistic, figure or datum point that differs from the other information collected. Outliers can cause problems when researchers are analysing data sets.

Participation   Participation as a concept within the literature is described as a continuum of involvement. In terms of research, some approaches allow participation in the whole research process whereas others dictate a more limited level of participation (Goodson and Phillimore 2012).

Participatory action research   An approach to research seeking to understand and improve the world by changing it. The process is both collective (involving researchers and community members) and uses self-reflection so that all of those involved can understand and improve their research practice. Action taken is linked to the local context in which the research is being done (Baum et al 2006).

Participatory impact   Banks et al (2017) define this as changes in the thinking, emotions and practices of those involved in participatory research. Examples include the development of research skills and new understandings, as well as increased confidence and empowerment. These changes are associated with the processes of participatory research.

Participatory research   Participatory research emphasises the participation and influence of non-academic researchers in the process of creating knowledge (Israel et al 1998). It is 'An umbrella term for a school of approaches that share a core philosophy of inclusivity and of recognising the value of engaging in the research process (rather than including only as subjects of the research) those who are intended to be the beneficiaries, users and stakeholders of the research' (Macaulay 2017:256).

Participatory video   'Participatory video aims to support an empowering process whereby community members engage in iterative cycles of shooting and reviewing videos to create video narratives that communicate what the participants want to communicate, in a manner they feel is appropriate' (Kindon 2003:143).

Partnership working   Partnership working refers to a broad range of activities and actions encompassed by two or more groups coming together to achieve a common purpose. Partnership approaches often underpin participatory research approaches (see earlier notes on CCPs).

Peer research   Peer research is research that is steered and conducted by people with lived experience of the issue being studied.

Philosophy   This can be designed as the study of knowledge, as well as a more general approach to studying/researching. Participatory research is underpinned by a core philosophy of inclusivity, involvement and engagement, so rather than including community members as subjects of the research, they become active participants (Macaulay 2017).

Photo elicitation   Photo elicitation is using photographs or other visual media in an interview to generate discussion.

Photovoice   Photovoice is 'a process by which people can identify, represent and enhance their community through a specific photographic technique' (Wang et al 2000:82).

Positivist   Positivism is the term used to describe an approach to research that seeks to understand the social world through scientific evidence. This underpins quantitative approaches to data collection including experiments and methods that generate statistical data. Participatory research designs can be positivist, because there is no preferred specific approach or methodology associated with them.

Power   Power is about working in a certain way and is discussed throughout the book because traditional research operates with different power dynamics when compared with participatory approaches. Participatory approaches try to mitigate against power dynamics in which the 'expert' researcher dominates by using dialogue, community capacity building and collaborative inquiry to work with 'non-experts'. In attempting to facilitate social change and achieve social justice, there is also broader concern with societal and political power across participatory models of research (Minkler and Wallerstein 2003).

Principles   Principles are a system of beliefs that guide action. Participatory research is governed by specific principles that include the involvement/participation of non-professional researchers, using a cooperative approach, supporting joint learning, aiming to build local capacity, facilitating empowerment and supporting action (Israel et al 2008).

Process evaluation   A process evaluation examines how an intervention is implemented and what was actually delivered, compared with what was intended to be implemented and delivered.

Qualitative research   There are various approaches to qualitative research but in general qualitative research uses techniques to collect, analyse and interpret data based on words and text. Qualitative data do not involve numbers or measurements.

Quantitative research   Quantitative approaches to research focus on measurement, and so often involve gathering data that are numerical. Quantitative approaches focus on data collection techniques, which create numerical data that can then be analysed via the application of statistical methods.

Randomised controlled trial (RCT)   The 'gold standard' or most rigorous experimental study design is the randomised controlled trial, in which participants are randomly allocated to one or more intervention or 'control' groups, in a process which is characterised by unpredictability.

Rapid participatory appraisal   Rapid participatory appraisal is used to provide qualitative information, especially about deprived urban areas, using key informants with knowledge of the area to identify problems and contribute to solutions.

Realist evaluation   A form of theory-driven evaluation, which aims to answer the question 'What works, for whom, in what respects, to what extent, in what contexts, and how?' (Pawson and Tilley 1997:7).

Reflexivity   This term has several meanings, but in relation to research it is used to describe the ways in which researchers reflect on their study; for example, reflecting on their data, their sampling, how their own approach and characteristics influenced the research process.

Representation   This term refers to the way in which data are used to illustrate (represent) findings, communities and their needs. Participatory approaches aim to involve community members in creating representations of such data through their involvement in the research processes as well as the articulation of their voices.

Research   Research is an active and systematic process of inquiry used to explore the social world and to gather information, to discover, interpret or revise facts, events, behaviours or theories.

Research methods   These are the procedures used to collect data in any research study. Quantitative research methods include surveys, census and administrative data. Qualitative methods include focus groups, in-depth interviews and more creative tools such as photovoice.

Sampling   Sampling is the process of selecting research participants from the target population being studied.

Social justice   This term is used to describe the equitable allocation of resources in society. For example, trying to achieve health equity is related to social justice, because health inequities reflect the unequal distribution of the resources that people need to stay healthy. Achieving social justice is an underpinning principle of participatory research approaches.

Steering group   Steering groups are usually made up of a number of people (professionals, community members, researchers) who offer advice and guidance on research projects, as well as being involved in the research process.

Theory of change   Theory of change is essentially a comprehensive description and illustration of how and why a desired change is expected to happen in a particular context. It is focused in particular on mapping out or 'filling in' what has been described as the 'missing middle' between what a programme or change initiative does (its activities or interventions) and how these lead to desired goals being achieved. www.theoryofchange.org/what-is-theory-of-change/

Third sector   The part of an economy or society comprising non-governmental and non-profit-making organisations or associations, including charities, voluntary and community groups, cooperatives and so on.

Values   Values are principles and beliefs, and these are discussed throughout the book in relation to participatory research because they underpin these approaches (see earlier points listed under principles).

Wicked   This term is often used in the fields of social policy, planning and research. It refers to a problem that is complicated and therefore difficult to both understand and deal with.

References

Acker, J., Barry, K. and Esseveld, J. (1983) 'Objectivity and truth: problems in doing feminist research', *Women's Studies International Forum*, 6(4): 423–35.

Adams, M. and Moore, G. (2007) 'Participatory action research and researcher safety', In Kindon, S., Pain, R. and Kesby, M. (eds) *Participatory action research approaches and methods: connecting people, participation and place*, London: Routledge, chapter 6.

Ahlin, T. and Fangfang L. (2019) 'From field sites to field events: creating the field with information and communication technologies (ICTs)', *Medicine, Anthropology and Theory*, 6(2): 1–24.

Ahmed, S. and Palermo, A. (2010) 'Community engagement in research: frameworks for education and peer review', *American Journal of Public Health*, 100(8): 1380–7.

Aleman, D. (2017) 'The three stages of data analysis: evaluating raw data', MethodSpace/Sage Publishing.

Alston, P. (2018) Statement on visit to the United Kingdom, by Professor Philip Alston, United Nations Special Rapporteur on extreme poverty and human rights, London, 16 November. www.ohchr.org/Documents/Issues/Poverty/EOM_GB_16Nov2018.pdf

Armstrong, A., Aznarez, M., Banks, S., Henfrey, T., Moore, H. and project participants (2011) *Community-based participatory research: ethical challenges*, Centre for Social Justice and Community Action, Durham University.

Arnstein, S.R. (1969) 'A ladder of citizen participation', *Journal of the American Planning Association*, 34(4): 216–24.

Askew, P. (2001) 'The university as a source for community and academic partnerships', *New Directions for Student Services*, 96: 61–82.

Ayers T.D. (1987) 'Stakeholders as partners in evaluation: a stakeholder–collaborative approach', *Evaluation and Program Planning*, 10: 263–71.

Azzarito, L. (2016) 'Moving in my world: from school PE to participants-centred arts exhibitions', *Journal of Teaching in Physical Education*, 35(1): 38–53.

Bach, M., Jordan, S., Hartung, S., Santos-Hövener, C. and Wright, M.T. (2017) 'Participatory epidemiology: the contribution of participatory research to epidemiology', *Emerg Themes Epidemiol*, 14(2). https://doi.org/10.1186/s12982-017-0056-4

Backett-Milburn, K. and McKie, L. (1999) 'A critical appraisal of the draw and write technique', *Health Education Research*, 14(3): 387–98.

Balandin, D. (2003) 'Happily ever after: communicating results to participants in research', *Journal of Intellectual & Development Disability*, 28(1): 87–9.

Banks, S., Armstrong, A., Carter, K., Graham, H., Hayward, P., Henry, A., Holland, T., Holmes, C., Lee, A., McNulty, A., Moore, N., Nayling, N., Stokoe, A. and Strachan, A. (2013) 'Everyday ethics in community-based participatory research', *Contemporary Social Science*, 8(3): 263–77.

Banks, S., Herrington, T. and Carter, K. (2017) 'Pathways to co-impact: action research and community organising', *Educational Action Research*, 24(4): 541–59.

Banks, S., Hart, A., Pahl, K. and Ward, P. (eds) (2019) *Co-producing research: a community development approach*, Bristol: Policy Press.

Barnes, J., Altimare, E., Farrell, P., Brown, R., Burnett, C., Gamble, L. and Davis, J. (2009) 'Creating and sustaining authentic partnerships with community in a systemic model', *Journal of Higher Education Outreach and Engagement*, 13(4): 15–29.

Basile, S., Asselin, H. and Martin, T. (2018) 'Co-construction of a data collection tool', *ACME: An International Journal for Critical Geographies*, 17(3): 840–60.

Bastida, E.M., Tseng, T.S., Mckeever, C. and Jack Jr, L. (2010) 'Ethics and community-based participatory research: perspectives from the field', *Health Promotion Practice*, 11(1): 16–20.

Baum, F., MacDougall, C. and Smith, D. (2006) 'Participatory action research', *J Epidemiol Community Health*, 60(10): 854–7, doi: 10.1136/jech.2004.028662.

Baum, H. (2000) 'Fantasies and realities in university-community partnerships', *Journal of Planning Education and Research*, 20(2): 234–46.

Beacon North East (2011) Co-inquiry toolkit. Community-university participatory research partnerships: co-inquiry and related approaches. Newcastle: Beacon North East. www.dur.ac.uk/socialjustice/toolkits/coinquiry/

Beacon North East (2012) Community toolkit. A guide to working with universities on research projects. Newcastle: Beacon North East. www.dur.ac.uk/socialjustice/toolkits/community/

Beebeejaun, Y., Durose, C., Richardson, J. and Richardson, L. (2013) 'Beyond text: exploring ethos and methods in co-producing research with communities', *Community Development Journal*, 49(1): 37–53.

Beebeejaun, Y., Durose, C., Rees, J., Richardson, J. and Richardson, L. (2015) 'Public harm or public value? Towards coproduction in research with communities', *Environment and Planning C*, 33(3): 552–65.

Bennett, M. (2004) 'A review of the literature on the benefits and drawbacks of participatory action research', *First Peoples Child and Family Review*, 1(1): 19–32.

Bindels, J., Baur, V., Cox, K., Heijing, S. and Abma, T. (2013) 'Older people as co-researchers: a collaborative journey', *Ageing and Society*, 34(6): 951–73.

Binet, A., Gavin, V., Carroll, L. and Arcaya, M. (2019) 'Designing and facilitating collaborative research design and data analysis workshops: lessons learned in the Healthy Neighborhoods Study', *International Journal of Environmental Research and Public Health*, 16(324), doi: 10.3390/ijerph16030324.

Black, G.F., Davies, A., Iskander, D. and Chambers, M. (2018) 'Reflection on the ethics of participatory visual methods to engage communities in global health research', *Global Bioethic*, 29(1): 22–38.

Blamey, A. and Mackenzie, M. (2007) 'Theories of change and realistic evaluation: peas in a pod or apples and oranges?', *Evaluation*, 13(4): 439–55.

Blumenthal, D. (2011) 'Is community-based participatory research possible?', *American Journal of Preventive Medicine*, 40(3): 386–89.

Boal, A. (2000) *Theatre of the oppressed*, London: Pluto Press.

Boase, J. and Humphreys, L. (2018) 'Mobile methods: explorations, innovations, and reflections', *Mobile Media & Communication*, 6(2): 153–62. doi. org/10.1177/2050157918764215

Bodison, S., Sankaré, I., Anaya, H., Booker-Vaughns, J., Miller, A., Williams, P. and Norris, K. (2015) 'Engaging the community in the dissemination, implementation, and improvement of health-related research', *Clinical and Translational Science*, 8(6): 814–19.

Boivin, A., Lehoux, P., Burgers, J. and Grol, R. (2014) 'What are the key ingredients for effective public involvement in health care improvement and policy decisions? A randomized trial process evaluation', *Milbank Quarterly*, 92: 319–50, doi: 10.1111/1468-0009.12060.

Bourke, L. (2009) 'Reflections on doing participatory research in health: participation, method and power', *International Journal of Social Research Methodology*, 12(5): 457–74.

Bowen, S. and Martens, P. (2005) 'Demystifying knowledge translation: learning from the community', *Journal of Health Services Research & Policy*, 10(4): 203–11.

Bowling, A. (2014) *Research methods in health: investigating health and health services* (4th edn), Maidenhead: Open University Press.

Bradding, A. and Horstman, M. (2009) 'Using the write and draw technique with children', *European Journal of Oncology Nursing*, 3(3): 170–5.

Braden, S. (1999) 'Using video for research and representation: basic human needs and critical pedagogy', *Journal of Educational Media*, 24(2): 117–29.

Braun, V. and Clarke, V. (2013) *Successful qualitative research: a practical guide for beginners*, London: Sage.

Bringle, R. and Hatcher, J. (2002) 'Campus-community partnerships: the terms of engagement', *Journal of Social Issues*, 58(3): 503–16.

British Academy (2008) *Punching our weight*, London, British Academy.

Brunger, F. and Wall, D. (2016) 'What do they really mean by partnerships? Questioning the unquestionable good in ethics guidelines promoting community engagement in Indigenous health research', *Qualitative Health Research*, 26(13): 1862–77.

Brunton, G., Caird, J., Stokes, G., Stansfield, C., Kneale, D., Richardson, M. and Thomas, J. (2015) *Review 1: Community engagement for health via coalitions, collaborations and partnerships – a systematic review*, London: EPPI Centre, University of London.

Brunton, G., Thomas, J., O'Mara-Eves, A., Jamal, F., Oliver, S. and Kavanagh, J. (2017) 'Narratives of community engagement: a systematic review-derived conceptual framework for public health interventions', *BMC Public Health*, 17(944). https://doi.org/10.1186/s12889-017-4958-4

Buchanan, D.R., Miller, F.G. and Wallerstein, N. (2007) 'Ethical issues in community-based participatory research: balancing rigorous research with community participation in community intervention studies', *Progress in Community Health Partnerships: Research, Education, and Action*, 1(2): 153–60.

Byrne, A., Canavan, J. and Millar, M. (2009) 'Participatory research and the voice-centred relational method of data analysis: is it worth it?', *International Journal of Social Research Methodology*, 12(5): 457–74.

Byrne, B. (2004) 'Qualitative interviewing', *Researching Society and Culture*, 2: 179–92.

Cade, B.W. (1982) 'Some uses of metaphor', *Australian Journal of Family Therapy*, 3(3): 135–40.

Cahill, C. (2007a) 'Participatory data analysis', In Kindon, S., Pain, R. and Kesby, M. (eds) *Participatory action research approaches and methods: connecting people, participation and place*, London: Routledge, chapter 21.

Cahill, C. (2007b) Doing research with young people: participatory research and the rituals of collective work, *Children's Geographies*, 5(3): 297–312, doi: 10.1080/14733280701445895

Cahill, C. and Torre, M.E. (2007) 'Beyond the journal article: representations, audience and the presentation of participatory action research', In Kindon, S., Pain, R. and Kesby, M. (eds) *Participatory action research approaches and methods: connecting people, participation and place*, London: Routledge, pp. 196–205.

CARE (Community Alliance for Research and Engagement) (no date) Beyond scientific publication: strategies for disseminating research findings, Yale Center for Clinical Investigation. https://ictr.wisc.edu/documents/beyond-scientific-publication-strategies-for-disseminating-research-findings/

Cargo, M. and Mercer, S.L. (2008) 'The value and challenges of participatory research: strengthening its practice', *Annu. Rev. Public Health*, 29: 325–50.

Carney, J.K., Maltby, H.J., Mackin, K.A. and Maksym, M.E. (2011) 'Community–academic partnerships: how can communities benefit?', *American Journal of Preventive Medicine*, 41(4): S206–13, doi: 10.1016/j.amepre.2011.05.020.

Castleden, H., Morgan, V. and Lamb, C. (2012) '"I spent the first year drinking tea": exploring Canadian university researchers' perspectives on community-based participatory research involving Indigenous peoples', *The Canadian Geographer/Le Géographe canadien*, 56(2): 160–79.

Catalani, C. and Minkler, M. (2010) 'Photovoice: a review of the literature in health and public health', *Health Education & Behavior*, 37(3): 424–51.

CCPH (Community-Campus Partnerships for Health) (2019) Principles of partnership: community-campus partnerships for health. www.ccphealth.org

Centre for Social Justice and Community Action (2012) Community-based participatory research: a guide to ethical principles and practice, Bristol: NCCPE.

Chambers, M., McAndrew, S., Nolan, F., Thomas, B., Watts, P. and Kantaris, X. (2016) 'Service-user involvement in the coproduction of a mental health nursing metric: the therapeutic engagement questionnaire', *Health Expectations*, 20: 871–7.

Charlton, J.I. (2000) *Nothing about us without us: disability oppression and empowerment*, Berkeley, CA: University of California Press.

Chen, P.G., Diaz, N., Lucas, G. and Rosenthal, M.S. (2010) 'Dissemination of results in community-based participatory research', *American Journal of Preventative Medicine*, 39(4): 372–8.

Cherry, D. and Shefner, J. (2004) 'Addressing barriers to university-community collaboration', *Journal of Community Practice*, 12(3–4): 219–33.

Chiles, P., Ritchie, L. and Pahl, K. (2019) 'Co-designing for a better future: Re-imagining the modernist dream at Park Hill, Sheffield', In Banks, S., Hart, A., Pahl, K. and Ward, P. (eds) *Co-producing research: a community development approach*, Bristol: Policy Press, chapter 5.

Clark, T. (2008) '"We're over-researched here!": exploring accounts of research fatigue within qualitative research engagements', *Sociology*, 42(5): 953–70, doi:10.1177/0038038508094573.

Cleaver, F. (2001) 'Institutions, agency and the limitations of participatory approaches to development', In Cooke, B. and Kothari, U. (eds) *Participation: the new tyrany?*, London: Zed Books, chapter 3.

Coan, S. and Witty, K. (2016) Campus to Community: Health Promotion Partnerships, Paper presented at 8th Nordic Health Promotion Research Conference (NHPRC), 20-22 June, Jyväskylä, Finland.

Coghlan, D. and Brydon-Miller, M. (2014) *The Sage encyclopedia of action research*, vol. 2, London: Sage, doi: 10.4135/9781446294406.

Connected Communities (2011) *Community-based participatory research: ethical challenges*, Centre for Social Justice and Community Action, Durham University. https://ahrc.ukri.org/documents/project-reports-and-reviews/connected-communities/community-based-participatory-research-ethical-challenges/

Connell, J.P., Kubisch, A.C., Schorr, L.B. and Weiss, C.H. (1995) *New approaches to evaluating community initiatives, vol. 1. Concepts, methods and contexts*, Washington, DC: Aspen Institute.

Cook, T., Boote, J., Buckley, N., Vougioukalou, S. and Wright, M. (2017) 'Accessing participatory research impact and legacy: developing the evidence base for participatory approaches in health research', *Educational Action Research*, 25(4): 473–88.

Cooper, E.J. and Drideger, S.M. (2018) 'Creative, strengths-based approaches to knowledge translation within indigenous health research', *Public Health*, 163: 61–6.

Copes, H., Tchoula, W., Brookman, F. and Ragland, J. (2018) 'Photo-elicitation interviews with vulnerable populations: practical and ethical considerations', *Deviant Behavior*, 39(4): 475–94.

Cornwall, A. and Jewkes, R. (1995) 'What is participatory research?', *Social Science and Medicine*, 41(12): 1667–76.

Coutts, P. (2019) *The many shades of co-produced evidence*, Dunfermline: Carnegie Trust.

Craig, P., Dieppe, P., Macintyre, S., Michie, S., Nazareth, I., Petticrew, M. and Medical Research Council Guidance (2008) 'Developing and evaluating complex interventions: the new Medical Research Council guidance', *BMJ* (Clinical research ed.), 337: a1655, doi:10.1136/bmj.a1655.

Creswell, J.W. (1998) *Qualitative inquiry and research design: choosing among five traditions*, Thousand Oaks, CA: Sage.

Cross, R.M. and Warwick-Booth, L. (2016) 'Using storyboards in participatory research', *Nurse Researcher*, 23(3): 8–12.

Crowe, S., Fenton, M., Hall, M., Cowan, K. and Chalmers, I. (2015) 'Patients', clinicians' and the research communities' priorities for treatment research: there is an important mismatch', *Research Involvement and Engagement*, 1(2). https://doi.org/10.1186/s40900-015-0003-x

Cyril, S., Smith, B.J., Possamai-Inesedy, A. and Andre, M.N.R. (2015) 'Exploring the role of community engagement in improving the health of disadvantaged populations: a systematic review', *Global Health Action*, 8: 1–12.

Danley, K. and Langer, E. (1999) *A handbook for participatory action researchers*, Boston, MA: Centre for Psychiatric Rehabilitation.

Danley, S. (2018) *A neighborhood politics of last resort. Post-Katrina New Orleans and the right to the city*, Montreal: McGill–Queen's University Press.

Darby, S. (2017) 'Making space for co-produced research 'impact': learning from a participatory action research case study', *Area*, 49(2): 230–7.

Davidson, L., Shaw, J., Welborn, S., Mahon, B., Sirota, M., Gilbo, P., McDermid, M., Fazio, J., Gilbert, C., Breetz, S. and Pelletier, J.F. (2010) '"I don't know how to find my way in the world": contributions of user-led research to transforming mental health practice', *Psychiatry*, 73(2): 1010–13.

Deacon, S.A. (2000) 'Creativity within qualitative research on families: new ideas for old methods', *The Qualitative Report*, 4(3): 1–11.

Debenham, M. (2001) 'Computer mediated communication and disability support: addressing barriers to study for undergraduate distance learners with long-term health problems', PhD thesis, The Open University.

Debenham, M. (2007) 'Epistolary interviews on-line: a novel addition to the researcher's palette', TechDis Website Resource, www.researchgate.net/publication/294718847_Epistolary_Interviews_On-line_A_Novel_Addition_to_the_Researcher's_Palate/citation/download

de Jager, A., Fogarty, A., Tewson, A., Lenette, C. and Boydell, K.M. (2017) 'Digital storytelling in research: a systematic review', *The Qualitative Report*, 22(10): 2548–82.

Delafield, R., Hermosura, A., Townsend, C., Hughes, C.K., Palakiko, D., Dillard, A., Kekauoha, P.B., Yoshimura, S.R., Gamio, S. and Kaholokula, J.K. (2016) 'A community-based participatory guided model for the dissemination of evidence-based interventions', *Progress in Community Health Partnerships: Research, Education, and Action*, 10(4): 585–95.

DeLuca, C., Bolden, B. and Chan, J. (2017) 'Systemic professional learning through collaborative inquiry: examining teachers', perspectives', *Teaching and Teacher Education*, 67: 67–78.

Denzin, N. and Lincoln, Y. (2011) *The Sage handbook of qualitative research*, Thousand Oaks, CA: Sage.

Dias, S., Gama, A., Simoes, D. and Mendao, L. (2018) 'Implementation process and impacts of a participatory HIV research project with key populations', *BioMed Research International*, 5845218, doi: 10.1155/2018/5845218.

Dodson, L., Piatelli, D. and Schmalzbauer, L. (2007) 'Researching qualitative inquiry through interpretive collaborations: shifting power and the unspoken contract', *Qualitative Inquiry*, 13(6): 821–43.

Drake, R.F. (1997) 'What am I doing here?', *Disability and Society*, 12: 643–5.

Durose, C. and Richardson, L. (2015) *Designing public policy for co-production*, Bristol: Policy Press.

Durose, C., Beebeejaun, Y., Rees, J., Richardson, J. and Richardson, L. (2011) *Towards co-production in research with communities*, Swindon: AHRC.

Durose, C., Mangan, C., Needham, C. and Rees, J. (2014) 'Evaluating co-production: pragmatic approaches to building the evidence base', Co-Production Panel Political Studies Association Conference, 14–16 April, Manchester.

Durose, C., Needham, C., Mangan, C. and Rees, J. (2017) 'Generating "good enough" evidence for co-production', *Evidence & Policy*, 13(1): 135–51.

Edensor, T. (2010) 'Walking in rhythms: place, regulation, style and the flow of experience', *Visual Studies*, 25(1): 69–79.

Elder, B.C. and Odoyo, K.O. (2018) 'Multiple methodologies: using community-based participatory research and decolonizing methodologies in Kenya', *International Journal of Qualitative Studies in Education*, 31(4): 293–311.

Emmel, N. (2008) Participatory mapping: an innovative sociological method. Real Life Methods, University of Leeds.

ESRC (Economic and Social Research Council) (2020a) What is impact? https://esrc.ukri.org/research/impact-toolkit/what-is impact/

ESRC (2020b) Lessons for collaborative research. https://esrc.ukri.org/collaboration/guidance-for-collaboration/lessons-for-collaborative-research/

Evans, R. (2016) 'Achieving and evidencing research "impact"? Tensions and dilemmas from an ethic of care perspective', *Area*, 48(2): 213–21.

Facer, K. and Enright, B. (2016) *Creating living knowledge: the Connected Communities Programme, community university relationships and the participatory turn in the production of knowledge*, Bristol: University of Bristol/AHRC Connected Communities. https://research-information.bris.ac.uk/en/publications/creating-living-knowledge-the-connected-communities-programme-com

Fenge, L., Jones, K. and Gibson, C. (2018) 'Meaningful dissemination produces the "long tail" that engenders community impact', *Qualitative Research Journal*, 18(1): 45–54.

Fine, M., Weis, L., Weseen, S. and Wong, M. (2000) 'For whom? Qualitative research, representations and social responsibilities', In Denzin, N. and Lincoln, Y. (eds) *The Sage handbook of qualitative research*, Thousand Oaks, CA: Sage, pp. 167–207.

Finley, S. (2008) 'Arts-based research', In Knowles, J.G. and Cole, A.L. (eds) *Handbook of the arts in qualitative research*, London: Sage, pp. 71–82.

Fischer, F. (2000) *Citizens, experts and the environment: the politics of local knowledge*, Durham NC: Duke University Press.

Fisher, P. (2016) 'Co-production: what is it and where do we begin?', *Journal of Psychiatric and Mental Health Nursing*, 23(6–7): 345–46.

Fisher, P., Warwick-Booth, L., Coan, S., Cross, R. and Kinsella, K. (2017) *Evaluation of co-production in the Weaving the Web Project Rape Crisis England and Wales* (RCEW), [internal report], Leeds: Leeds Beckett University.

Flicker, S., Savan, B., McGrath, M., Kolenda, B. and Mildenberg, M. (2007) '"If you could change one thing …" What community-based researchers wish they could have done differently', *Community Development Journal*, 43(2): 239–53.

Flinders, M., Wood, M. and Cunningham, M. (2016) 'The politics of co-production: risks, limits and pollution', *Evidence & Policy*, 12: 261–79

Flyvberg, B. (2001) *Making social science matter: why social inquiry fails and how it can succeed again*, Cambridge: Cambridge University Press.

Foot, J. and Hopkins, T. (2010) *A glass half-full: how an asset approach can improve community health and wellbeing*, London: IDeA.

Franz, N. (2013) 'The data party: involving stakeholders in meaningful data analysis', *Journal of Extension*, 51(1): 67–77.

Fraser, S. (2018) 'What stories to tell? A trilogy of methods used for knowledge exchange in a community-based participatory research project', *Action Research*, 16(2): 207–22.

Freeman, E., Brugge, D., Bennett-Bradley, W., Levy, J. and Carrasco, E. (2006) 'Challenges of conducting community-based participatory research in Boston's neighborhoods to reduce disparities in asthma', *Journal of Urban Health*, 83(6): 1013–21.

Freire, P. (1970) *The pedagogy of the oppressed*, New York: Herder and Herder.

Frey, B.B. (ed.) (2018) *The SAGE encyclopedia of educational research, measurement, and evaluation*, Thousand Oaks, CA: Sage.

Fulbright-Anderson, K., Kubisch, A. and Connell, J. (eds) (1998) *New approaches to evaluating community initiatives, vol 2. Theory, measurement, and analysis.* Washington, DC: Aspen Institute.

Furman, E., Singh, A.K., Wilson, C., D'Alessandro, F. and Miller, Z. (2019) '"A space where people get it": a methodological reflection of arts-informed community-based participatory research with nonbinary youth', *International Journal of Qualitative Methods*, 18, ID: 1609406919858530.

Gambone M.A. (1998) 'Challenges of measurement in community change initiatives', In Connell, J. Kubish, A.C. and Fulbright-Anderson, K. (eds) *New approaches to evaluating community issues. Volume two. Theory, measurement and analysis*, Washington, DC: Brookings Institution Press, pp. 149–63.

Garcia, R., Melgar, P and Sorde, T. in conversation with Cortes, L., Santiago, C. and Santiago, S. (2013) 'From refusal to getting involved in Romani research', In Mertens, M., Cram, F. and Chilisa, B. (eds) *Indigenous pathways into social research: voices of a new generation*, Walnut Creek, CA: Left Coast Press, pp. 367–80.

Garnett, B.R., Wendel, J., Banks, C., Goodridge, A., Harding, R., Harris, R., Hacker, K. and Chomitz, V.R. (2015) 'Challenges of data dissemination efforts within a community-based participatory project about persistent racial disparities in excess weight', *Progress in Community Health Partnerships: Research, Education, and Action*, 9(2): 289–298.

Gaventa, J. and Cornwall, A. (2008) 'Power and knowledge', In Reason, P. and Bradbury, H. (eds) *The Sage handbook of action research: participative inquiry and practice* (2nd edn), pp. 172–89.

Gibson, S. (2013) The lived experience of co-producing research. www.invo.org.uk/the-lived-experience-of-co-producing-research/

Gillard, S., Turner, K., Lovell, K., Norton, K., Clarke, T., Addicott, R., McGivern, G. and Ferlie, E. (2010) 'Staying native: coproduction in mental health services research', *International Journal of Public Sector Management*, 23(6): 567–77.

Gillard, S., Simons, L., Turner, L., Lucock, M. and Edwards, C. (2012) 'Patient and public involvement in the coproduction of knowledge: reflection on the analysis of qualitative data in a mental health study', *Qualitative Health Research*, 22: 1126–37.

Glaser, B.G. and Strauss, A.L. (2017) 'Theoretical sampling', In N. Denzin (ed.) *Sociological methods: a sourcebook*, London/New York: Routledge, pp. 105–14.

Glassman, M. (2019) 'The internet as a context for participatory action research', *Education and Information Technologies*, 25: 11–21.

Glaw, X., Inder, K., Kable, A. and Hazelton, M. (2017) 'Visual methodologies in qualitative research: autophotography and photo elicitation applied to mental health research', *International Journal of Qualitative Methods*, 16(1), ID: 1609406917748215.

Goodman, L.A., Thomas, K.A., Nnawulezi, N., Lippy, C., Serrata, J.V., Ghanbarpour, S., Sullivan, C. and Bair-Merrit, M.H. (2018) 'Bringing community based participatory research to domestic violence scholarship: an online toolkit', *Journal of Family Violence*, 33(2): 103–7.

Goodson, L. and Phillimore, J. (2012) 'Community research: opportunities and challenges', In Goodson, L. and Phillimore, J. (eds) *Community research for participation: from theory to method*, Bristol: Policy Press, pp. 3–20.

Gov.uk (2019) Guide to writing a memorandum of understanding (MOU). www.gov.uk/government/publications/setting-up-school-partnerships/guide-to-writing-a-memorandum-of-understanding-mou

Grant, J. and Hinrichs, S. (2015) *The nature, scale and beneficiaries of research impact*, London: Higher Education Council for England.

Green, G., Grimsley M., Syolcas, A., Prescott, M., Jowitt, T. and Linacre R. (2000) *Social capital, health and economy in South Yorkshire coalfield communities*, Sheffield: Centre for Regional Economic and Social Research, Sheffield Hallam University.

Green, J. and South, J. (2006) *Evaluation: key concepts for public health practice*, London: Sage.

Greenberg, J., Howard, D. and Desmond, S. (2003) 'A community-campus partnership for health: the Seat Pleasant–University of Maryland health partnership', *Health Promotion Practice*, 4(4): 393–401.

Greenhalgh, T., Raftery, J., Hanney, S. and Glover, M. (2016) 'Research impact: a narrative review', *BMC Medicine*, 14(1): 78–94.

Greve, J. (1975) 'Research and the community', In Jones, D. and Mayo, M. (eds) *Community work: two*, London/Boston: Routledge and Kegan Paul.

Grieb, D.D., Eder, M., Smith, K.C., Calhoun, K. and Tandon, D. (2015) 'Qualitative research and community-based participatory research: considerations for effective dissemination in the peer-reviewed literature', *Progress in Community Health Partnerships: Research, Education, and Action*, 9(2): 275–82.

Grimes, D.A. and Schulz, K.F. (2002) 'An overview of clinical research: the lay of the land', *The Lancet*, 359(9300): 57–61.

Grover, S. (2004) '"Why won't they listen to us?" On giving power and voice to children participating in social research', *Childhood*, 11(1): 81–93.

Guba, E.G. (1978) *Toward a methodology of naturalistic inquiry in educational evaluation*, 'CSE monograph series in evaluation', No. 8., Los Angeles, CA: Center for the Study of Evaluation, UCLA.

Guba E.G. and Lincoln Y.S. (1989) *Fourth generation evaluation*, Newbury Park, CA: Sage.

Gust, S. and Jordan, C. (2007) 'The community impact statement: a prenuptial agreement for community-campus partnerships', *Journal of Higher Education Outreach and Engagement*, 11(2): 155–69.

Guta, A., Flicker, S. and Roche, B. (2013) 'Governing through community allegiance: a qualitative examination of peer research in community-based participatory research', *Critical Public Health*, 23(4): 432–51.

Hacker, K. (2013) *Community-based participatory research*, London: Sage.

Halcomb, E.J. (2016) 'Understanding the importance of collecting qualitative data creatively', *Nurse Researcher*, 23(3): 6–7.

Halcomb E. and Hickman L. (2015) 'Mixed methods research', *Nurs Stand*, 29: 417, doi: 10.7748/ns.29.32.41.e8858.

Hall, B., Tandon, R. and Tremblay, C. (2015) *Strengthening community university research partnerships: global perspectives*, University of Victoria, Canada.

Hall, J. and Lavrakas, P. (2008) 'Cross-sectional survey design', In *Encyclopedia of survey research methods*, Thousand Oaks, CA: Sage, pp. 172–3.

Harper, D. (2002) 'Talking about pictures: a case for photo elicitation', *Visual Studies*, 17(1): 13–26.

Hart, A. and Wolff, D. (2006) 'Developing local 'communities of practice', through local community – university partnerships', *Planning Practice and Research*, 21(1): 121–38.

Hart, A., Maddison, E. and Wolff, D. (2007) *Community-university partnerships in practice*, Leicester: National Institute of Adult Continuing Education.

Hart, R. (1992) 'The meaning of children's participation', In Hart, R. *Children's Participation from Tokenism to Citizenship* (Innocenti Essays No 4) Florence: UNICEF. www.unicef-irc.org/publications/pdf/childrens_participation.pdf

Hartel, J. (2014) 'An arts-informed study of information using the draw-and-write technique', *Journal of the Association for Information Science and Technology*, 65(7): 1349–67.

Haver, A., Akerjordet, K., Caputi, P., Furunes, T. and Magee, C. (2015) Measuring mental well-being: A validation of the short Warwick–Edinburgh mental well-being scale in Norwegian and Swedish. *Scandinavian journal of public health*, 43(7): 721–7.

Hayes, K. and Tanner, T. (2015) 'Empowering young people and strengthening resilience: youth-centred participatory video as a tool for climate change adaptation and disaster risk reduction', *Children's Geographies*, 13(3): 357–371.

Heckler, M. (1985) *Report of the secretary's task force on black and minority health*, Washington, DC: US Department of Health and Human Services.

HEFCE (Higher Education Funding Council for England) (2016) REF impact. www.hefce.ac.uk/rsrch/REFimpact/

Heinsch, M., Gray, M. and Sharland, E. (2015) 'Re-conceptualising the link between research and practice in social work: a literature review on knowledge utilisation', *Int J Soc Welfare*, doi: 10.1111/ijsw.12164.

Heron, J. (1996) *Co-operative inquiry: research into the human condition*, London: Sage.

Hickey, G. (2018) 'The potential for coproduction to add value to research', Editorial, *Health Expectations*, 21: 693–4.

Hickey, G., Brearley, S., Coldham, T., Denegri, S., Green, G., Staniszewska, S., Tembo, D., Torok, K. and Turner, K. (2018) *Guidance on co-producing a research project*, Southampton: INVOLVE.

Hilger-Kolb, J., Ganter, C., Albrecht, M., Bosle, C., Fischer., J.E., Schilling, L., Schlufter, C., Steinisch, M. and Hoffman, K. (2019) 'Identification of starting points to promote health and wellbeing at the community level – a qualitative study', *BMC Public Health*, 19(1), doi: 10.1186/s12889-019-6425-x.

Hills, M. and Mullett, J. (2000) 'Community-based research: creating evidenced-based practice for health and social change', Paper presented at the Qualitative Evidence-Based Practice Conference, Coventry University, 15–17 May.

Hillstrom, K., Ruelas, V., Peters, A., Gedebu-Wilson, T. and Iverson, E. (2014) 'A retrospective analysis of the capacity built through a community-based participatory research project addressing diabetes and obesity in south east Los Angeles', *Health*, 6: 1429–35.

Hind, M. (2014) *What is inclusive research?*, London: Bloomsbury Academic.

Holland, S., Renold, E., Ross, N. and Hillman, A. (2008) 'Rights, 'right on', or the right thing to do? A critical exploration of young people's engagement in participative social work research', NCRM Working Paper Series 07/08. http://eprints.ncrm.ac.uk/460/1/0708%2520critical%2520exploration.pdf

Holmes, B.J. (2017) On the co-production of research: why we should say what we mean, mean what we say, and learn as we go [blog]. https://blogs.lse.ac.uk/impactofsocialsciences/2017/09/21/on-the-co-production-of-research-why-we-should-say-what-we-mean-mean-what-we-say-and-learn-as-we-go/

Horn, K., McCraken, L., Dino, G. and Braybot, M. (2008) 'Applying community-based participatory research principles to the development of a smoking-cessation program for American Indian teens: "telling our story"', *Health Education and Behaviour*, 44: 44–69.

Hubbell, K. and Burman, M. (2006) 'Factors related to successful collaboration in community-campus partnerships', *Journal of Nursing Education*, 45(12): 519–22.

Ilustre, V., López, A.M. and Moely, B.E. (2012) 'Conceptualizing, building, and evaluating university practices for community engagement', *Journal of Higher Education Outreach & Engagement*, 16(4): 129.

Ingram, M., Murrietta, L., de Zapien, J.G., Herman, P.M. and Carvajal, S.C. (2015) 'Community health workers as focus group facilitators: a participatory action research method to improve behavioral health services for farmworkers in a primary care setting', *Action Research*, 13(1): 48–64.

Involve (2018) Guidance on co-producing a research project. www.invo.org.uk/wp-content/uploads/2019/04/Copro_Guidance_Feb19.pdf

Involve (2019) About Involve. www.involve.org.uk/about/about-involve

Israel, B.A., Schultz, A.J., Parker, E.A. and Becker, A.B. (1998) 'Review of community based research: assessing partnership approaches to improve public health', *Annual Review of Public Health*, 19: 173–202.

Israel, B.A., Parker, E.A., Rowe, Z. et al. (2005a) 'Community-based participatory research: lessons learned from the Centers for Children's Environmental Health and Disease Prevention research', *Environmental Health Perspectives*, 113: 1463–71.

Israel, B., Eng, E., Schultz, A.J. and Parker, E.A. (2005b) *Methods in community-based participatory research for health*, San Francisco, CA: Jossey-Bass.

Israel, B.A., Schultz, A.J., Parker, A.E., Becker, A.B., Allen, A.J. and Guzman, J.R. (2008) 'Critical issues in developing and following CBPR principles', In Minkler, M. and Wallerstein, N. (eds) *Community-based participatory research for health: from process to outcomes* (2nd edn), San Francisco, CA: Jossey-Bass, pp. 47–62.

Israel, B.A., Coombe, C.M., Cheezum, R.R., Schulz, A.J., McGranaghan, R.J., Lichtenstein, R., Reyes, A.G., Clement, J. and Burris, A. (2010) 'Community-based participatory research: a capacity-building approach for policy advocacy aimed at eliminating health disparities', *American Journal of Public Health*, 100(11): 2094–102.

Israel, B.A., Eng, E., Schultz, A.J. and Parker, E.A. (2013) *Methods in community-based participatory research for health* (2nd edn), San Francisco, CA: Jossey-Bass.

Jackson, S. (2008) 'A participatory group process to analyse qualitative data', *Progress in Community Health Partnerships: Research, Education, and Action*, 2(2): 161–70.

Jagosh, J., Macaulay A.C., Pluye P., Salsberg J., Bush P.L., Henderson J., Sirett E., Wong G., Cargo M., Herbert C.P., Seifer S.D., Green L.W. and Greenhalgh T. (2012) 'Uncovering the benefits of participatory research: implications of a realist review for health research and practice', *Milbank Quarterly*, 90(2): 311–46.

Jagosh, J., Bush, P.L., Salsberg, J., Macaulay, A., Greenhalgh, T., Wong, G., Cargo, M., Green, L.W., Herbert, C.P. and Pluye, P. (2015) 'A realist evaluation of community-based participatory research: partnership synergy, trust building and related ripple effects', *BMC Public Health*, 15(725), doi: 10.1186/s12889-015-1949-1.

James, A. (2007) 'Giving voice to children's voices: practices and problems, pitfalls and potentials', *American Anthropologist*, 109(2): 261–72.

Jamshidi, E., Morasae, E.K., Shahandeh, K., Majdzadeh, R., Seydali, E., Aramesh, K. and Abknar, N.L. (2014) 'Ethical considerations of community-based participatory research: contextual underpinnings for developing countries', *International Journal of Preventative Medicine*, 5(10): 1328–36.

Jasanoff, S. (ed.) (2004) *States of knowledge: the co-production of science and the social order*, London: Routledge.

Jennings, H., Slade, M., Bates, P., Munday, E. and Toney, R. (2018) 'Best practice framework for Patient and Public Involvement (PPI) in collaborative data analysis of qualitative mental health research: methodology development and refinement', *BMC Psychiatry*, 18: 213, doi.org/10.11867/s12888-018-1794-8.

Johnson Butterfield, A. and Soska, T. (2004) 'University–community partnerships', *Journal of Community Practice*, 12(3–4): 1–11.

Jorian, T.J. and Nicolazzo, Z. (2017) 'Bringing our communities to the research table: the liberatory potential of collaborative methodological practices alongside LGBTQ participants', *Educational Action Research*, 25(4): 594–609.

Kagan, C. (2007) *Making a difference: participation, well-being and levers for change*, Liverpool, RENEW [intelligence report].

Kagan, C. (2012) 'La ricerca-azione partecipata e la psicologia di comunità Rome' [Participatory action research and community psychology], In Zani, B. (ed.) *Psicologia di comunità: Prospettive, idee, metodi*, Carocci Editore. www.compsy.org.uk/PAR%20kagan%20final%20for%20web.pdf

Kagan, C. (2013) 'Co-production of research: for good or ill?', Paper presented to Research Conference, Edge Hill University, 8 July.

Kania, J. and Kramer, M. (2011) *Collective impact*, Stanford: Stanford Social Innovation Review.

Kaptani, E. and Yuval-Davis, N. (2008) Participatory theatre as a research methodology: identity, performance and social action among refugees. *Sociological Research Online*, 13(5): 1–12.

Kara, H. (2015) *Creative methods in the social sciences: a practical guide*, Bristol: Policy Press.

Kara, H. (2017) Academic taboos #1: what cannot be said. https://helenkara.com/tag/ethics/

Kara, H. (2018) *Research ethics in the real world. Euro-Western and Indigenous perspectives*, Bristol: Policy Press.

Kara, H. (2020) Research methods to consider in a pandemic. https://helenkara.com/2020/05/20/research-methods-to-consider-in-a-pandemic/

Katon, W., Unutzer, J., Wells, K. and Jones, L. (2010) 'Collaborative depression care: history, evolution and ways to enhance dissemination and sustainability', *General Hospital Psychiatry*, 32(5): 456–464.

Kavanagh A., Daly J. and Jolley D. (2002) 'Research methods, evidence and public health', *Australian and New Zealand Journal of Public Health*, 26(4): 337–42.

Kawulich, B. and Ogletree, T. (2012) 'Ethics in community research: reflections from ethnographic research with First Nations people in the US', In Goodson, L. and Phillimore, J. (eds) *Community research for participation: from theory to method*, Bristol: Policy Press, pp. 201–14.

Kendall, E., Marshall, C.A. and Barlow, L. (2013) 'Stories rather than surveys: a journey of discovery and emancipation', *International Journal of Qualitative Methods*, 12: 258–71.

Kiernan, C. (1999) 'Participation in research by people with learning disability: origins and issues', *British Journal of Learning Disabilities*, 27: 43–7.

Kindon, S. (2003) 'Participatory video in geographic research: a feminist practice of looking?', *Area*, 35: 142–53.

Kindon, S., Pain, R. and Kesby, M. (eds) (2007) *Participatory action research approaches and methods: connecting people, participation and place*, London: Routledge.

Knerr, S., Hohl, S.D., Molina, Y., Neuhoser, M.L., Li, C.I., Coronado, G.D., Fullerton, S.M. and Thompson, B. (2016) 'Engaging study participants in research dissemination at a centre for population health and health disparities', *Progress in Community Health Partnerships: Research, Education, and Action*, 10(4): 569–76.

Komaie, G., Goodman, M., McCall, A., McGill, G., Pattersone, C., Hayes, C. and Sanders Thompson, V. (2018) 'Training community members in public health research: development and implementation of a community participatory research pilot project', *Health Equity*, 2(1): 282–7, doi: 10.1089/heq.2018.0043.

Koster, R., Baccar, K. and Lemelin, R. (2012) 'Moving from research ON, to research WITH and FOR Indigenous communities: a critical reflection on community-based participatory research', *The Canadian Geographer/Le Géographe canadien*, 56(2): 195–210.

Kramer, S., Amos, T., Lazarus, S. and Seedat, M. (2012) 'The philosophical assumptions, utility and challenges of asset mapping approaches to community engagement', *Journal of Psychology in Africa*, 22(4): 537–44

Krimerman, L. (2001) 'Participatory action research: should social inquiry be conducted democratically?', *Philosophy of the Social Sciences*, 31(1): 60–82.

Kwan, C. and Walsh, C.A. (2018) 'Ethical issues in conducting community-based participatory research: a narrative review of the literature', *The Qualitative Report*, 23(2): 369–386.

Kyneswood, B. (2018) 'Co-production as a new way of seeing: using photographic exhibitions to challenge dominant stigmatising discourses', In Banks, S., Hart, A., Pahl, K. and Ward, P. (eds) *Co-producing research: a community development approach*, Bristol: Policy Press, chapter 8.

Lambert, J. (2009) 'Where it all started: the center for digital storytelling in California'. In J. Lambert and K. McWilliam (eds), *Story circle: digital storytelling around the world*, Chichester: Wiley-Blackwell, pp. 77–90.

Laverack, G. (2006) 'Improving health outcomes through community empowerment: a review of the literature', *J Health Popul Nutr*, 24(1): 113–20

Lee, J. and Ingold, T. (2006) 'Fieldwork on foot: perceiving, routing, socializing, In Coleman, S. and Collins, P. (eds) *Locating the field: space, place and context in anthropology*, Oxford: Berg, pp. 67–86.

Lee-Treweek, G. and Linkogle, S. (2000) *Danger in the field*, London: Routledge.

Lewin, K. (1948) *Resolving social conflicts: selected papers on group dynamics*, New York: Harper and Row.

Lobe, B., Morgan, D. and Hoffman, K.A. (2020) 'Qualitative data collection in an era of social distancing', *International Journal of Qualitative Methods*, https://doi.org/10.1177/1609406920937875

Locock, L. and Boaz, A. (2019) 'Drawing straight lines along blurred boundaries: qualitative research, patient and public involvement in medical research, co-production and co-design', *Evidence and Policy*, 15(3): 409–22.

Locock, L., Kirkpatrick, S., Brading, L., Sturmey, G., Cornwell, P., Churchill, N. and Glenn, R. (2019) 'Involving service users in the qualitative analysis of patient narratives to support healthcare quality improvement', *Research Involvement and Engagement*, 5(1), doi.10.1186/s40900-018-0133-z.

Loeffler, E. and Bovaird, T. (2016) 'User and community co-production of public services: what does the evidence tell us?', *International Journal of Public Administration*, 39(13): 1006–19.

Loh, P., Sugerman-Brozan, J., Wiggins, S., Noiles, D. and Archibald, C. (2002) From asthma to AirBeat: community-driven monitoring of fine particles and black carbon in Roxbury, Massachusetts', *Environmental Health Perspectives*, 110(suppl 2): 297–301.

London, J.K., Mirel Zagofsky, T., Huang, G. and Saklar, J. (2011) 'Collaboration, participation and technology: the San Joaquin Valley Cumulative Health Impacts Project', *Gateways: International Journal of Community Research & Engagement*, 4: 12–30. https://doi.org/10.5130/ijcre.v4i0.1780

Long, J.W., Ballard, H.L., Fisher, L. and Belskey, J.M. (2016) 'Questions that won't go away in participatory research', *Society and Natural Resources*, 29: 250–63.

Love, K. (2011) 'Little known but powerful approach to applied research: community-based participatory research', *Geriatric Nursing*, 32(1): 52–4.

Lupton, D. (2020) Doing fieldwork in a pandemic [crowd-sourced document]. https://nwssdtpacuk.files.wordpress.com/2020/04/doing-fieldwork-in-a-pandemic2-google-docs.pdf

Lushey, C.J. and Munro, E.R. (2015) 'Participatory peer research methodology: an effective method for obtaining young people's perspectives on transitions from care to adulthood?', *Qualitative Social Work*, 14(4): 522–37. https://doi.org/10.1177/1473325014559282

Macaulay, A. (2017) 'Participatory research: what is the history? Has the purpose changed?', *Family Practice*, 34(3): 256–8.

MacLeod, M.A. and Emejulu, A. (2014) 'Neoliberalism with a community face? A critical analysis of asset-based community development in Scotland', *Journal of Community Practice*, 22(4): 430–50.

Macpherson, H., Davies, C., Hart, A., Eryigit-Madzwamuse, S., Rathbone, A., Gagnon, E., Buttery, L. and Dennis, S. (2017) 'Collaborative community research dissemination and networking: experiences and challenges', *Gateways: International Journal of Community Research and Engagement*, 10: 298–312.

Maiter, S., Simich, L., Jacobsen, N. and Wise, J. (2008) 'Reciprocity. An ethics for community-based participatory action research', *Action Research*, 63(3): 305–25.

Mand, K. (2012) 'Giving children a "voice": arts-based participatory research activities and representation', *International Journal of Social Research Methodology*, 15(2): 149–60.

Mannay, D., Staples, E., Hallett, S., Roberts, L., Rees, A., Evans, R. and Andrews, D. (2019) 'Enabling talk and reframing messages: working creatively with care experienced children and young people to recount and re-present their everyday experiences', *Child Care in Practice*, 25(1): 51–63.

Manzo, L. and Brightbill, N. (2007) 'Toward a participatory ethics', In Kindon, S., Pain, R. and Kesby, M. (eds) *Participatory action research approaches and methods: connecting people, participation and place*, London: Routledge, pp. 33–40.

Martin, S. (2010) 'Co-production of social research: strategies for engaged scholarship', *Public Money and Management*, 30(4): 211–18.

McDavitt, B., Bogart, L.M., Mutchler, M.G., Wagner, G.L., Green, H.D., Lawrence, S.J., Mutepfa, K.D. and Nogg, K.A. (2016) 'Dissemination as dialogue: building trust and sharing research findings through community engagement', *Preventing Chronic Disease*, 13, doi: 10.5888/pcd13.150473

Merzel, C., Burrus, G., Davis, J., Moses, N., Rumley, S. and Walters, D. (2007) 'Developing and sustaining community–academic partnerships: lessons from downstate New York Healthy Start', *Health Promotion Practice*, 8(4): 375–83.

Metz, A., Boaz, A. and Robert, G. (2019) 'Co-creative approaches to knowledge production: what next for bridging the research to practice gap?', *Evidence and Policy*, 15(3): 331–7.

Mey, E. and van Hoven, B. (2019) 'Managing expectations in participatory research involving older people: what's in it for whom?', *International Journal of Social Research Methodology*, 22(3): 323–34.

Milgram, S. (1963) 'Behavioral study of obedience', *Journal of Abnormal and Social Psychology*, 67: 371–78.

Minkler, M. (2004) 'Ethical challenges for the "outside" researcher in community-based participatory research', *Health Education and Behaviour*, 31: 684–97.

Minkler, M. (2010) Linking science and policy through community-based participatory research to study and address health disparities, *American Journal of Public Health*, 100(S1): S81–7.

Minkler, M. and Wallerstein, N. (eds) (2003) *Community-based participatory research for health*, San Francisco, CA: Jossey-Bass.

Minkler, M. and Wallerstein, N. (2008) 'Introduction to community-based participatory research: new issues and emphases', In Minkler, M. and Wallerstein, N. (eds) *Community-based participatory research for health: from process to outcomes* (2nd edn), San Francisco, CA: Jossey-Bass, pp. 5–24.

Minkler, M., Fadem, P., Perry, M., Blum, K., Moore, L. and Rodgers, J. (2002) 'Ethical dilemmas in participatory action research: a case study from the disability community', *Health Education and Behaviour*, 29(1): 14–29.

Minkler, M., Garcia, A., Rubin, V. and Wallerstein, N. (2012) 'Community-based participatory research: a strategy for building healthy communities and promoting health through policy change', Oakland, CA: PolicyLink, www.policylink.org/resources-tools/building-healthy-communities-and-promoting-health-through-policy-change

Mitchell, D. and Staeheli, L. (2005) 'The complex politics of relevance in geography', *Annals of the Association American Geographers*, 95(2): 357–72.

Mohatt, N.V. and Beehler, S. (2018) 'Application of community engaged and community based participatory research to support military families', Paper commissioned for the Committee on the Well-being of Military Families, Washington DC, National Academics of Science, Engineering and Medicine.

Mooney, S.J. and Pejaver, V. (2018) 'Big data in public health: terminology, machine learning, and privacy', *Annual Review of Public Health*, 39: 95–112.

Morton, K. (1995) 'The irony of service: charity, project and social change in service-learning', *Michigan Journal of Community Service Learning*, 2: 19–32. http://search.ebscohost.com.ezproxy.leedsbeckett.ac.uk/login.aspx?direct=true&db=eric&AN=EJ552424&site=eds-live&scope=site

Mosavel, M., Ferrell, D. and LaRose, J.G. (2016) 'House chats as a grassroots engagement methodology in community-based participatory research: the WE Project, Petersburg', *Progress in Community Health Partnerships: Research, Education, and Action*, 10(3): 391.

Mosavel, M., Winship, J., Ferrel, D. and Larose, J.G. (2019) 'Data dissemination in CBPR: accountability and responsiveness', *Collaborations: A Journal of Community-Based Research and Practice*, 2(1): 1–11.

Murray, S., Tapson, J., Turnbull, L., McCallum, J. and Little, A. (1994) 'Listening to local voices: adopting rapid appraisal to asses health and social needs in general practice', *BMJ*, 308: 698–70.

Myers, P. and Barnes, J. (2004) 'Sharing evaluation findings: disseminating the evidence', London: NESS, Birkbeck University of London. www.ness.bbk.ac.uk/support/GuidanceReports/documents/647.pdf

N8/ESRC (N8 Research Partnership/Economic and Social Research Council) (2016) *Knowledge that matters: realizing the potential of co-production*, N8/ESRC Research Programme, Manchester: N8 Research Partnership, www.n8research.org.uk/media/Final-Report-Co-Production-2016-01-20.pdf

Nelson, D. (2017) 'Participatory action research: a literature review', Working Paper. www.researchgate.net/publication/321398218_Participatory_Action_Research_A_Literature_Review

Nesta (2012) *People powered health co-production catalogue*, London: Nesta. https://media.nesta.org.uk/documents/co-production_catalogue.pdf

NFHEPG (National Forum on Higher Education for the Public Good) (2005) *Higher education collaboratives for community engagement and improvement*, Ann Arbor, MI: School of Education, University of Michigan.

Nguyen, A., Christensen, C., Taylor, J. and Brown, B. (2020) 'Leaning on community-based participatory research to respond during COVID-19', *AIDS and Behavior*, 24(10): 2773–5.

Nind, M. (2011) 'Participatory data analysis: a step too far?', *Qualitative Research*, 11(4): 349–63.

Nind, M. (2017) 'The practical wisdom of inclusive research', *Qualitative Research*, 17(3): 278–88.

Nind, M. and Vinha, H. (2016) 'Creative interactions with data: using visual and metaphorical devices in repeated focus groups', *Qualitative Research*, 16(1): 9–26.

Nolan, M., Grant, G., Keady, J. and Lundh, U. (2003) 'New directions for partnership: relationship centered care', In Nolan, M., Lundh, U., Grant, G. and Keady, J. (eds) *Partnership in family care: understanding the caregiving career*, Maidenhead/Philadelphia, PA: Open University Press, pp. 257–91.

Noland, C.M. (2006) 'Auto-photography as research practice: identity and self-esteem research', *Journal of Research Practice*, 2(1): M1.

Northmore, S. and Hart, A. (2011) 'Sustaining community-university partnerships', *Gateways: International Journal of Community Research & Engagement*, 4: 1–11. https://doi.org/10.5130/ijcre.v4i0.2356

O'Connell, B. (2005) *Ethical considerations for research on housing-related health hazards involving children*, Washington DC: National Academies Press.

OECD (Organisation for Economic Cooperation and Development) (2011) *Together for better public services: partnering with citizens and civil society*, Paris: OECD.

Oliver, K., Kothari, A. and Mays, N. (2019) 'The dark side of coproduction: do the costs outweigh the benefits for health research?', *Health Research Policy and Systems*, 17(33), https://doi.org/10.1186/s12961-019-0432-3

O'Mara-Eves, A., Brunton, G, McDaid, D., Oliver, S., Kavanagh, J., Jamal, F., Matosevic, T., Harden, A. and Thomas, J. (2013) 'Community engagement to reduce inequalities in health: a systematic review, meta-analysis and economic analysis', *Public Health Research*, 1(4), www.ncbi.nlm.nih.gov/books/NBK262817/

O'Mara-Eves, A., Brunton, G., Oliver, S., Kavanagh, J., Jamal, F. and Thomas, J. (2015) 'The effectiveness of community engagement in public health interventions for disadvantaged groups: a meta-analysis', *BMC Public Health*, 15(129), https://doi.org/10.1186/s12889-015-1352-y

O'Neill, M. and Hubbard, P. (2010) 'Walking, sensing, belonging: ethno-mimesis as performative praxis', *Visual Studies*, 25(1): 46–58.

O'Neill, M., Erel, U., Kaptani, E. and Reynolds, T. (2018) *Participatory theatre and walking as social research methods: a toolkit*, http://eprints.ncrm.ac.uk/4120/

ONS (Office for National Statistics) (2019) Exploring the UK'S digital divide, www.ons.gov.uk/peoplepopulationandcommunity/householdcharacteristics/homeinternetandsocialmediausage/articles/exploringtheuksdigitaldivide/2019-03-04#how-does-digital-exclusion-vary-with-age

Orr, K.M. and Bennett, M. (2009) 'Reflexivity in the co-production of academic-practitioner research', *Qualitative Research in Organisations and Management*, 4: 85–102.

Osborne, P., Radnor, Z. and Strokosch, K. (2016) 'Co-production and the co-creation of value in public services: a suitable case for treatment?', *Public Management Review*, 18(5): 639–53.

Ostrander, S. (2004) 'Democracy, civic participation, and the university: a comparative study of civic engagement on five campuses', *Nonprofit and Voluntary Sector Quarterly*, 33(1): 74–93.

Ostrom, E. (1996) 'Crossing the great divide: co-production, synergy and development', *World Development*, 24(6): 1073–88.

Pain, R. (2014) 'Impact: striking a blow or walking together', *ACME*, 13(1): 19–23.

Pain, R., Whitman, G. and Milledge, D. (2011) 'Participatory action research toolkit. An introduction to using PAR as an approach to learning, research and action', Department of Geography, Durham University. http://communitylearningpartnership.org/wp-content/uploads/2017/01/PARtoolkit.pdf

Pain, R., Askins, K., Banks, S., Cook, T., Crawford, G., Crookes, L., Darby, S., Heslop, J., Holden, A., Houston, M., Jeffes, J., Lambert, Z., McGlen, L., McGlynn, C., Ozga, J., Raynor, R., Robinson, Y., Shaw, S., Stewart, C. and Vanderhove, D. (2015) *Mapping alternative impact. Alternative approaches to impact from co-produced research*, Centre for Social Justice and Community Action, Durham University. www.dur.ac.uk/resources/beacon/MappingAlternativeImpactFinalReport.pdf

Pankaj, V., Welsh, M. and Ostenso, L. (2011) *Participatory analysis. Expanding stakeholder involvement in evaluation*, Washington DC: Innovation Network.

Papineau, D. and Kiely, M.C. (1996) 'Participatory evaluation in a community organization: fostering stakeholder empowerment and utilization', *Evaluation and Program Planning*, 19(1): 79–93.

Parrado, E.A., McQuiston, C. and Flippen, C.A. (2005) 'Integrating community collaboration and quantitative methods for the study of gender and HIV risks among Hispanic migrants', *Sociological Methods & Research*, 34(2): 204–39

Patton, M. (2010) *Developmental evaluation: applying complexity concepts to enhance innovation and use*, New York: Guilford Press.

Pawson, R. and Tilley, N. (1997) *Realistic evaluation*, London: Sage.

Peters, D.H., Tran, N.T. and Adam, T. (2013) *Implementation research in health: a practical guide*, Geneva: Alliance for Health Policy and Systems Research/WHO.

PHE (Public Health England)/NHS England (2015) *A guide to community-centred approaches for health and wellbeing*, London: PHE publications.

Picciotto, R. (2015) 'Democratic evaluation for the 21st century', *Evaluation*, 21(2): 150–66.

Pink, S. (2008) 'Mobilising visual ethnography: making routes, making place and making images', In *Forum Qualitative Sozialforschung/Forum: Qualitative Social Research*, 9(3).

Plush, T. (2009) 'Video and voice: how participatory video can support marginalized groups in their efforts to adapt to a changing climate', Unpublished Master's synthesis paper.

Pohl, C., Rist, S., Zimmermann, A., Fry, P., Gurung, G.S., Schneider, F. and Wiesmann, U. (2010) 'Researchers' roles in knowledge co-production: experience from sustainability research in Kenya, Switzerland, Bolivia and Nepal', *Science and Public Policy*, 37(4): 267–81.

Pope, C. and Allen, D. (2020) 'Observational methods', in Pope, C. and Mays, N. (eds) *Qualitative Research in Health Care* (4th edn), Chichester/Hoboken, NJ: John Wiley & Sons, pp. 67–81.

Porter, L. (2010) *Unlearning the colonial cultures of planning*, Surrey: Ashgate.

Protz, M. (1998) 'Video, gender and participatory development', In Guijt, I. and Kaul Shah, M. (eds) *The myth of community: gender issues in participatory development*, Rugby: Practical Action Publishing, pp. 165–77.

Public Profit (2019) *Dabbling in the data. A hands-on guide to participatory analysis*, Oakland, CA: Public Profit. www.publicprofit.net/Dabbling-In-The-Data-A-Hands-On-Guide-To-Participatory-Data-Analysis

Pufall, E.L., Jones, A.Q., McEwan, S.A., Lyall, C., Peregrine, A.S. and Edge, V.L. (2011) 'Community-derived research dissemination strategies in an Inuit community', *International Journal of Circumpolar Health*, 50(5): 532–41.

Quigley, D. (2006) 'A review of improved ethical practices in environmental and public health research: case examples from native communities', *Health Education and Behaviour*, 33(2): 130–47.

Ramgard, M., Forsgren, A. and Avery, H. (2017) 'PHR in health and social care for older people – regional development through learning within and across organisations', *Educational Action Research*, 25(4): 506–24.

Reeves, S., Kuper, A. and Hodges, B.D. (2008) 'Qualitative research methodologies: ethnography', *BMJ*, 337, p.a1020.

Riger, S. (1992) 'Epistemological debates, feminist voices: science, social values and the study of women', *American Psychologist*, 47(6): 730–40.

Rink, E. (2016) 'An evaluation of the interaction of place and community-based participatory research as a research methodology in the implementation of a sexually transmitted infection intervention for Greenlandic youth', *International Journal of Circumpolar Health*, 75(1), doi: 10.3402/ijch.v75.32239.

Rippon S. and Hopkins, T. (2015) *Head, hands and heart: asset-based approaches in health care*, London: Health Foundation.

Rix, E., Wilson, S., Sheehan, N. and Tujague, N. (2018) 'Indigenist and decolonizing research methodology', In Liamputtong, P. (ed.) *Handbook of research methods in health social sciences*, Singapore: Springer, pp. 1–15.

Ronzi, S., Puzzolo, E., Hyseni, L., Higgerson, J., Stanistreet, D., Hugo, M.N.B., Bruce, N. and Pope, D. (2019) 'Using photovoice methods as a community-based participatory research tool to advance uptake of clean cooking and improve health: the LPG adoption in Cameroon evaluation studies', *Social Science & Medicine*, 228: 30–40.

Samrova, D.P. and Cummings, C.E. (2017) 'Participatory action research (PAR) with children and youth: an integrative review of methodology and PAR outcomes for participants, organizations and communities', *Children and Youth Services Review*, 8(1): 400–412.

Sanders, D., Labonte, R., Baum F. and Chopra, M. (2004) 'Making research matter: a civil society perspective on health research', *Bull World Health Organ*, 82: 757–63.

Schulz, A., Israel, B. and Lantz, P. (2003) 'Instrument for evaluating dimensions of group dynamics within community-based participatory research partnerships', *Evaluation and Program Planning*, 26(3): 249–62.

Sclove, R. (1997) 'Research by the people, for the people', *Futures*, 29(6): 541–9.

Sclove, R.E., Scammell, M.L. and Holland, B. (1998) *Community-based research in the United States: an introductory reconnaissance, including twelve organizational case studies and comparison with the Dutch science shops and the mainstream American research system*, Amherst, MA: The Loka Institute.

Scott-Samuel, A., Birley, M. and Ardern, K. (2001) *The Merseyside guidelines for health impact assessment* (2nd edn), Liverpool: International Health Impact Assessment Consortium, ISBN 1 874038 56 2.

Seifer, S. (1998) 'Service-learning: community-campus partnerships for health professions education', *Academic Medicine*, 73(3): 273–7.

Selener, D. (1997) *Participatory action research and social change*, Ithaca, NY: Cornell University Press.

Sense, A. (2006) 'Driving the bus from the rear passenger seat: control dilemmas of participative action research', *International Journal of Social Research Methodology*, 9(1): 1–13.

Shallwani, S. and Mohammed, S. (2007) 'Community-based participatory research. A training manual for community-based researchers', www.livingknowledge. org/fileadmin/Dateien-Living-Knowledge/Dokumente_Dateien/Toolbox/ LK_A_Training_manual.pdf

Sherriff, S.L., Miller, H., Williamson, A., Eades, S. and Haynes, A. (2019) 'Building trust and sharing power for co-creation in Aboriginal health research: a stakeholder interview study', *Evidence and Policy*, 15(3): 371–92.

Shorten, A. and Smith, J. (2017) 'Mixed methods research: expanding the evidence base', *Evidence-Based Nursing*, 20: 74–5.

Sime, D. (2008) 'Ethical and methodological issues in engaging young people in poverty with participatory methods', *Children's Geographies*, 6(1): 63–78.

Simister, N. (2017) 'Developmental evaluation'. M&E Universe, INTRAC. www. intrac.org/wpcms/wp-content/uploads/2017/01/Developmental-evaluation. pdf

Singh, A.A., Richmond, K. and Burnes, T.R. (2013) 'Feminist participatory action research with transgender communities: fostering the practice of ethical and empowering research designs', *International Journal of Transgenderism*, 14(3): 93–104.

Smith, C. (2013) 'Becoming a Kaupapa Maori researcher', In Mertens, D., Cram, F. and Chilisia, B. (eds) *Indigenous pathways into social research: voices of a new generation*, Walnut Creek, CA: Left Coast Press, pp. 89–99.

Soska, T. and Butterfield, A. (2012) *University-community partnerships*, Hoboken, NJ: Taylor and Francis.

South, J., Meah, A., Bagnall, A.M., Kinsella, K., Branney, P., White, J. and Gamsu, M. (2010) *People in public health: a study of approaches to develop and support people in public health roles*, Project report, Leeds Metropolitan University. http://eprints. leedsbeckett.ac.uk/id/eprint/837/

Spears Johnson, C.R., Kraemer, A.E. and Arcury, T.A. (2016) 'Participation levels in 25 community-based participatory research projects', *Health Education Research*, 31(5): 577–86.

Springett, J. (2017) 'Impact in participatory health research: what can we learn from research on participatory evaluation?', *Educational Action Research*, 25(4): 560–74.

St Leger, A.S., Schnieden, H. and Wadsworth-Bell, J.P. (1992) *Evaluating health services' effectiveness*, Milton Keynes: Open University Press.

Staley, K. (2015) '"Is it worth doing?", Measuring the impact of patient and public involvement in research', *Research Involvement and Engagement*, 1(6). https://doi. org/10.1186/s40900-015-0008-5

Staley, K. and Elliot, J. (2017) 'Public involvement could usefully inform ethical review, but rarely does: what are the implications?', *Research Involvement and Engagement*, 3(30). https://doi.org/10.1186/s40900-017-0080-0

Stalker, K. (1998) 'Some ethical and methodological issues in research with people with learning disabilities', *Disability and Society*, 13: 5–19.

Stern, N. (2016) *Building on success and learning from experience and independent review of the Research Excellence Framework*, London: Department for Business, Energy and Industrial Strategy. https://assets.publishing.service.gov.uk/government/uploads/system/uploads/attachment_data/file/541338/ind-16-9-ref-stern-review.pdf

Stevenson, M. (2014) 'Participatory data analysis alongside co-researchers who have Down syndrome', *Journal of Applied Research in Intellectual Disabilities*, 27: 23–33.

Stewart-Brown, S., Tennant, A., Tennant, R., Platt, S., Parkinson, J. and Weich, S. (2009) 'Internal construct validity of the Warwick-Edinburgh mental well-being scale (WEMWBS): a Rasch analysis using data from the Scottish Health Education population survey', *Health and Quality of Life Outcomes*, 7(1): 15.

Stoecker, R. (2013) *Research methods for community change. A project-based approach* (2nd edn), London/Thousand Oaks, CA: Sage.

Strand, K.J., Cutworth, N., Stoecker, R. and Marullo, S. (2003) *Community-based research and higher education: principles and practices*, New York: John Wiley & Sons.

Strang, J.F., Klomp, S.E., Caplan, R., Griffin, A.D., Anthony, L.G., Harris, M.C., Graham, E.K., Knauss, M. and van der Miesen, A.I.R. (2019) 'Community-based participatory design for research that impacts the lives of transgender and/or gender-diverse autistic and/or neurodiverse people', *Clinical Practice in Pediatric Psychology*, 7(4): 396–404.

Strier, R. (2010) 'The construction of university-community partnerships: entangled perspectives', *Higher Education*, 62(1): 81–97.

Stringer, E.T. (1996) *Action research. A handbook for practitioners*, London: Sage.

Stuart, C.A. (1998) 'Care and concern: an ethical journey in participatory action research', *Canadian Journal of Counselling/Revue canadienne de counseling*, 32(4): 298–314.

Suarez, P., Ching, F., Ziervogel, G., Lemaire, I., Turnquest, D., de Suarez, J.M. and Wisner, B. (2008) 'Video-mediated approaches for community-level climate adaptation', *IDS Bulletin*, 39(4): 96–104.

Suarez-Balcazar, Y., Harper, G. and Lewis, R. (2005) 'An interactive and contextual model of community-university collaborations for research and action', *Health Education & Behavior*, 32(1): 84–101.

Sushama, P., Ghergu, C., Meershoek, A., de Witte, L., van Schayck, O. and Krumeich, A. (2018) 'Dark clouds in co-creation, and their silver linings', *Global Health Action*, 11(1), doi: 10.1080/16549716.2017.1421342.

Tamariz, L., Medina, H., Taylor, J., Carrasquillo, O., Kobetz, E. and Palacio, A. (2015) 'Are research ethics committees prepared for community-based participatory research?', *Journal of Empirical Research on Human Research Ethics*, 10(5): 488–95.

Tamí-Maury, I., Brown, L., Lapham, H. and Chang, S. (2017) 'Community-based participatory research through virtual communities', *Journal of Communication in Healthcare*, 10(3): 188–94.

Tendulkar, S.A., Chu, J., Opp, J., Geller, A., DiGirolamo, A., Gandelman, E. and Hacker, K. (2011) 'A funding initiative for community-based participatory research: lessons from the Harvard Catalyst Seed Grants', *Progress in Community Health Partnerships: Research, Education, and Action*, 5(1): 35–44, doi: 10.1353/cpr.2011.0005.

Terry, L. (2016) *Refreshing perspectives. Exploring the application of peer research with populations facing severe and multiple disadvantage*, London: Revolving Doors Agency/Lankelly Chase.

Teti, M., Murray, C., Johnson, L. and Binson, D. (2012) 'Photovoice as a community-based participatory research method among women living with HIV/AIDS: ethical opportunities and challenges', *Journal of Empirical Research on Human Research Ethics*, 7(4): 34–43.

Teufel-Shone, N., Schwartz, A., Hardy, L., de Heer, H., Williamson, H., Dunn, D., Polingyumptewa, K. and Chief, C. (2018) 'Supporting new community-based participatory research partnerships', *International Journal of Environmental Research and Public Health*, 16(1): 44.

Thomas, N. and O'Kane, C. (1998) 'The ethics of participatory research with children', *Children and Society*, 12: 336–48.

Thompson, L., Story, M. and Butler, G. (2003) 'Use of a university-community collaboration model to frame issues and set an agenda for strengthening a community', *Health Promotion Practice*, 4(4): 385–92.

Timmins, F. (2015) 'Disseminating nursing research', *Nursing Standard*, 29(48): 34–9.

Trickett, E. and Beehler, S. (2017) 'Participatory action research and impact: an ecological ripples perspective', *Educational Action Research*, 25(4): 525–40.

Trinidad, S.B., Ludman, E., Hopkins, S., James, R.D., Hoeft, T.J., Kinegak, A., Lupie, H., Kinegak, R., Boyer, B.B. and Burke, W. (2015) 'Community dissemination and genetic research: moving beyond results reporting', *American Journal of Medical Genetics Part A*, 167(A): 1542–50.

Unicef (2018) How we protect children's rights with the UN Convention on the Rights of the Child. www.unicef.org.uk/what-we-do/un-convention-child-rights/

University of Delaware (2016) What is the difference between community-based research/creative scholarship and traditional scholarship? https://cpb-us-w2.wpmucdn.com/sites.udel.edu/dist/7/4457/files/2016/08/differenceschart-yj3bij.pdf

Urdarn, T.C. (2010) *Statistics in plain English*, Mahwah, NJ: Lawrence Erlbaum, chapter 7.

Van Blerk, L. and Ansell, N. (2007) 'Participatory feedback and dissemination with and for children: reflections from research with young migrants in Southern Africa', *Children's Geographies*, 3(3): 313–24.

Vaughn, N.A., Jacoby, S.F., Williams, T., Guerra, T., Thomas, N.A. and Richmond, T.S. (2013) 'Digital animation as a method to disseminate research findings to the community using a community-based participatory approach', *Am J Community Psychology*, 51: 30–42.

Vigurs, K. and Kara, H. (2017) 'Participants' productive disruption of a community photo-elicitation project: improvised methodologies in practice', *International Journal of Social Research Methodology*, 20(5): 513–23.

Visser, M. (2012) 'Participation in community research: experiences of community researchers undertaking HIV research in South Africa', In Goodson, L. and Phillimore, J. (eds) *Community research for participation: from theory to method*, Bristol: Policy Press, chapter 8.

Wallerstein, N. and Duran, B. (2010) 'Community-based participatory research contributions to intervention research: the intersection of science and practice to improve health equity', *American Journal of Public Health*, 100(Suppl.1): S40–6.

Wallerstein, N., Duran, B., Oetzel, J.G. and Minkler, M. (2008) 'On community-based participatory research', In Minkler, M. and Wallerstein, N. (eds) *Community-based participatory research for health: from process to outcomes* (2nd edn), San Francisco, CA: Jossey-Bass.

Wallerstein, N., Giatti, L.L., Bogus, C.M., Akerman, M., Jacobi, P.R., Ferraz de Toledo, R., Mendes, R., Acioli, S., Bluehorse-Anderson, M., Frazier, S. and Jones, M. (2017) 'Shared participatory principles and methodologies: perspectives from the USA and Brazil – 45 years after Paulo Freire's "Pedagogy of the oppressed"', *Societies*, 7(2): 6, https://doi.org/10.3390/soc7020006

Walmsley, J. (2004) 'Involving users with learning difficulties in health improvement; lessons from inclusive learning disability research', *Nursing Inquiry*, 11: 54–64.

Walmsley, J. and Johnson, K. (2003) *Inclusive research with people with learning disabilities: past, present and futures*, London: Jessica Kingsley.

Walters, K., Stately, A., Evans-Campbell, T., Simoni, J., Duran, B., Schultz, K., Stanley, E., Charles, C. and Guerrero, D. (2009) '"Indigenist" collaborative research efforts in Native American communities', In Stiffman, A.R. (ed.) *The field research survival guide*, Oxford: Oxford University Press, pp. 146–73.

Wang, C.C. and Redwood-Jones, Y.A. (2001) Photovoice ethics: perspectives from Flint Photovoice, *Health Education & Behavior*, 28(5): 560–72.

Wang, C.C., Cash, J.L. and Powers, L.S. (2000) 'Who knows the streets as well as the homeless? Promoting personal and community action through photovoice', *Health Promotion Practice*, 1(1): 81–9.

Wang, K.H., Racy, N.J., Berg, D.N., Greene, A.T., Lucas, G., Harris, K., Carroll-Scott, A., Tinney, B. and Rosenthal, M.S. (2017) 'Using community-based participatory research and organizational diagnosis to characterize relationships between community leaders and academic researchers', *Preventative Medicine Reports*, 7: 180–6.

Warwick-Booth L. (2007) 'Being involved in community based research: lessons from the Objective 1 South Yorkshire context', *Journal of Community Work and Development*, 9: 67–85.

Warwick-Booth L. (2008) 'Locally directed policy and the fostering of social capital within regeneration: the case of Objective 1 South Yorkshire', *Social Policy and Society*, 7(1): 53–63.

Warwick-Booth, L. and Coan, S. (2020) Using creative qualitative methods in evaluating gendered health promotion interventions, *SAGE Research Methods Cases*, doi:10.4135/9781529707281.

Waterman H., Tillen D., Dickson R. and de Koning K. (2001) 'Action research: a systematic review and guidance for assessment', *Health Technology Assessment*, 5(23): iii–157, PMID: 11785749.

Watters, J., Comeau, S. with Restrall, G. (2010) 'Participatory action research: an educational tool for citizen-users of community mental health services', University of Manitoba, http://umanitoba.ca/rehabsciences/media/par_manual.pdf

Wehrens, R. (2014) 'Beyond two communities – from research utilization and knowledge translation to co-production?', *Public Health*, 128: 545–51.

Wenger, E. (1998) *Communities of practice: learning, meaning and identity*, Cambridge: Cambridge University Press.

Westbrook, R.B. (1992) 'John Dewey and American democracy', *The American Historical Review*, 97(3): 919–20.

Wetton, N.M. and McWhirter, J. (1998) 'Images and curriculum development in health education', In Prosser, J. (ed.) *Image-based research: a sourcebook for qualitative researchers*, London: Falmer Press, pp. 263–83.

Whitehead, D., Taket, A. and Smith, P. (2003) 'Action research in health promotion', *Health Education Journal*, 62: 5–22, doi: 10.1177/001789690306200102.

Whitmore, E. (2001) 'Evaluation and empowerment: it's the process that counts', *Empowerment and Family Support Networking Bulletin* (Cornell University Empowerment Project), 2(2): 1–7.

WHO (World Health Organization) (1984) The Ottawa Charter for Health Promotion. www.who.int/healthpromotion/conferences/previous/ottawa/en/

WHO (2019) Ageing and life-course. Knowledge translation. www.who.int/ageing/projects/knowledge_translation/en/

Wilkins, C.H. (2011) 'Communicating results of community-based participatory research', *American Medical Association Journal of Ethics*, 13(2): 81–5.

Williams, G. (2012) 'The discipling effects of impact evaluation practices: negotiating the pressures of impact within an ESRC-DFID project boundary crossings', *Transactions of the Institute of British Geographers*, NS 37: 489–95.

Wilson, E., Kenny, A. and Dickson-Swift, V. (2018a) 'Ethical challenges in community-based participatory research: exploring researchers' experience', *International Journal of Social Research Methodology*, 21(1): 7–24.

Wilson, E., Kenny, A. and Dickson-Swift, V. (2018b) 'Ethical challenges in community-based participatory research: a scoping review', *Qualitative Health Research*, 28(2): 189–99.

Wimpenny, K. (2013) 'Using participatory action research to support knowledge translation in practice settings', *International Journal of Practice-Based Learning in Health and Social Care*, 1(1): 3–14.

Winter, R. and Munn-Giddings, C. (eds) (2001) *Handbook for action research in health and social care*, London: Routledge.

Wisdom, J. and Creswell, J.W. (2013) *Mixed methods: integrating quantitative and qualitative data collection and analysis while studying patient-centered medical home models*, Rockville, MD: Agency for Healthcare Research and Quality, publication no. 13-0028-EF.

Wolff, M. and Maurana, C. (2001) 'Building effective community: academic partnerships to improve health', *Academic Medicine*, 76(2): 166–72.

Wolfson, M., Wagoner, K.G., Rhodes, S.D., Egan, K.L., Sparks, M., Ellerbee, D., Song, E.Y., Debinski, B., Terrillion, A., Vining, J. and Yang, E. (2017) 'Coproduction of research questions and research evidence in public health: the study to prevent teen drinking parties', *BioMed Research International*, ID: 3639596, doi: 10.1155/2017/3639596.

Wong, D. and Baker, C. (1988) Pain in children: comparison of assessment scales. *Pediatric Nursing*, 14(1): 9–17.

Woodall, J., Woodward, J., Witty, K. and McCulloch, S. (2013) 'An evaluation of Calderdale's toothbrushing in schools scheme', Leeds: Leeds Metropolitan University.

Woodall, J., Woodward, J., Witty, K. and McCulloch, S. (2014) 'An evaluation of a toothbrushing programme in schools', *Health Education*, 114(6): 414–34.

Woodall, J., Kinsella, K., Cross, R., Bunyon, A.M.B. and Inspiring Change Manchester's Peer Researchers (2016) 'Service users' experiences of inspiring change, Manchester', Leeds: Leeds Beckett University.

Woodall, J., Cross, R., Kinsella, K. and Bunyon, A.M.B. (2018) 'Using peer research processes to understand strategies to support those with severe, multiple and complex health needs', *Health Education Journal*, 78(2): 176–88.

Wright, M.T., Salsberg, J. and Hartung, S. (2018) 'Editorial: impact in participatory health research', *BioMed Research International*, ID: 3907127.

Young, I. (2000) *Inclusion and democracy*, Oxford: Oxford University Press.

Yuffrey-Wijne, I. and Butler, G. (2009) 'Co-researching with people with learning disabilities: an experience of involvement in qualitative data analysis', *Health Expectations*, 13: 174–84.

Index

Note: Page locators in *italics* refer to figures or tables.

www.ingramcontent.com/pod-product-compliance
Lightning Source LLC
Chambersburg PA
CBHW080556030426
42336CB00019B/3210